How India Became Territorial

SERIES EDITORS

Amitav Acharya, Chief Editor
American University

David Leheny, Chief Editor
Princeton University

Alastair Iain Johnston
Harvard University

Randall Schweller
The Ohio State University

INTERNATIONAL BOARD

Rajesh M. Basrur
Nanyang Technological University

Brian L. Job
University of British Columbia

Barry Buzan
London School of Economics

Miles Kahler
University of California, San Diego

Victor D. Cha
Georgetown University

Peter J. Katzenstein
Cornell University

Thomas J. Christensen
Princeton University

Khong Yuen Foong
Oxford University

Stephen P. Cohen
The Brookings Institution

Byung-Kook Kim
Korea University

Chu Yun-han
Academia Sinica

Michael Mastanduno
Dartmouth College

Rosemary Foot
University of Oxford

Mike Mochizuki
The George Washington University

Aaron L. Friedberg
Princeton University

Katherine H. S. Moon
Wellesley College

Sumit Ganguly
Indiana University, Bloomington

Qin Yaqing
China Foreign Affairs University

Avery Goldstein
University of Pennsylvania

Christian Reus-Smit
Australian National University

Michael J. Green
Georgetown University

Varun Sahni
Jawaharlal Nehru University

Stephan M. Haggard
University of California, San Diego

Etel Solingen
University of California, Irvine

G. John Ikenberry
Princeton University

Rizal Sukma
CSIS, Jakarta

Takashi Inoguchi
Chuo University

Wu Xinbo
Fudan University

Studies in Asian Security

The Studies in Asian Security book series promotes analysis, understanding, and explanation of the dynamics of domestic, transnational, and international security challenges in Asia. The peer-reviewed publications in the Series analyze contemporary security issues and problems to clarify debates in the scholarly community, provide new insights and perspectives, and identify new research and policy directions. Security is defined broadly to include the traditional political and military dimensions as well as nontraditional dimensions that affect the survival and well-being of political communities. Asia, too, is defined broadly to include Northeast, Southeast, South, and Central Asia.

Designed to encourage original and rigorous scholarship, books in the Studies in Asian Security series seek to engage scholars, educators, and practitioners. Wide-ranging in scope and method, the Series is receptive to all paradigms, programs, and traditions, and to an extensive array of methodologies now employed in the social sciences.

How India Became Territorial

FOREIGN POLICY, DIASPORA, GEOPOLITICS

Itty Abraham

STANFORD UNIVERSITY PRESS
Stanford, California

Stanford University Press
Stanford, California

© 2014 by the Board of Trustees of the Leland Stanford Junior University.
All rights reserved.

No part of this book may be reproduced or transmitted in any form or by any means, electronic or mechanical, including photocopying and recording, or in any information storage or retrieval system without the prior written permission of Stanford University Press.

Printed in the United States of America on acid-free, archival-quality paper

Library of Congress Cataloging-in-Publication Data
Abraham, Itty, 1960- author.
    How India became territorial : foreign policy, diaspora, geopolitics / Itty Abraham.
        pages cm — (Studies in Asian security)
    Includes bibliographical references and index.
    ISBN 978-0-8047-9163-2 (cloth : alk. paper) |
    ISBN 978-1-5036-0841-2 (pbk. : alk. paper)
    1. India—Boundaries. 2. Territory, National—India. 3. India—Foreign relations. 4. East Indian diaspora. 5. Geopolitics—India. 6. India—Politics and government—1947– I. Title. II. Series: Studies in Asian security.
    DS448.A4343 2014
    327.54—dc23
                                                           2014004017

ISBN 0-978-8047-9268-4 (electronic)

Typeset by Thompson Type in 10.5/13.5 Bembo

For My Mother and My Father

Contents

Acknowledgments	*xi*
Preface	*xiii*
Introduction	1
1 Territory and Foreign Policy	19
2 A Brief International History of the Nation-State	46
3 Diaspora as Foreign Policy	73
4 Geopolitics as Foreign Policy	107
Conclusion	141
Notes	*165*
Bibliography	*191*
Index	*207*

Acknowledgments

The first draft of this book was written in Hyderabad, India, while I was on leave from the University of Texas at Austin. My sincere thanks to my former dean, Randy Diehl, for his encouragement and support in allowing me this time to transition successfully from my administrative responsibilities as director of UT's South Asia Institute back to full-time research. For some of this period (2011–2012), I was also supported financially by a Nehru-Fulbright senior fellowship. I am extremely grateful to the Fulbright Commission and especially their India office for all their help and assistance. My time in Hyderabad was made enormously productive entirely due to the unstinting efforts of my dear comrade-in-arms Arati Vidyasagar, who made it possible for me to work uninterrupted and in the most congenial of environments. Without her and the salubrious Gagan Mahal, this book would have taken far longer to complete. Willem van Schendel, Tina Harris, Sanjib Barua, Xonzoi Barbora, Turan Kayaoglu, Latha Vardarajan, Sankaran Krishna, and Srirupa Roy graciously agreed to read early drafts of individual chapters that, as a result, needed to be changed substantially. They helped in more ways than they possibly realize. Draft chapters were also presented at a seminar at the School of International Studies, JNU, over the course of three lectures in Kolkata, and at a workshop at the University of Oregon, Eugene. I would like to acknowledge the generosity of Varun Sahni, Samir Kumar Bose, and Bryna Goodman in organizing those events and to Achin Vanaik and Ranabir Samaddar for their insightful questions. Tan See Seng and I collaborated to organize a workshop on "How Asia Became Territorial" at the second Inter-Asia Conference organized by the Social Science Research Council and National University of Singapore. Participants at that workshop, especially Carolyn Cartier, Siba Grovogui, Turan Kayaoglu, L. M. H. Lee, David Ludden, and Ken MacLean helped me clarify my thinking on territoriality and introduced me to important scholarship that I was unfamiliar with. David Magier went out of his way to procure a copy of the Indian Home Rule petition for me and later invited me to present a paper at the Columbia South Asia Seminar: my thanks. The first complete version of the manuscript was taken apart, chapter-by-chapter, at a mini-workshop convened at the Asia Research Institute (ARI) while I was in residence as senior visiting fellow in early 2012. My sincere thanks to all those who helped in that most productive deconstruction, including Kanti Bajpai, Ian Chong, Janice Bially Mattern, C. Raja Mohan, James Sidaway, Sinderpal Singh, and, especially, ARI director Prasenjit Duara. Prasenjit has not only engendered an extremely vibrant intellectual atmosphere at ARI that I have benefited hugely from; he has been for me personally a solid pillar of support in so many ways. The latter set of individuals mentioned above have since become my colleagues, and it is in no small part due to their, and Goh Beng Lan's, welcoming presence that I have been so comfortable in my new home at the National University of Singapore. Finally, it has also been a distinct pleasure working with Stanford University Press and the Studies in Asian Security series. Amitava Acharya, in particular, David Leheny, and Geoffrey Burn have from the outset been very supportive partners in the uncertain process of getting a manuscript from early draft to final product. My thanks to them and their faith in the intellectual value of this project.

Singapore, December 2013

Preface

This project effectively began over a decade ago when I started work on a series of articles on the historic Bandung conference of 1955, seen from the vantage point of its fiftieth anniversary. I had always taken for granted that Bandung was a singular moment in world history: the moment when newly independent leaders of Asia and Africa collectively articulated their own path to world peace in the face of global resistance. Once I began to read the primary documents related to this event, I was surprised to find that the first Asia-Africa conference was much more—and less—than its dominant representation. Bandung is usually positioned in relation to the *future*, as the event that led to the founding of the nonaligned movement. I came to the opposite conclusion. Not only was it an event where disagreement and conflict told us more than agreement, its significance could not be fully appreciated until set in the context of prior multicultural political gatherings I was only barely aware of. Fault lines—ethnic, religious, racial, and civilizational—made visible through the conference discussions went well beyond the usual tropes of Cold War politics and China's arrival on the world scene and pointed to structures of hierarchy and exclusion that conventional accounts of international relations rarely addressed. I began to see Bandung as the *culmination* of a series of little-known "international" events that sought to confront and overcome global political subjection and racial division. I started to read more widely in the international history of the immediate postwar period, only to find myself going back into the Dark Ages of the twentieth century until I reached World

War I. That was the moment, I realized, when the current topography of what I was now beginning to think of as a new international scale was set in place.

It was not until a few years ago that I was able to synthesize these readings into a revised understanding of Indian foreign policy. Crucial to this end were the conceptual innovations and revisionist writings coming out of critical geography and postcolonial legal studies that helped me clarify the political stakes involved in coming to grips with a territorialized world of states and their interactions. That said, I began this project under the impression that I was writing an article addressing the one constant of Indian foreign policy behavior, namely New Delhi's seemingly endless search for international status, position, and, respect: in a word, *recognition*. Beginning from international recognition as an independent variable that I thought explained state behavior, I ended up with recognition as a dependent variable, a concept that itself needed to be explained. Captured in that complete turnaround is my own gradual realization of the complexity of the implications of a territorialized foreign policy. This turned out to be far more than just thinking about prestige and respect as drivers of international behavior. It also meant coming to terms with how foreign policy profoundly shapes domestic politics. My efforts to deal with this complexity have led what was to be an article into this book.

It will soon become apparent that this is not a conventional study of Indian foreign policy. This study does not try to establish realist, idealist, or constructivist frames with which to understand international relations and the state. It does not periodize Indian foreign policy behavior and change in relation to political leadership, for example, the Nehruvian moment, the Janata interregnum, or the BJP transformation. It neither focuses on bilateral relations between India and a now-familiar bestiary of Dragons, Bears, and Eagles, nor does it offer a microanalysis of Indian diplomacy in foreign capitals or the intricacies of bureaucratic infighting in South Block. Examples of these staples of Indian foreign policy analysis are to be found throughout this book but do not appear in their usual places.[1] Nevertheless, this book is centrally concerned with questions basic to the study of foreign policy, while at the same time questioning the conventional parameters of that field.

Perhaps the most visible divergence of this study from the conventional study of Indian foreign policy is the challenge to its familiar starting point. Indian foreign policy is typically assumed to begin in 1947 for the "obvious" reason that before August 15 of that year, there was no "India." If India as a sovereign state dates from 1947, the logic goes, so must its foreign policy. By contrast, I treat the beginning of the twentieth century as a more appropriate beginning for the study of "Indian foreign policy." I am not suggesting that India had complete autonomy in its foreign policy decision making from as early as, say, 1919, but it is clear that on certain issues, particularly the movement and protection of overseas Indians and the maintenance of strategic hegemony in an extended region that stretched from Aden to Singapore, it was able to make decisions based on what was good for Delhi and did not necessarily conform to London's interests. Incomplete sovereignty, moreover, shaped future behavior in important ways. Delinking 1947 from the beginnings of Indian foreign policy permits the tracing of important continuities between colonial and postcolonial ways of thinking and acting across a number of foreign policy domains. What is genuinely new and different about sovereign India's foreign policy thereby becomes much clearer.[2]

By tracing the genealogies of territory and its attendant inclusions and exclusions, this study demonstrates that foreign policy is much more than the habitual practice of a modern state embedded in and engaged with an international system. Understood as a boundary-making practice, foreign policy becomes central to what we understand by modern citizenship. Social as much as political boundaries are constituted through the institutionalization of difference. Once delinked from an unproblematized notion of territory, the exercise of "foreign policy" produces an uneven domestic space. The "body politic" comes to be internally divided and hierarchically organized on political, social, and economic lines through the boundary making actions of foreign policy. Internal fissures, including the boundaries that mark majorities and minorities and that exclude populations from the national center on the basis of ethnicity, class, religion, gender, and civilization, are found to follow inevitably from the particular political intersection of territory and sovereignty that is dominant today. Unequal citizenship, this study argues, is endemic to the modern nation-state.

Although this is a book primarily about India (and by extension, China and Pakistan), my hope is that it also offers useful insights and approaches to scholars interested in the large set of countries that joined and remade the international system during the twentieth century. Often lumped under the label of "postcolonial," this study is also very much about the travails of these new states entering an international order where the rules were already established and the reception from established states was less than warm and welcoming. By approaching this problem through a revisionist historical account, my intent is to also go beyond some of the intellectual stasis that has plagued recent debates on postcolonial, feminist, and poststructural theories as applied to international relations (IR). As an insurgent approach dating back to the seminal work of Richard Ashley, Rob Walker, Mike Shapiro, Cynthia Enloe, Ann Tickner, Sankaran Krishna, Siba Grovogui, and others—and with which I wholly identify—feminist, critical, and postcolonial theories have proved immensely useful in offering a sustained and robust critique of mainstream approaches to international relations. Where these approaches have been less than successful is in offering an alternative approach to the study of IR, a self-imposed limit that in my opinion comes from not fully taking on the project of entirely rewriting the histories and geographies of states and people in international space.

This book takes a small step in that direction. It does so in the introduction by first sketching an outline of the meaning and making of the "international" itself, a necessary condition for beginning this major empirical-theoretical project. I argue that international space should be seen as an unstable space produced by constant struggle between status quo and insurgent forces. What this means, among other things, is to see international space as "naturally" populated by entities other than states, as well as a space that is undergoing constant transformation through the dialectic of control and resistance. Drawing on the insights of Michel Foucault, this allows me to propose that international space is not an extra-domestic "level of analysis," as IR would have it, but is best understood as a political field, a *regime*.

A second major objective of this study is to bring the findings of human geography into the study of IR. It is ironic that a field that accepts territoriality as one of the key foundations of its scholarly apparatus has spent so little time understanding the theoretical foundations of territory and why it matters as much as it does. Human and political geographers have been concerned with precisely these questions for decades now, and it is important for scholars of IR to learn from and internalize the common sense of their debates. Much of the first chapter seeks to bring territory "in" and to show what it means for the study of international relations. This "territorial turn," I show in the second half of the book, offers us important new tools for the study of classic themes of international relations, notably for geopolitics and diaspora, and demonstrates how the intersection of the nation and IR becomes central in shaping the contours of modern citizenship.

The final objective of this study is to offer a constructive way of thinking about a "real-world" problem that is likely to become a flashpoint for international conflict, namely interstate territorial disputes. In my view, it is also not unreasonable to criticize postcolonial approaches to the study of IR for the relatively small number of studies that take on the big issues of our times—nuclear weapons, international power transitions, "humanitarian" interventions, international and ethnic conflict, to name a few of the most obvious ones. The task of understanding and offering ways of thinking about these issues have been ceded, for the most part, to mainstream approaches, which are then roundly (and rightly) criticized for their reductionist and positivist framing of problem(s). While it may even be correct to castigate the mainstream for being complicit in the reproduction of the unequal and unjust structure of contemporary international relations, giving up this ground too soon permanently relegates critical approaches to the margins of intellectual discourse where they continue to mutter, "I told you so." Although not being in the least bit naïve about the willingness of mainstream discourse to accept points of view that offer truly alternative perspectives on current problems of world politics, it is ducking a considerable responsibility, in my view, not to take on these and other "big questions" centrally and to try, as much as possible, to get critical perspectives taken seriously.

In this study I offer a new way of understanding one of the foremost problems of Indian and, for that matter, Asian, foreign policies, namely, interstate territorial disputes. Indian foreign policy has long been shaped by protracted and deeply emotive disputes with its immediate neighbors over contested lands, notably Pakistan over Kashmir and China over Arunachal Pradesh and Aksai Chin. It would not be an overstatement to say that until these disputes are resolved to the mutual satisfaction of all parties, they remain the most likely causes of interstate conflict—old-fashioned war—in the South Asia region. To understand the general phenomenon of interstate territorial disputes, however, it is not enough to explore the origins of particular disputes. That is precisely what the forensic approach of international law does and, in the same moment, demonstrates its limits. For me, the answer lies with the fluid and contentious concept of the nation, a still incomplete formation. Bringing competing spatial imaginaries of the nation and the emotive power of territorial nationalism together allows me to explain why some disputes become highly contentious and protracted while others do not. Not seeing the nation as the critical mediating factor in producing interstate contentions over territory leads us to see territorial loss as a loss of state power and hence something to be avoided at all costs. The more pertinent question is: Why is territorial loss overwhelmingly construed as a loss of state power when, as we know, territory has been given up in the past without leading to the breakdown of the state?

The answer begins from the conjuncture of nation, state, and territory at a particular moment in world history, the end of World War I, when the call for national self-determination was proclaimed as a universal global standard.

Aspirations for political freedom were now, and for the first time, defined solely in terms of collective membership of a sovereign territorial nation-state. This was a moment when most nations of the world lacked political freedoms and were held subordinate as the colonial possessions of imperial powers. To be recognized as sovereign, subjugated peoples seeking freedom had to meet the new standard of national self-determination: they needed to conform to the identity of one nation–one state–one territory. Few subordinated entities could conform to that impossible standard due to ambiguities over the boundaries of nations and borders of states. Given this radical uncertainty, political control over a defined territory—that is, territorial sovereignty—became the practical condition from which peoples seeking freedom could make a legitimate claim to sovereignty and recognition. Once territorial control had become the *fons et origo* for a state to claim international legitimacy and recognition, a loss of territory became equivalent to the loss of state power. The burning question for us today is whether there is a way out of this "territorial trap"? I believe there is and spell out my thinking in the conclusion to this book.

Even if my conclusion is relatively optimistic, the overall picture I sketch in this book is not. This is a study that sees hierarchy as a structural feature of international relations, an outcome that is hardly surprising in a world created by the extension of colonial difference to the global stage. The original fear of the postcolonial nations—that the new international order would never be more than a two-tier world with what Vijay Prashad calls the "darker nations" in its outer perimeter—has been shown to be well founded. This book argues that the world-historical project of decolonization is a struggle that is far from over. Standing firmly in its way are the territorial foundations of modern political life and identity.

How India Became Territorial

Introduction

This study explores the relationship between decolonization and postcolonial political outcomes.[1] To do so means not only having to overcome the ontologically suspect (but patriotically privileged) break between the colonial past and the postcolonial present; it also means bridging the gulf between an international arena where anarchy is said to prevail and a domestic zone assumed to be an endogenously ordered political space. There are no small disciplinary and political investments in keeping these domains—colonial/international and postcolonial/domestic—separate. Not transcending these conventional boundaries of time and space, however, I argue, makes it impossible to understand how international forces consequentially shaped the political possibilities available to newly arrived postcolonial subjects.

Decolonization was never just a demand for political freedoms "at home." It was always also a claim to fully recognized and legitimate membership in the existing "family of nations." For the first generation of soon-to-be postcolonial states and existing members of international society alike, this was a fraught and uncertain process. Colonial elites were all too aware that the Great Powers had long used racial and civilizational criteria to exclude legally sovereign and independent states such as Turkey and Siam from full international personhood. Imperial powers that dominated the contemporary international system feared the inclusion of former colonies for the potential disruption of their carefully crafted and structurally unequal global order. Colonies may unquestionably have had moral power on their side in their demands for freedom, but the intensity of that feeling did not equate to convincing the Great Powers that the time had come either to give up their colonial possessions or to move the international order toward a more just and democratically organized arrangement. The first generation of new entrants into the postwar international system thus faced the daunting prospect of establishing the terms for full international personhood—external sovereignty—with little historical precedent, while also remaining deeply aware that international recognition was being negotiated with powerful states deeply resistant to changing the status quo.

What was not questioned by new states was the absolute necessity of joining the contemporary international system, warts and all. Whether because pragmatism demanded it, in the form of access to much-needed loans, capital, food, technology, or resources, or because it was the only conceivable means through which reform of an unjust international order could be initiated, the call for political independence was also always a demand for international recognition. Yet the bitter truth is that the necessity of gaining and retaining external sovereignty was a poisoned chalice: in practice it meant learning that change in the international system was not going to come easily, if at all, and that long-established privileges were not going to be given up without a fight. However, what was barely appreciated at all, and this insight marks the point of departure for this study, was that the means to external sovereignty would also have far-reaching domestic political implications.

To rephrase in more specific terms: this is a book about India's encounter with the world as it sought to free itself of colonial rule and the effects of that encounter on postcolonial Indian citizenship. It highlights the struggles faced by the people of the "darker nations" in being recognized as full and legitimate members of the international system, the constraints they had to overcome, and the compromises they had to make to participate as fully fledged international persons.[2] But the story does not end there. This bruising encounter with the world also left an enduring mark in a "domestic" arena typically assumed to be distant from foreign affairs. In particular, the quality of postcolonial citizenship bears the scars of India's encounter with the world, stripping some Indian subjects of full participation in the newly formed nation-state and denying other Indian nationals the weight of state protections they had every right to expect. These political outcomes are neither occasional aberrations nor unintended products of poor policy making. Rather, I will argue, uneven and unequal forms of citizenship are structural features of the territorially bound nation-state.

In the process of explaining these two related outcomes, this book interrogates a number of assumptions familiar to students of international relations and foreign policy studies. The most basic is the assumption that what we mean by "foreign policies" are restricted to a set of bounded actions that take place beyond state borders. Foreign policy, in this book, is shown to have a direct impact in shaping the topos of political life within the "domestic" borders of the state. Rather than begin from a taken-for-granted difference between "domestic" and "foreign," as is commonplace, I follow the lead of Rob Walker, Sankaran Krishna, and David Campbell in arguing that foreign policy is best understood as a boundary-making technology.[3] From this perspective, a firm separation of the foreign and the domestic is the desired *end* of a complex set of spatializing processes that are consolidated under the sign of foreign policy. Establishing the boundary between domestic and foreign is a modern state imperative; however, this distinction is never fixed or permanent but is constantly being reproduced through practices, performances, and regulations that seek to produce the "state effect" of an ontological difference between inside and outside.[4] But that is not all. This study also complements and extends the work of Indian historians and scholars of nationalism and domestic politics by opening up a domain of enquiry that has remained largely absent from their scholarship, the international arena. In this study, I will argue for the importance of understanding how new nations coped with the pressures of international forces insofar as they shaped unequal domestic political arrangements that still stand today as deeply sobering reminders of the limits of Indian democracy.

Understanding the international-historical context within which new states emerged, I argue, is the first step to understanding the "domestic" political and organizational choices made by new entrants to the international order. To understand these political outcomes, however, we cannot assume that we all know what is meant by the term *international*. My use of the term supplements conventional notions of the international as the space produced by interstate interactions with the presence and circulation of transnational forces, nonstate actors, ideas, material flows, and people and locates the emergence of international space in historical terms. I argue that a critical aspect of what we term *international relations* today is best understood as the efforts of states to monopolize extradomestic space for themselves, seeking to regulate and/or exclude these other forces and unrecognized actors. As the following section details, I propose that we need to understand the international as always a heterogeneous and unstable space of struggle.

The importance of seeing international space as a field of struggle follows from the claim that the meanings of political freedom for colonized peoples included demands to access, participate in, and shape the world beyond the domestic arena. Seeing the international in these terms also helps us localize a very different image of the "foreign" produced by state boundary-making practices. Once states seek to create hard borders between home and abroad—foreign policy—the foreign is typically produced as a site of fear and anxiety. But it cannot be forgotten that the international was, and remains, also a zone of novelty, potential, and attraction. (In other words, difference may not always be a site of social abjection). We can only retain both meanings of the foreign—attraction and anxiety—if we start from the international as a heterogeneous and unstable space.

To sustain this view conceptually, I draw on the idea of scale as deployed by human geographers. Following the discussion of the "new international scale," I offer an outline of the book, highlighting the main arguments of each chapter. This book is effectively divided into two parts, the first two chapters addressing India's encounter with the world; the third and the fourth chapter exploring the outcomes of that encounter on "domestic" political life. If much of this study is devoted to offering a new perspective on foreign policy and territory, that is not all it offers. The practical, dare I even say "policy-relevant," consequences of this conceptual revision are spelled out in the conclusion. Appreciating "how India became territorial" leads, I argue, to an entirely new way of understanding two long-standing political problems that are structurally related: the difficulty of resolving interstate territorial disputes, and why Pakistan remains a foundational problem for Indian foreign policy.

The "Space" of the International

Rather than imagined as an ontologically stable zone that borders the domestic "level of analysis," the international should be understood as an emergent space of struggle. Such a view alters entirely the conventional historical narrative in the field of International Relations that views the early twentieth century as a period of gradual transition from the age of empire to the era of the nation-state. The decades-long process of the dissolution of most of the world's empires and the emergence of the nation-state as the preeminent political unit of our times must not be reduced to a misleading teleology of the replacement of one form of political organization by another, superior, one. What I want to highlight is the process of *struggle* between entrenched formations and new forces that created a space marked—both then and now—by the copresence of empires; semisovereign nations; fully and partially recognized states, people, transnational institutions, and corporations; and nongovernmental agencies. Together, these entities and institutions working across multiple geographic scales jointly constitute an international space, the boundaries of which are constantly undergoing change. To make sense of this argument requires drawing on a spatial concept very familiar to human geographers but still largely absent from international relations, namely, "scale."

Political scientists have long conceptualized the international in relation to "levels of analysis."[5] Such a formulation tacitly identifies with a governmentalized organization of territorial space by normalizing a discrete hierarchy of administrative units, from the smallest locality through the district and province, "up" to the largest, the nation-state. In the level of analysis schema, the international is deemed to be what lies beyond the nation-state level; for most IR scholars, the international is constituted through unequal power relations between nation-states, the highest form of modern political organization.[6] States constantly seek to normalize the logic of "levels of analysis" that makes, for example, the province, the district, and the village appear as natural and inevitable divisions of political space. This is no small task. It takes considerable effort and resources to marginalize the other social relations that cut across these "levels" to make this familiar division of space appear normative. Space, however, is not a synonym for "place" or "location," as is implied in commonly used phrases such as a description of Kashmir as a "space of conflict." Space is an outcome, not a prior foundational condition. Seen in this way, "Space no longer appears as a static platform of social relations, but rather as one of their constitutive dimensions, itself historically produced, reconfigured, and transformed."[7]

By contrast, critical geographers prefer to identify political spaces in terms of "scales," a formulation that makes it much easier to identify and explain the expression and mobility of power relations working across state administrative "levels," made visible through the everyday functioning of practices, institutions, ideas, and material flows.[8] Spaces are produced by the dialectic of "de- and reterritorialization" across multiple scales; scales, in turn, are emergent and dynamic spatial relations that are the "provisional geographical resolutions of power struggles."[9] Translating these definitions into what we mean by "international space" takes the meaning of the international from a fixed and bounded stage on which states play into a zone of struggle produced by processes of conflict that seek to shape, order, resist, and transform this space. Lost in this translation is the privileged position of the state. States now become actors seeking to shape international space and to regulate its content and boundaries through their resources and the power of their interactions. The "international" of International Relations is a regime.

Expressing the international in terms of the outcome of a multiscalar process is vital to understanding the rapidly changing shape of the space lying outside the bounds of territorially defined communities—the "domestic" arena—in the turbulent decades following the fin de siècle. But, before getting there, it is important to affirm that this is not an argument that proposes that "international space" did not exist prior to the end of the nineteenth century. Far from it. An international arena had been very much an identifiable space since at least a century before, though of a size far smaller than it would become.[10] Prior international space was produced and regulated by a handful of states located in Europe and North America through a succession of collective agreements variously deemed "Peaces," "Concerts," and "Conventions" that sought to channel interstate interactions into directions such that the frequency of war was reduced and, when it did occur, was managed through rules that sought to reduce the devastation of combat, especially against civilians and nonbelligerents.[11] This interstate space was founded in the aftermath of the decline of the authority of the Holy See, during a period when hundreds of semisovereign political entities in Europe began to be absorbed into larger bodies; when diplomatic texts began to shape memory, obligations, and interactions between states; and when mercantile empires were giving way to direct and indirect forms of territorial rule over contiguous and overseas possessions.[12] Participants in early international space were far from uniform, a pattern that continues into the present. By the late nineteenth century, these would include more or less nationally constituted states such as Sweden; principalities in regions that would become Italy and Germany; metropolitan representatives of global empires, such as Britain or France; and declining imperial monarchies such as the Austro-Hungarian Empire, as well as rising immigrant settler republics such as the United States. But, also, this international space was shaped by the existence of transnational entities of which the most prominent was probably the International Committee of the Red Cross, founded in 1863, as well as the social movements such as the antislavery societies that successfully lobbied for the passing of the British Slavery Abolition Act of 1833.[13]

This profusion of novel, contradictory, and customary modes of interaction that made up international space was, during the nineteenth century, ordered and codified by the votaries of so-called positive international law, exemplified by such figures as the American Henry Wheaton, the Englishman John Westlake, and the German-American L. F. L. Oppenheim. This distinctive legal approach sought above all to regularize and regulate a limited international order by elevating sovereign states over other political entities, Euro-Americans over the colored races, and power over principle.[14] Their objective was to establish firm boundaries around and to define the rules of the international system; their method was a process of vigorous intellectual justification of selective amnesia, racial exclusion, and subservience to the might of military force. Ironically, their greatest influence would come just when the prevailing international order was on the cusp of radical change brought about by the immense human conflagrations of the early twentieth century, namely, World War I and the social revolutions that led to the formation of the Soviet Union. It should also be noted in passing that disabling, albeit partially, the unequal and illiberal norms of positive international law would be among the most important early projects taken on by the United Nations due to pressures from what would become the nonaligned countries and movement.[15]

If international space is best defined at the end of the nineteenth century as a small and mutually reinforcing concert of Euro-American states, the walls surrounding this exclusive club soon began to crumble under the multiple onslaughts of transformative political events leading to mass mobilization of subordinated people on a scale never seen before. One "international" event in particular stands out for its global impact. For the rest of the world, and especially Asia, the space lying beyond the domestic took on new meaning with the news of the Japanese naval victory over Russian forces at Port Arthur in 1905. Notwithstanding Japan's own desires to emulate Western imperial glory, the event circulated as a racialized discourse: the first major victory of an Asian power over a Western one. The imputed meaning of this event gave heart to anticolonialists and nationalists across Asia and beyond; it seemed clearly to imply that the power of European states was not without limits.[16]

If the Japanese victory was symbolic of future change that was now imaginable as possible, these feelings were more than complemented by domestic social transformations taking place across Asia due to the impact of modern technologies that brought what were once imaginaries of the future into tangible experience. In a few short decades, asphalted highways, electric trams, steel bridges, electric light, photographs and moving pictures, bicycle and motorcycle clubs, sewing machines, irrigation canals, modern sewage systems, new medicines for old diseases, microscopes and fingerprints, radio waves and telephone lines became part of the, especially, urban landscape in colonial societies. Each of these technologies brought with it elements of a modern cosmopolitan habitus that made even the recent past appear hopelessly outmoded.[17] But, also, for colonial societies familiar with the deployment of foreign technologies as "the measure of man"[18] instrumentally reinforcing the political and economic distance between colonizer and colonized, technologies of consumption coming from new sites, notably the United States and Japan, represented a modernity that was for the first time recognizably plural. Symbolically and materially, colonial societies were experiencing the boundary between the domestic and the external altogether differently. The international became, for the colonial subject, a zone of possibility as much as a source of military threat and political subjugation.

Although there is no question that particular domestic idioms of "tradition" and aesthetic practice would have to work overtime to come to terms with this invasion of experience,[19] such a reinscription of the domestic–foreign boundary meant that transformative change was not always seen primarily as alien or threatening, even if this possibility has been largely ignored by theorists of nationalism. Pheng Cheah's concept of "spectral promises" seeks to expand on this theme, imagining a transnational space not entirely dominated either by the nation or by capital, the limiting conditions of domestic and international life.[20] This welcoming of the new international space is also visible, ironically, in the emergence of new languages of political freedom typically couched as nationalism yet deeply inflected by the foreign. Benedict Anderson has reminded us how often core anticolonial nationalist texts were written and initially disseminated in a location external to the object of liberation.[21] So many of what we might call the first generation of nationalist ideologues—José Rizal, Sun Yat-Sen, Mohandas K. Gandhi, Tan Malaka, Jamal al-din Al-Afghani, to mention only a few of the best known—would politically come of age overseas and would find their overseas experience a vital resource in developing their critiques of colonial and imperial order. Writing in the context of Gandhi in South Africa, Faisal Devji goes so far as to say, "The struggles of minorities in diverse parts of the empire might serve to define what it meant to be Indian far better than anything that was possible in the mother country."[22] There were a number of reasons for these foreign epiphanies, including the opportunity of seeing the imperial racial order upended in various ways, the possibility of sharing and learning from stories, critiques, and theories from other like-minded souls across colonial lines, as well as the forging of new alliances with movements and organizations dedicated to the emancipation of subjugated peoples and an end to imperialism. These encounters were predicated on new means and possibilities of long distance travel, means that were now increasingly available and at lower cost, and possibilities shaped by class position, which also helps explain why radicals were disproportionately middle-class figures. In the last instance, however, claims on the international were also claims of entitlement to the universal, an unquestioned condition of political freedom.

Starting in the twentieth century, the variety of events and occasions that brought together people who had hitherto rarely had a chance to meet and discuss their respective political fates was little short of extraordinary. While the Paris Peace Conference of 1919 has long exemplified the moment when interstate diplomacy was made subject to global public attention and even some scrutiny, it was hardly the only moment when nonstate political actors sought to draw international attention to their causes and plight.[23] An incomplete list of meetings that rejected the existing world order in some way would include the Universal Races Conference, London, 1911; the Baku Congress of Peoples of the East, 1920; the Bierville Peace Conference of 1926; and the 1927 anticolonial conference held in Brussels, which brought together 180 delegates from thirty-four countries and would lead to the formation of the Berlin-based League Against Imperialism.[24] It was at Baku, for instance, that the Indian Communist M. N. Roy first articulated his thesis on the dangers of supporting anticolonial nationalism in opposition to the Leninist line that saw bourgeois revolutions in the colonial world as potential tools in the global struggle against capitalism.[25] Regionally focused meetings included the first Pan-Asiatic Congress at Nagasaki in 1926; the Pan-Asiatic Conference in Shanghai in 1927; the All-Asia Education Conference, Benares, 1930; the All-Asia Women's Conference, Lahore, 1931; and the Pan-Asiatic Labour Congress, Colombo, 1934.[26] At these meetings, Asian nationalists were able to meet each other as well as supporters of their causes from Europe and the United States, offering them the ability to develop cosmopolitan critiques of imperialism that exceeded national boundaries and adopted an explicitly transnational scale.

As the scales, origins, and content of transnational and cross-border flows increased and multiplied in the new century, the social and economic landscapes of colonial and metropolitan worlds began to change markedly. On the one hand, metropolitan advances in areas as different as botanical knowledge, public health, urban sanitation, disease eradication, criminology, anthropology, fingerprinting, pharmaceuticals, and even educational curricula had long been a product of the monopolized imperial relationship with the colony.[27] Modern Western national consciousness itself could best be seen in relation to the imperial encounter, as Hannah Arendt would suggest: "The truth was that only far from home could a citizen of England, Germany or France be nothing but an Englishman, German, or Frenchman."[28] On the other hand, imperial boundaries that had kept metropole from colony and colonies from each other now began to break down under the pressures of rapidly moving global capital and a flood of new ideas that spoke to the illegitimacy of political and social relationships hitherto considered unquestionable. If what it meant to be a Spanish

Catholic had once been largely shaped by the decisions of colonial administrators in South America,[29] if the goods available in Indian shops were once almost entirely produced in Britain and its dependencies,[30] if no small part of French scientific knowledge was once shaped by its explorations and scientists working in its Indochina colonies,[31] none of these conditions was any longer obvious. The diminished ability to keep empires apart would most vividly (and for some, disturbingly) be expressed by colonial soldiers from Africa and Asia fighting in Europe during World War I. The proximity of these subalterns to the local populations they were defending would lead inevitably to the violation of one of the greatest taboos of colonial order, namely, the sexual barrier between white women and black men.[32]

Along with the dissolution of older political and economic boundaries; the increasing movement of people, goods, and ideas; and the growth of what we now call international civil society movements, other entities would take their place in defining the international. After World War I and the proclamation of a new liberal-global norm of national self-determination, a proliferation of new entities began to shape the new international scale. These included entirely new countries carved out of the defeated Ottoman and Austro-Hungarian empires, as well as novel political spaces variously called protectorates, dependencies, and territories, entities with considerably different degrees of formal and recognized sovereignty. Joining the still familiar, if constitutionally different, political entities now shaping the international scale were a new set of transnational institutions that emerged as a result of the formation of the League of Nations, the first genuinely transnational organization of states ever created.[33] In retrospect, the League may be less important for its failings as an institution devoted to promoting collective security and world peace and remembered more for the technical agencies created under its aegis, some of which are still part of the transnational landscape today. The International Labor Organization, the World Health Organization, and the Food and Agriculture Organization in particular would stand as transnational supplements to national governments in the provision of basic services and social infrastructure by offering novel biopolitical standards and know-how in an effort to enable all populations to reach minimum standards of working dignity, nutrition, and health.[34] Their experts and reports would influence and shape global standards and "best practices" in these and other areas, often with a strong bias for state-run organizations over the private sector, influenced heavily by a humanitarian and noncapitalist ethos. Moreover, the staffs of these organizations were not drawn solely from the Western world but also included personnel from the colonies and newly independent nation-states, even if often at different rates of emolument.[35] A further set of transnational technical agencies offering international public goods, such as railway track gauges, wireless communications, posts and telegraphs, civil aviation, scientific terms, standards, and measurements continued to grow and become stronger during this period. Olympic Games and Nobel Prizes would each affirm the primacy of the nation-scale while also working to reinforce the idea of a scale beyond the state where national desires could receive expression. Finally, an International Court of Justice was created at the Hague: although the court, given its subordination to the states that created it, may have been relatively toothless in practice, it nonetheless reinforced the symbolic possibility of a Kantian cosmopolitan liberalism where the injustices of the past would receive redress. Even as these emergent political formations came to be more visible, victorious empires moved swiftly to expand, in some cases, and to consolidate their existing territorial possessions, in others. Some empires may have been defeated, but the remaining others took steps to ensure their continued existence, including by offering a larger quotient of political rights and entitlements to their subjugated populations.[36]

The link between a rapidly transforming international system and domestic political arrangements lies in the conceptual and spatial conjunction of nation, state, and territory. Historians may debate exactly when this moment became dominant; for my argument, it is sufficient to remember that this three-way intersection is a historical moment. From the point of view of the former colonial world, the Paris Peace Conference of 1919 is generally accepted as the moment when U.S. President Woodrow Wilson's call for national self-determination was broadly accepted as a universal standard for political freedom, even if it was not intended to address them at all. For the first time, aspirations to political freedom were defined solely in terms of—and limited to—membership of a sovereign, physically bounded territorial nation-state. At once, political projects around the world had no choice but to be redefined in these terms. To be free, subjugated peoples now had to meet the new standard of national self-determination: they had to conform to the identity of one people–one land–one state to be accepted as having a legitimate claim to political personhood. That meeting these standards was next to impossible; that nations were beyond unambiguous definition; that colonial administrative boundaries separated kin, peoples, and cultures; and that practically no existing state conformed to these strictures was hardly the point. From the point of view of those seeking to overcome political unfreedom, a new mandate had been proclaimed, however imprecise and contradictory. As the history of the twentieth century makes only too clear, the imperative of national self-determination could become the contradictory justification for both the division of nations across more than one state as well as the creation of territorial states comprised of more than one nation.

National self-determination may have sounded to some as the apogee of an enlightened liberalism. To most others, even ostensible beneficiaries, this call immediately took on a far more ominous tone. Historian Mark Mazower records a resident of the Polish city of Lvi'v, speaking to an American visitor in 1919: "You see these little holes? We call them here 'Wilson's Points.' They have been made with machine guns; the big gaps have been made with hand grenades. We are now engaged in self-determination, and God knows what and when the end will be."[37] Colonies like India did not immediately descend into violent conflict, as did much of Eastern and Central Europe and Asia Minor after Wilson's call for self-determination, but the dilemmas facing colonial subjects seeking political independence were of no small order. First of all, multinational and diasporic—in other words, normal—countries like India hardly conformed to the impossible standard of one people–one land–one state. As we shall see in Chapter 2 of this volume, this gap between prescription and diagnosis led Indian nationalists into discursive convolutions trying both to meet and to reject the new prescriptions for political independence.

In the absence of any possibility of meeting the newly sanctified standard of national self-determination, colonial nationalists sought to redefine the prime criterion for independent statehood as unified political control over a defined piece of land, or territorial sovereignty. This eminently pragmatic move had grave unintended consequences. Once territorial sovereignty was established as the way out of the impossible one land–people–state trinity, the loss of state territory could become nothing less than the loss of state power. Defining the right to sovereignty through territorial control thus carried with it the seeds of two kinds of future conflict. The first may be summarized as territorial disputes between states; the second concerns the political effects of dividing territories internally. Foreign policy, the boundary-making technology that separates inside from outside, is, we realize, first and foremost a problem of territoriality.

Outline of the Study

I have already flagged a number of concepts and themes that are addressed in more detail in the following chapters. Regardless, the starting point for this discussion is territory, the "hyphen," to borrow anthropologist Arjun Appadurai's apposite formulation, that both joins and divides nation and state, incompletely and ambivalently, with complex political consequences.[38] But territory is not just land, just as territory is not just terrain. Territory, geographer Stuart Elden argues, is "something that is both [land and terrain] and more than these."[39] Territory involves power: it is a political claim over land and terrain by social groups. Territoriality, as will be explained in more detail in the next chapter, is a spatial strategy that ties together space and society through political investments in particular places.[40] Territorial disputes, in other words, cannot be reduced to interstate competition over land or terrain. If territory were just about the natural resource of land, it would be possible—if not necessarily easy—to find forms of equivalence or compensation that would permit the exchange of lands between states to resolve outstanding territorial disputes. The difficulty of even imagining what such a trade might look like only reinforces the need to think of territory in more complex ways.

This task is undertaken in the first chapter. Beginning with a discussion of territorial sovereignty as it is conventionally understood in International Relations, we find that the core concepts of territory and territoriality receive little critical attention, to the considerable detriment of analysis. Drawing on work in human geography, the chapter then summarizes the scholarship that allows us to make sense of the complex interrelation of space and territory. To place these general concerns in concrete detail, the chapter then turns to a review of literature on the spaces of Indian nationalism. At once, the uneven character of the national landscape becomes clear, with territorial divisions separating the different Indian religious communities in the effort to define the nation. The following section turns to a discussion of foreign policy, understood as a state territorial practice seeking to stabilize the shifting meanings of territory. In their effort to distinguish national and state spaces unambiguously, foreign policy practices territorialize much more than land. The chapter closes with a discussion of the territorialization of women's bodies as a means to fix notions of national patriarchal honor and to compensate for the loss of land at the moment when the Indian state became sovereign.

The second chapter takes a more historical turn in addressing the character of the international system leading up to Indian independence. It takes as a starting point the Paris Peace Conference of 1919 insofar as it deals with questions of race and national self-determination. This historic conference also exposed as never before the racial underpinnings of the contemporary international order, as even Japan, the only nonwhite Great Power, eventually came to realize. "India" played a double role at this conference. It was both an official delegate as well as an insurgent presence seeking entry to demand freedom from colonial rule. Indian efforts to garner support for its independence are contrasted with Ireland's effort to do the same, showing how the common idea of national self-determination produced very different discourses of freedom from Britain's biggest and closest colonies, respectively. Both tendencies lead to the same outcome. Claiming territorial sovereignty would turn out to be a necessary means by which to resolve the problems of incomplete international personhood and India's lack of conformity to the ideal type of nation-state. This discussion shows that international recognition—external sovereignty—is best understood as a rule that governs and conditions the entrance of new states into the international order. To meet the elusive conditions of international recognition, India would come to reterritorialize its national body to exclude persons of Indian origin living outside state borders.

Bringing the findings of both chapters together allows new insight into one of Asia's endemic problems, interstate territorial disputes. These disputes are both protracted and charged because they are about much more than a simple loss or gain of a property relation (territory as land) or a politico-strategic relation (terrain). The additional constraint begins from the emotional and affective meaning invested in territory deemed national by the state and its people. Territorial disputes become contentious when they involve the (loss or regain of) space of the nation. Territory seen as national space makes compensation for the loss of territory beyond the reach of normal diplomacy. The core problem with territorial loss is that it opens the door to an excavation of the relationship of state and nation. It exposes the nation as a historically contingent formation and brings into question the state's claim to represent this nation, now and in the past. Territorial disputes are, to borrow a Freudian metaphor, the spatial unconscious of the state: the return of this repressed historical memory brings back to life interred possibilities of other plausible political futures.

That said, what further complicates matters is that national space need not be fixed in time, be limited by standard cartographic categories, or even be materially identifiable. Disputes have broken out over islands that have temporarily emerged from river silt formations and volcanic eruptions, lands have been claimed on the basis of myth and legend, and imaginary homelands such as Lemuria are believed to lie under water.[41] Moreover, national space is unevenly distributed across state territories; that is, not all land or terrain lying within state boundaries matters to the same extent. To make matters worse, not all state territories include space that belongs to the nation, and not all national spaces are controlled by the national state. Yet, with all this, it also cannot be forgotten that state territories have been given away in the past without necessitating the perceived loss of national space and without producing hostile popular nationalist reactions. For all their seeming intractability, territorial disputes can and have been resolved.

What this farrago of confused categories and contradictory relations adds up to is that the general phenomenon of territorial disputes cannot be understood via a forensic analysis of the origins of particular disputes. Such an approach, prominent in legal and diplomatic discourses, cannot explain why some territorial disputes become contentious and protracted and others do not. Nor do these approaches explain why some disputes can be resolved by the withdrawal of official state claims to lost lands, while others cannot. I have already pointed to the importance of the national investment in land and terrain as the complicating factor in understanding the meaning of territory; to understand how this territorial "surplus" became political space involves an entirely different approach.

Understanding territorial disputes begins by appreciating how the relationship between sovereignty and territory came to be so intertwined and naturalized such that not only is state sovereignty conflated with territorial control, but also how the loss of territory came to be identified as a crisis of state sovereignty. Given the highly emotive popular reaction to territorial disputes, understanding territorial disputes also requires understanding how some nationals come to identify so much with the territorial equation of state power that the intensity of their celebration of territorial gain can only be matched by the extent of their shock at the loss of territory, leading to its public representation as a form of state treason. Subjecting the territory–sovereignty equation to a critical historical examination, the object of the first chapter, allows us to see why some national territories matter and others do not and why some disputes become protracted while others do not. The historical contingency of the territory–sovereignty relation points to possible resolutions of this problem; it allows for the possibility of reimagining the relation of land, territory, nation, and state in ways other than the simple possessive equation characteristic of state territorial sovereignty.

The third and fourth chapters of this book turn to the spatial practices of foreign policy: how nation and state come to be joined through territory. India is a country where the boundaries of nation and state have never explicitly coincided. Given this unsettled starting point, the final objective of the territorializing practices of foreign policy is to bind nation and state through territory such that there is a unique identification of a nation with a state and its territory. The particular foreign policy practices—how territorial sovereignty is made "on the ground"—addressed in this book are glossed as diaspora and geopolitics respectively. Diaspora is a state practice that separates the territorially bound nation from its overseas community. It produces "insiders without," namely, nationals who live beyond the state's territorial borders. Geopolitics is a practice that, in the process of creating state borders that are defensible and secure, results in the creation of "outsiders within," nonnationals who live within recognized state borders. Diaspora foreign policy practices changed radically before and after independence and are now in the process of changing again. The practices of postcolonial geopolitics turn out to be wholly consistent with imperial strategies of defending and extending colonial Indian territorial boundaries.

Foreign policy as *diaspora* traces the shifting boundary that divides the global Indian nation. Foreign policy at the moment of independence territorialized what was once a global nation into mutually exclusive political categories: citizens of territorial India and an overseas population without recourse to political rights and protections guaranteed by the Indian state. This division took place in spite of the close involvement of a globally dispersed diaspora with the struggle for Indian independence to assuage the fears of India's Asian neighbors, among other reasons. In recent years, the boundary between a territorial state and a global nation has been substantially relocated. The diaspora has now been brought much closer to India through new regimes of deterritorialized citizenship. These shifts are best explained by seeing the inscription of boundaries within the global Indian nation in terms of class and caste. If earlier representations of overseas Indians produced the *girmitiya*, economically poor and socially inferior, making it relatively easy for upper-caste elites to draw a line between "India" and them at the moment of independence, such a view did not hold by the end of the twentieth century. The overseas Indian could now be represented as an upper-caste, middle-class person who had left India for reasons of "discrimination" and loss of economic mobility. This social flight was produced by a socialistically inclined state and exacerbated by the expansion of political participation among India's "backward" castes and "untouchable" Dalits. A deeply conservative class-based and antidemocratic critique of "reservations," the Indian term for affirmative action, underwrites territorial India's return to its diaspora in the last two decades. With the economic success of Indians overseas it became possible to attempt to restore the hierarchy of the Hindu social order through this "objective" proof that upper-caste talents were not dependent on inherited privilege. Nonresident Indians could now be celebrated as exemplars of the new global Indian, with India now understood in deterritorialized terms. What needs to be stressed is that what changed in the fifty years between Indian independence in 1947 and the end of the twentieth century is not "India" but dominant representations of India's diaspora.

Foreign policy as *geopolitics* also inscribes boundaries between state and nation, but very differently. India's territorial boundaries had long been in a state of flux due to a century of subordination to imperial strategic imperatives. Over the nineteenth and twentieth centuries, the area of the territorial state repeatedly shifted, expanding as new territories were incorporated and contracting as other territories were granted autonomy from Calcutta and then New Delhi (for example, the Straits Settlements and Burma). These imperatives had led to the mapping of Indian territory in relation to a strategic logic that inscribed a hierarchy of spaces within the Indian state. There was a territorial heartland, the ultimate object of state protection, and extended strategic peripheries that included protectorates, dependencies, and suzerainties, bordered by unsettled frontiers and uncivilized "buffers." British Indian geopolitics, ostensibly a spatial catalogue of territorial divisions for national security, was reinforced by civilizational boundaries. The colonial gaze justified the systematic political exclusion and marginalization of residents of culturally liminal but geopolitically significant borderlands in terms of their alleged lack of civilization, creating a space of exception at the eastern limits of the country. With sovereignty in 1947, fluid imperial boundaries became the fixed borders of the nation-state. These borders now incorporated territories and peoples that could not be easily identified as culturally "Indian" and, who, moreover, soon came to define themselves in opposition to a predatory Indian nation-state. The exceptional status of the Northeast as a site of irreducible difference now works, perversely, to normalize the rest of India. Foreign policy as geopolitics created national boundaries *within* the Indian territorial state.

Seen as a boundary-making practice, foreign policy becomes central to our understanding of modern citizenship. Once territory becomes a necessary but historically contingent and unstable hyphen joining nation and state, foreign policy practices produce a sharply uneven domestic topos. The "body politic" comes to be internally divided and hierarchically organized through the spatialization of difference. Territorial practices created boundaries that produced permanent majorities and minorities and that excluded populations from the national center on the basis of ethnicity, class, religion, gender, and putative civilizational status. Political difference is endemic to the particular intersection of territory and sovereignty that is hegemonic today under the sign of the nation-state. Unequal and uneven forms of citizenship, I argue, are structural features of the territorially bound nation-state.

This interpretation of Indian foreign policy offers important insights into the process of decolonization. The diaspora chapter demonstrates how the new nations of Southeast Asia had completely internalized the logic of national self-determination. That logic played itself out by normalizing the concepts of national homeland, demographic majority, and ethnic minority as structural features of new Asian nation-states. Overnight, amnesia overcame this region's long and polyglot histories of social inclusion, popular mobility, and cultural hybridity. Countries that had once represented social diversity in all respects now became redefined in oppositional terms: *bumiputra*, an autochthonous and unmarked majority, and others: distinct ethnic and cultural minorities. Minorities were understood to be of two kinds. Emigrants from large and powerful neighbors, who were too new to be assimilated to the nation-state; and indigenous "tribal" people, who were too old.

Placing together the findings from this discussion of diaspora and geopolitics offers us an altogether novel view of India's historically vexed relations with its closest neighbor, Pakistan. The Muslim-majority state of Pakistan that now interrupts colonial India's northwestern strategic frontier can be seen as the spatial intersection of both geopolitics and diaspora: in both cases, it also stands as their ultimate negation. The people of Pakistan are India's closest diaspora yet are also, because they are predominantly Muslim, an alien corpus that can never be incorporated into the national body. The Pakistani state occupies a territory that, due to its sovereignty, highlights the breakdown of the colonial geopolitical scheme that India long relied on for its military security by extending its frontiers far beyond its national heartland. The existence of Pakistan—people and territory—defies the logic of the structures that underpin the Indian nation-state's foreign policies of diaspora and geopolitics. That is why, unless India unterritorializes its way of thinking and seeing the world, Pakistan can never be seen as anything but a fundamental crisis. Pakistan's continued existence represents an ongoing contradiction of the territorially bound and imagined Indian nation-state.

1

Territory and Foreign Policy

My primary concern, to recapitulate, is to understand how the path taken to Indian decolonization had profound but poorly appreciated political consequences. As the introduction details, my understanding of the impact of external forces on postcolonial outcomes is developed in two parts, the first examining the character of India's encounter with the world, the second focusing on the effects of that foreign encounter on its domestic political futures. This chapter and the next outline India's encounter with the world. Taken together, the first half of this book offers a new understanding of how territorial disputes have come to raise such intense passions among elites and domestic publics, even if the land involved is economically and politically worthless, and also of why the exchange of territory between states is almost always portrayed as a net loss to state power even when the objective benefits of resolving territorial disputes include a mutual improvement in bilateral relations and greater regional peace and stability.

The extensive scholarly discussion of interstate territorial disputes begins from the very practical concern that struggles over territory are a grave danger to the maintenance of international order.[1] A higher order concern justifies extreme reactions to territorial loss because such loss brings state sovereignty into question. Both concerns are entirely sensible but beg the larger question. Few scholars stop to ask why the loss or gain of territory should raise such intense emotions and generate such serious political challenges. Fewer still stop to consider what territory entails and what these entailments mean. By not exposing the concept of territory to a more critical examination, prevailing scholarship ends up reinforcing the very relation that this chapter seeks to bring into question, namely the historical and political contingency of the link between territorial possession and modern state power. To find answers to these important questions requires untangling the meanings and significance of the relationship of territory, state, and, as I shall argue, nation.

This is no easy task, as the conjoined meanings of these concepts are now so interwoven that it seems impossible to imagine the modern state without reference to "its" territory.[2] What territory is to the state is not unlike the relation between history and the nation: a self-reinforcing bond that leads to the replacement of the subject with the object.[3] Not only does it appear that territory has always been the basis of state power, it also seems impossible today to imagine modern political authority without reference to exclusive territorial control. No matter how ubiquitous these beliefs, such a formulation turns the larger problematic of territory and sovereignty entirely around. The question ought to be: How did relations between territory and nation-state come to be so dominated by the idea of sovereignty as exclusionary control that no other possibility seems politically viable? Territorial sovereignty, the first half of this book will argue, became a universal condition only when former colonies like India achieved independence and found they had little choice but to define themselves in territorial terms. It was only when postcolonial states accepted preexisting colonial administrative borders that territorial sovereignty became the universal norm it appears to be today.

The starting point for this chapter is the contemporary difficulty of imagining modern political life without the prior condition of territorial possession and control. It seeks, in other words, to address the mystification of the command of territory as a precondition for political life and state existence through an interrogation of the core concepts of this study: territory and foreign policy. The need to return to the obscured origins of the coproduction of territory and sovereignty is suggested by Henri Lefèbvre when he notes, "Each state claims to produce a space wherein something is accomplished—a space even, where something is brought to perfection: namely, a unified and hence homogenous society."[4] Bringing "something" to perfection is a claim about how the political field seamlessly joins the spatial: it requires understanding territory's ability to give the nation-state, in Paul Allies's words, "a physical basis which seems to render it inevitable and eternal."[5] "Accomplishment" for Lefèbvre means that territorial sovereignty, the unity of nation, state, and territory, should appear to have no history; it should seem to be as if this trinity has always been in place. This appearance is necessary for the state to generate the official fiction that it has always been and is the only legitimate organizer of political life within a particular place. Such a fiction both enables and requires the state to resist any threat to the stability of the nation-state-territory trinity at any cost.

In the familiar conjunction "territorial sovereignty," the qualifier *territory*, if addressed at all, is usually taken to be homogenous, fixed, bounded, ahistorical, and singular. Yet the discussion that follows draws precisely the opposite conclusions. As human geographers have long argued, territory is neither stable nor fixed but inherently variable and includes much more than just land and terrain. This unstable and multisited view of territory opens the door to understanding foreign policy as the geopolitical equivalent of David Harvey's idea of the "territorial fix."[6] Foreign policy, this chapter will argue, is a state response to the fluidity of territory and is best understood as a set of enactive and performative practices that seek to stabilize territorial uncertainty. States invest territory with epistemic and material stability to appear to stand as irreplaceable and inevitable conditions of modern political life; in other words, state space as accomplishment, even perfection.

To explore these issues, this chapter is divided into the following sections. The first section offers an overview of debates in IR on territorial sovereignty. It shows that dominant conceptions of territorial sovereignty are conceptually and historically inadequate, necessitating a closer examination of the concepts of territory and territoriality. Drawing on work in critical geography allows us to understand territoriality as a set of practices—technologies—that seek to control and define space and thus to appreciate how territory emerges as an uneven, hierarchical, and divided political outcome. Exploring techniques of mapping and visualizing space in colonial India drives this point home. We find the anticolonial nationalist imaginary produces a territorial vision of India as a fissured and uneven space that ranks Hindus, as rightful owners, above Muslims, seen as an "irreducible alterity."

Foreign policy, the following section proposes, is best understood as a state territorial practice concerned primarily with stabilizing the fluidity of territory through boundary making. In general, foreign policies seek to institute ontic boundaries between home and abroad, a distinction that equally establishes the psychic difference between safe and unsafe. Although typically understood to be in operation beyond the state's geophysical limits, this section works through what happens in the contradictory effort to engender regions of absolute "domestic" safety, namely, the production of deep internal fissures and hierarchies *within* the domestic community. Foreign policy boundaries enunciated across national and state spaces produce hierarchies and unevenness both within as well as across national and state territories. The chapter closes with a symptomatic account of "foreign" policy's effort to engender separate and stable domains of security and insecurity. Through a reading of the narratives of "abducted women" during the formation of India and Pakistan in 1947, it becomes clear how the violent territorialization of women's bodies was a necessary step to securing and restoring a masculinized sense of honor under threat of being swept away by a feminized condition of shame and violation.

Demystifying Territorial Sovereignty

Discussions of territorial sovereignty rarely expose the term *territory* to critical scrutiny. Sovereignty is the focus of attention, and the rise of territorial sovereignty as a global norm is the main object of analysis. Before analyzing the variable meanings of *territory* and their consequential political implications, this section reminds us of the lack of agreement over the origins of the so-called norm of territorial sovereignty. Political geographer John Agnew has long criticized "fields such as international relations and political geography [for operating] very much as if sovereign territorial states and the modern state system associated with them have not only been around from time immemorial [but] will continue to do so indefinitely."[7] Political theorist Rob Walker proposes that by not considering how a sovereign approach to land emerged historically and became the dominant and normalized meaning of territory, international relations mistakenly allocates political space a prior ontological existence.[8] Historian James Sheehan weighs in to note, "The state is an important part of this history [of territorial sovereignty], but not its natural or inevitable culmination."[9] IR scholar John Ruggie forthrightly states not only that "systems of rule need not be territorial . . . [and] systems of rule need not be territorially fixed . . . [but also] the prevailing concept of territory need not entail mutual exclusion."[10] Before turning to how territory—understood as an exclusive and sovereign space—has become the sine qua non of modern state existence, the following discussion highlights the weak historical and conceptual foundations of prevailing understandings of territorial sovereignty in IR.

The views quoted in the preceding paragraph are far from typical. Much more commonplace in IR is the assumption of territorial acquisition as an unquestioned good, a belief that is held to have been dominant since the Treaty of Westphalia (1648). Westphalia is proclaimed as the moment when the idea of territorial sovereignty became hegemonic, coterminous with the emergence of the modern state as the primary unit of international life.[11] As Mark Zacher states confidently, "In . . . [the] early years of the Westphalian order, territory was the main factor that determined the wealth and security of states, and thus the protection and acquisition of territory were prime motivations of foreign policy"; hence, it is implied, it is no surprise that states fight over territory.[12] Daniel Philpott's account of modern sovereignty makes complementary claims regarding the arrival of the modern state and the primacy of territorial conceptions of sovereignty. He argues that the significance of Westphalia, following the earlier Treaty of Augsburg, comes from the shift of political authorities that reduced internecine wars among European Christian principalities and marked the end of the "supraterritorial government" of the Holy Roman Empire. After Westphalia, he argues, "States were virtually uninhibited in their authority over internal matters," a reading that implies both the equation of "internal" with "territorial" and the replacement of empire by state as the preeminent international actor.[13]

Recent scholarship, however, has questioned these assertions in multiple ways.[14] First of all, the treaty's association with an understanding of sovereignty as exclusive control has been examined and rejected as a view that conflates legal jurisdiction with supreme control. In his well-known counterreading of Westphalia, Stephen Krasner argues persuasively that the treaty matters less for the onset of ideas of exclusive territorial sovereignty and more because it forced princes to accept limits to their sovereignty in the form of protections for religious minorities living within their spatial jurisdiction.[15] To the extent that Westphalia was even universally accepted as a binding constraint on royal behavior, in other words, it indexes a conception of sovereignty that is far from exclusive and points, additionally, to the heterogeneity of the "people" living within a political jurisdiction. Moreover, Edward Keene argues that, well after Westphalia, sovereignty in practice often remained partial and divisible. Land in one sovereign's realm could be the property of individuals subject to another, physically distant, sovereign.[16]

Second, there is little evidence that territory was the "main factor" determining state wealth at this time. Proponents of this view often quote approvingly Charles Tilly's famous statement about the reduction of the number of states in Europe from "500 to about 25" over the course of three centuries.[17] This datum makes it appear that absorption of smaller units into larger ones is best explained by the centrality of territory to prevailing conceptions of wealth and power. Tilly's classic account, however, suffers from serious problems of both functionalism and what might be called evolutionism. Starting by seeking an explanation of why the modern state acquired its preeminence in the modern era, he looks backward to propose that this form of political organization was the most functionally equipped to survive the challenges of the period, putting, in effect, the conceptual cart before the empirical horse. Moreover, it is difficult to describe the twenty-five remaining entities in nineteenth-century Europe as "states" with any degree of accuracy. Most, including the richest—Britain, France, and the Netherlands—were hybrid political entities that combined features of the modern state with respect to governmentality with zones of indirect and illiberal rule within a global imperial organization, a political formation that Jane Burbank and Frederick Cooper call "empire states."[18] Others, including the Austro-Hungarian and German systems, combined aspects of noncontiguous imperial rule with confederal systems of allegiance and domination. Finally, even if it is conceded that territory was the prime source of wealth in Western Europe between the seventeenth and nineteenth centuries, it does not follow that territorial sovereignty preceded legal understandings of state existence. Sheehan reinforces this point, noting that changing legal powers shaped understandings of modern sovereignty, not vice versa: "The expansion of the legal system was not just an instrument of an expanding sovereign authority, it was the process itself."[19] Meanings of European sovereignty were still very much in flux at this time rather than fixed around territory.

Perhaps the most stinging critique of the equation of Westphalia with territorial sovereignty and the rise of the modern state comes from legal historians. Much of the IR scholarship seems unaware that one of the founding works of modern sovereignty, Jean Bodin's *On Sovereignty*, "is notable for its utter lack of attention, and even mention, of territory." Legal historian Lauren Benton goes to say, "Bodin did not omit territory as a category through some oversight. His view was consistent with an early modern construction of sovereignty as spatially elastic. Because subjects could be located anywhere, and the tie between sovereign and subject was defined as a legal relationship, legal authority was not bound territorially." Her work demonstrates that, from the seventeenth century onward, territorial sovereignty was more often than not segmented, partial, fragmented, and divided. By conflating long-running struggles over legal jurisdictions with uniform territorial control, most studies of sovereignty explain the rise of a territorial sovereign state as functionally superior to other forms of political organization.[20] Not only does this view not address the ambiguous condition of rule over physically forbidding regions such as mountains, it ignores nonterritorial forms of rule that were a characteristic feature of European power in the period of overseas empires.[21] Emerging conceptions of sovereignty, rights, legitimacy, wars, and justice not only had to grapple with states and people, they were often driven by the actions of "nonstate actors" such as trading companies, freebooters, and pirates.[22] In short, what Westphalia "means" remains far from settled.

Turan Kayaoglu has recently summarized the literature on Westphalia to show that "many norms and institutions attributed to the Peace of Westphalia emerged much later, in the eighteenth and nineteenth centuries."[23] Westphalia, for him, becomes a means by which IR narrates a history for itself that privileges the European origins of the international system. Other scholarship points to the serious conceptual problems that arise from treating the European continent—notably its western edges—as history's great exception, based on the unconvincing premise of its geographic exclusivity.[24] The general disciplinary unwillingness to see Europe's political transformations in a larger spatial context has long plagued our understandings of the emergence of modern conceptions of sovereignty. The systematic exclusion of vital connections between Europe and the rest of the world makes it impossible to appreciate that imperial and colonial encounters were central to understanding how modern territorial sovereignty came to dominate other understandings of spatial organization. While the next chapter spells out how European "positive" international law emerged through engagement with ideas of natural law and customary practice already well established in Asia, there are numerous other examples to draw on. Anthony Pagden and Nicolas Way Gomez, for example, have explored the debates surrounding definitions of the New World as *terra nullis* and resulting conceptions of property, humans, and legal rights "back home" in the European heartland.[25]

The evidence from other world regions offers very different equations of resources and state power. In Southeast Asia and Africa, state power was not necessarily enhanced by the capture of territory. Achille Mbembe uses the term *itinerant territoriality* to describe patterns of political power in areas of precolonial West Africa that were long-lasting but never adopted fixed geopolitical boundaries of rule and control,[26] while James Scott states bluntly that "the concentration of manpower was the key to political power in premodern Southeast Asia."[27] In areas of labor shortage, capturing people, not land, was the great prize for kingdoms seeking not just to increase their power but also to survive. Sovereignty itself, he argues, was often best understood in terms of concentric circles, with state power declining rapidly outside a core settled area. This meant that regions lying on the borders of two or more kingdoms often had considerable autonomy, a condition they would use to their advantage, leading to a situation where "sovereignty was ambiguous, plural, shifting, and often void altogether."[28] Territorial possession did not necessarily equate to wealth and power, and state sovereignty was rarely defined in terms of exclusive control analogous to the private ownership of property.

The limits of prevailing conceptions of territory, state, and sovereignty do not end here. Although recent scholarship has shown how technologies such as mapmaking played a critical role in making possible the imagination of territory as a homogenous state space, the issue goes well beyond that.[29] Not only are dominant accounts of the emergence of territorial sovereignty between Westphalia and the Treaty of Vienna (1815) shot through with conceptual and historical flaws, the study of the period that follows is equally problematic. The place of territory as an indispensable element of state formation begins to change in commentaries on the eighteenth and nineteenth centuries, when the idea of the nation-state first makes its appearance. What becomes apparent at this moment is that territory, once the preeminent foundation of the modern Western state, is no longer considered a stable, uniform, and fixed analytic category. The implications of this conceptual shift are profound.

Consider Kalevi J. Holsti's well-known account of the territorial foundations of state sovereignty. Holsti is concerned to understand a long-running puzzle, the so-called norm of antiterritorial revision, namely, the relative stability of most international boundaries during the last century in spite of massive change in the international order.[30] He explains the power of the norm by highlighting how the meanings of territory have changed from Westphalia to the modern period. Holsti argues that popular sovereignty was the turning point. After the French Revolution, territory was no longer merely a "piece of real estate," as it was treated under the rule of despotic sovereigns, but became the physical and emotional basis of a "political community." The argument runs as follows: Once despotic sovereignty was replaced by a conception of sovereignty that drew on popular assent, state territories became redefined as national homelands.[31] This enduring emotional bond between people and land becomes an inertial force preventing boundaries from changing. From a historical standpoint, the critical event took place when "territory . . . became the most obvious marker of a people and their identity." State ownership of land is supplanted by culture. When "nationalism and Romanticism" became "grafted" onto territory, it becomes a national homeland.[32] In this account, popular sovereignty is a function of nationalism; national identity requires a territorial homeland; hence, territory takes on the meaning of homeland through the people who identify with it. This description of the process by which territory—allegedly the "most obvious marker" of identity—becomes the expression and embodiment of a people while also being the precondition for their identification is circular. In Marxist terminology, the explanation is entirely "mystified." Holsti identifies but fails to appreciate the full implications of a conception of territory that changes meanings—from real estate to homeland—over time by conflating it with a simultaneous shift in meanings of sovereignty: from despotic to popular.

The French Revolution has long been acknowledged as the critical turning point in the formation of a national people. Yet even this seminal shift to popular sovereignty did not include a unique attachment to a national homeland. Instead, it drew into question the very idea of a homogenous "nation." Historians have long argued that the attachment of people in French-speaking territories for "France" remained quite tenuous as late as the twentieth century.[33] Among the first acts of the new revolutionary government was to impose restrictions on movement of "foreigners," defined as French citizens whose domiciles were other than Paris, dividing the French nation on the basis of privileged location.[34] Under Napoleon Bonaparte, not only was "France" an extremely heterogeneous space, including as it did parts of Germany while excluding the Vendée, but what we mean by the "French nation" under Napoleon was also being "built in the non-European parts of the Empire."[35] (And, it might be pointed out, the inheritors of liberty, equality, and fraternity moved swiftly to restore slavery to Haiti, the first colony to claim freedom for itself).[36] Burbank and Cooper argue that post-Revolutionary France is best understood in terms of a core and a periphery, a proposition that reshapes conceptions of equal, uniform, homogenous state territory into a differentiated and hierarchical landscape of land and terrain divided by political authorities.[37] They argue that, when seen on a global scale, it is far more appropriate to use the term *empire-state*, rather than *nation-state*, for countries like France, England, and the Netherlands, a term that confounds the normative ideals of a homogenous national people, a uniform state space and contiguous territorial sovereignty. Once territory is neither uniform nor conceptually stable, it throws into doubt its other political dependents, including people, state, and sovereignty. When it comes to conceptualizing territorial sovereignty, and the even more practical question of why countries go to war over territory, if what we mean by *territory* is not a homogenous political space but rather a hierarchically organized space that from its onset divided citizens from each other, privileged one region over another, was divided between competing authorities, had unstable boundaries that changed with differing historical contexts and representational practices, then clearly the term *territory* rests on very shaky intellectual foundations.

Territory as Technology: Visualizing Colonial India

Territory, geographer Stuart Elden argues, cannot be reduced to land or terrain. It is more than economic relations (land as property) or strategic relations (terrain as power), while remaining "something that is both of these, and more than these."[38] John Agnew argues for the historicity of the idea of political territoriality, which he defines as a particular "organization and exercise of power, legitimate or otherwise, over blocs of space."[39] Territoriality "entails . . . total mutual exclusion"; or, political space becomes identified with singular control and possession. Uncritically accepting the "territorial trap" of conflating the state with a clearly defined territory, Agnew and Corbridge argue, leads to the false metaphor that territory is the property of the state. Elden dismisses familiar conceptions of territoriality that have associations with biological drives and social needs and seeks to return political space to analytic center stage.[40] He argues that to appreciate territory as a "historical question: produced, mutable, and fluid" foregrounds *practices*, "rendering . . . the emergent concept of space as a political category: owned, distributed, mapped, calculated, bordered, and controlled."[41] Territory, far from being natural or obvious, should be understood as the spatial outcome of a specific set of territorializing practices.[42] Collectively, these views contest the view that political authority, under any name, will naturally gravitate to a form of power that has no choice but to treat the space under its control in a territorial way.

Elden's emphasis on the idea of territory as the spatial outcome of particular practices—territorialization as a political technology—points to the importance of measurement, mapping, and calculations in the making of modern political space. Among the most conventional techniques for territorializing space is the production of maps. Modern maps are of course much more than cartographic representations of space; they are congealed representations of knowledge deeply shaped by power relations. The apparent legibility and transparency of maps produced by the expertise of cartographic science, Irit Rogoff reminds us, "mask the interests that bring them into being." Maps, she says, "translate all the power relations and material and political realities and fantasmatic relations into a benign language of geographical taxonomies."[43] In what follows, changing techniques of mapping are seen to correspond to a shift from what Edward Soja calls a "social definition of territory to a territorial definition of society."[44] Entirely different conceptions of territory are produced when the techniques of measurement change, driven by entirely different interests, as illustrated by the shift in the transition from precolonial to colonial conceptions of Indian political space.

Take mapping in precolonial India. Once the English East India Company transformed from a trading company to a landed power, it soon realized the need to conduct surveys of their properties to "defend frontiers, chart inland and river trade routes, ascertain the extent and revenue potentials of cultivated lands and ensure the safety and regularity of communications."[45] Company maps emerged from the need to know better, and thereby better control, their newly acquired territories. Preexisting Indian maps could not be used for this purpose, for they obscured the project of control with all manner of other, less-than-relevant, information for the aspiring English ruler. C. A. Bayley divides the maps of this period into "a purely empirical idiom, an idiom of spiritual anthropology, 'moral ecology' and genealogy."[46] Mughal route maps contained reams of practical information for an army on the move but lacked precise scalar coordinates and cadastral specificity that would have helped more efficient revenue extraction. Other maps in circulation included genealogies of royal families, information about pilgrimage sites and temples, and the location of tradable goods, producing "an epicurean landscape including mangoes, guavas, bullocks, rice, pickle and medicines." Premodern maps often combined cosmological features like the mythical Mount Meru with details of the "real" world, confirming Orientalist skepticism over the value of Indian knowledge practices, even though the English had relied heavily on, especially, Indian maritime maps for conquest.[47] The immense Trigonometrical Survey of India begun in the waning years of the eighteenth century took this desire to know—to ascertain, ensure, and secure—to its logical extreme. Company officers could believe, however mistakenly, they were "constructing a single, complete, truthful, and ordered archive of geographical knowledge for their empire."[48] The belief that such an immense project was possible and the faith in the technology of triangulation speak to the heart of what would eventually become the colonial enterprise.[49] The epistemic differences between Indian and English maps during the period of Company rule point to very different ways of conceiving and visualizing the spatial world and its relation to human action, reflecting very different interests, in a narrow sense, and, more important, understandings of the meaning of territory.

In the process of fixing external boundaries through technologies of territorialization, it is important to realize that the spatial "interior" is going through its own changes of signification and meaning. Even as the territorial techniques involved may seek to invest the interior with an ahistorical homogeneity and spatial stability, mapping also produces internal instability and unevenness. A particular kind of unevenness emerges when territory becomes invested with a variety of social and cultural meanings that carry powerful affective dimensions. Popular forces acting on territory and incorporating passion, love, and devotion, as well as dread, threat, and insecurity, produce a political field that transforms the internal contours of territory. They lead to the privileging of some places over others and the elevation of some peoples over others.

Among the many sites of contestation between Indian nationalist forces and the British colonial state was the spatial-visual field. Possibly the most vivid example of such contestation emerged through a representation of the national body in the form of the figure of a sari-clad woman that would become sacralized as *Bharat Mata* (Mother India). In historian Sumathi Ramaswamy's recent book-length exploration of the *Bharat Mata* icon, we are introduced to an extraordinary array of images of "India" figured simultaneously as a cartographic map and a Hindu goddess, overlaid with a variety of "supplemental" images and signs that work to reinforce a composite image of visual nationalism. Ramaswamy argues that, for Indian nationalists, a mere cartographic map was "not an adequate representational device for picturing their country as homeland and motherland." The scientifically precise map of the country needed to be "supplemented" by something more: Echoing Benedict Anderson, she asks, how could the patriot be asked to "die for what were after all [mere] lines drawn on a piece of paper?"[50] Although it might appear that the overlay of the map with the goddess undermines and subverts the power of colonial knowledge in the form of scientific cartography, Ramaswamy makes precisely the opposite argument: "For once the world is carto-graphed . . . all discourses of territory, especially nonscientific, sentimental, and sacral ones, have to necessarily contend with . . . the scientific map form." It is in relation to the cartographic map of India, in other words, that other supplemental images have to locate themselves against and within. Even as the visual spectacle of India would be revisioned by anticolonial nationalists working in a variety of idioms, the political and cartographic boundaries of the territorial map of the country would be reinforced as the primary scale through which to visualize India.

One aspect of Ramaswamy's discussion in particular needs to be highlighted. By foregrounding the visual aspect of the territorializing *Bharat Mata* icon, she points to a representational aporia that "even the most pluralist or secular of her devotees have been unable to overcome." Although *Bharat Mata* tries to

> ... secure a plural and religiously diverse body politic ... the rational science of cartography itself ironically becomes complicit in picturing India as essentially and eternally Hindu ... Mother India's body thus functions as a microcosm of the nation's plural religious history, even as it is used to signal what can—and cannot—be included within its ample fold. Her carto-graphed form is pictured to suggest that members of India's diverse religious communities are co-dwellers of the Indian geo-body, but some more intimately than others.[51]

This visual marginalization of populations long resident in India through the territorial image of *Bharat Mata* reinforces Rogoff's claim that territorialization through mapping is hardly a neutral or benign process. The national body produced by *Bharat Mata* is unevenly Indian: the specter of populations located within but not of India is a deeply threatening trope that continues to haunt Indian territorial practices. Making the national body safe, in other words, cannot come solely from securing the dangerous outside; it must work on the "intimate enemy" lying within the national boundaries at the same time.[52]

Mapping is only one, albeit powerful, technique of territorialization. In a landmark study, Manu Goswami has outlined how the colonial state and its "moderate" critics among the Indian intelligentsia came to territorialize India.[53] The "production of colonial state space," as she puts it, came through the incorporation of a number of novel technologies, including the "institution and working of a massive web of transportation and irrigation structures," extending the reach of the railways across the country; pedagogical practices ranging from new forms of vocational education to disseminating new maps and teaching geography; and a raft of bureaucratic reforms, notably in budgeting and other fiscal matters.[54] The success of the British state between 1858 and 1920 in homogenizing and bounding Indian national space through various territorializing processes engendered its own critical reaction from Indian protonationalists, most publicly in the realm of public finance. Dadabhai Naoroji's critique of colonial financial practices had the effect of putting the colonial government permanently on the defensive as it sought to counter his well-documented arguments based on the colonial state's own reports that as much as 200 million pounds sterling were being "drained" away from India and transferred to Britain annually.[55]

Complementing the visualization of India as *Bharat Mata* and a mercantilist economy, Indian intelligentsia reworked the colonial space of British India to produce "a conception of Bharat as a real, enduring, spatially bounded national entity."[56] *Bharat* was a reimagining of India that emerged, according to Goswami, in northern and northwestern India in the late nineteenth century. Drawing from the epic literature of the *Puranas* when Bharat was the nominal territorial presence of what would later be termed India, intellectuals such as Raja Shiva Prasad worked to restore Bharat to the center of the territorial imaginary of colonial India. The discourse of Bharat acted on multiple registers, seeking continuity between a glorious classic past and modern India while joining "history, territory and collective identity," to effect the possibility of a noncolonized future.[57] Following Gyan Prakash's examination of the ways in which colonized elites used science to rewrite their particular condition in universal terms, we can read the turn to *Bharat* as a "return of the archaic" and, hence, as a "space of translation."[58] This move is important, for Prakash reminds us that the copresence of past and present breaks the desired organic link between history and the nation and represents the modern nation as "estranged and distorted."[59] The break that led to glorious Indian pasts being alienated from the colonial present is written through the trope of invasion, specifically Muslim invasions.

In her analysis of vernacular geography textbooks, Goswami demonstrates how the invocation of Bharat produces a plural (in regional, linguistic, and cultural terms) Indian social-scape, but with the following political fault line. Muslims were marked as an "irreducible alterity" whose lack of faith in India came from their status as "supranational and superterritorial" subjects who first came to India as an invading force. Permanently invaders and outsiders to the national body, Muslims help identify the true inheritor and occupant of Bharat as the unmarked figure of the upper-caste Hindu.[60] We find that the imagination of a unified politico-cultural geo-body, represented through political economy, history writing, geography textbooks, songs, and images of *Bharat Mata*—the nationalist counterpoint to colonial representations of Indian space—was at its very inception fissured by its inability to incorporate all of India into this territorial imaginary. What is critically important to remember is that Goswami is not analyzing the discourse of Hindu right-wing extremists that organized themselves around a hypernationalist anti-Muslim ideology. Her protagonists are nationalist moderates, elites working within the colonial apparatus, but who nonetheless found themselves unable to go beyond a spatial vision of India that began from an upper-caste Hindu worldview in which Muslims in particular had no place.[61] Imagining Indian "territory" as a national space, regardless of the techniques used, produced a political field divided on the basis of the religion of its residents: Hindus were the natural inheritors of India; Muslims were latecomers and permanent outsiders.

Territory is both prior to *and* an emergent condition of space, engendered through particular state practices. Territory is not reducible to "land," "sea," or "terrain," though it incorporates these and other geophysical entities, but is a particular spatial outcome working through relations of property, strategy, and technologies of measurement. Territorial practices seek to fix state boundaries even as they work to homogenize the national interior with an eye to making it appear that these boundaries and the state that controls the lands and people they encompass have always been there. This genealogical approach to the emergence of territorial sovereignty in India shows that once territorializing practices are foregrounded, the uneven production of "domestic" space is too obvious to be ignored.[62] The historic shift from precolonial Mughal maps to British Company maps revalues and reorients the meaning of land altogether to make it more amenable to state control; the nationalist affect of sacralizing territory as a response to the hegemonies of colonial rule brings with it the separation of Hindus and Muslims and the representation of the latter as an "irreducible alterity." Territorializing practices produce social, political, economic, cultural, and military boundaries both at the limits of state territory and within it.

Foreign Policy

Foreign policy has a special place in the portfolio of state territorial practices because its primary purpose is to produce the effect of a boundary deemed essential by the modern state.[63] This is the boundary that divides inside from outside or home from abroad.[64] The separation of inside and outside is much more than the demarcation of the territorial limits of the national homeland or the establishment of an international border. Inside/outside, home/abroad, domestic/foreign are different ways of saying "us" and "them," the distinction that lies at the heart of the foreign policy problematic. Foreign policy is about bounding the state by defining the national body in, ideally, unequivocal terms. What Walker describes as "defense" policy applies as much to foreign policy: "[It] is usually understood in relation to the securing of boundaries from external threat. It is at least as important to understand it as a practice intended to inscribe the boundaries of 'normal' politics, a patrolling of the borders at home, a disciplining of the claims to sovereign authority and national identity within."[65] For Walker, foreign policy is central to the set of practices and performances that enables the state to claim it is sovereign. The existence of a "foreign" policy is a claim that the state commands *national* space, rather than the conventional meaning of the term, which begins from the existence of the sovereign state and then institutes a "foreign" policy in the extraterritorial realm beyond its sovereign reach.[66]

When Walker argues that the "inside" is a space absent threat, marked by normal politics, where sovereignty reigns, it follows that this reassuring outcome requires a counterpoint, an "outside," a threatening, non-normal, anarchic space, against which these categories can be measured. This formulation implies that these binaries—inside/outside, home/abroad—are loaded with a conceptual and emotional freight far beyond the geophysical coordinates of the nation-state and what lies beyond it. David Campbell develops this insight further to ask what "is at stake in the attempt to screen the strange, the unfamiliar, and the threatening associated with the outside from the familiar and safe, which are linked to the inside?"[67] He argues that the inseparability of foreign policy from "discourses of danger" requires that the practice of foreign policy "be understood as giving rise to a [special kind of] boundary."[68] The boundary invoked here is not the familiar physical and literal international border of international relations; rather it begins with "the disciplining of ambiguity, the containment of contingency" and ends by seeking to impose a permanent distinction between safe and unsafe/home and abroad/national and alien.[69]

Foreign policy, Campbell argues, should be understood as "practices of differentiation" and "modes of figuration" produced in the confrontation between self and other. Identity and difference, in other words, are centrally implicated in the making of foreign policy:

> The construction of social space that emerges from practices associated with the paradigm of sovereignty thus exceeds a simple geographic partitioning: it results in a conception of divergent *moral* spaces. In other words, the social space of inside/outside is both made possible by and helps constitute a moral space of superior/inferior, which can be animated, in terms of any figurations of higher/lower.[70]

Foreign policy, understood as a core state boundary-making exercise, seeks to create and privilege, on the one hand, the reassurances of home, with all its attendant pleasures of security, comfort, and the absence of threat, even as, on the other hand, it demonizes the zone lying outside the domestic space as the representation of all that is to be feared and kept away. The spatial boundary that foreign policy seeks to institute and maintain is also a moral boundary, a hierarchical, even eschatological, ordering and separation of good and evil.

Conventional notions of foreign policy work through a battery of boundary-making institutions, practices, artifacts, and performances, including (but not limited to) passports, visas, national ID cards, border controls, customs and immigration agencies, international border lines and no-man's-land, border patrols and boundary walls, lines of actual control and cease-fire lines, official maps and survey reports, espionage and counterespionage, embassies and consulates, summit meetings and bilateral agreements, treaties, démarches, and diplomatic notes, nationalization procedures and extradition, to mention only the most obvious examples. What links the national ID card and the passport is that both are absolute forms of national distinction, allowing the state to distinguish between citizen and alien. The national ID card is intended to have meaning "domestically," the passport "abroad." The imputed difference between these two artifacts is what produces the effect of a difference between home and abroad, not the other way around. Juxtaposition of these foreign policy artifacts engenders the effect of an ontic spatial distinction between domestic space and the world outside—foreign policy. Hence, foreign policy should be understood as a set of state territorializing practices that produce the "state effect" of an absolute distinction between two kinds of space, home and abroad, safety and danger, loyalty and treason, by seeking to mark unambiguous differences between the figures of citizen and alien, national and foreigner, denizen and sojourner.[71]

As the most visible of foreign policy performances take place at the physical limits of domestic space, at border crossings and customs checkpoints, there is a mistaken tendency to assume that foreign policy works only at "land's end." Territorial borders do not singularly correspond to ontic boundaries. As much recent, especially anthropological work has shown, borders are fluid, shifting, and mobile spaces of human action.[72] State "border games" seek to transform this fluidity and mobility into a fixed and unchanging form, namely the permanent international border between countries.[73] Boundary-making practices, by contrast, work across the body of the nation, not only at the territorial limits of the state. Because the primary function of foreign policy is to police the divide between safety and danger, loyalty and treason, citizen and alien, there is no necessary connection between foreign policy and geophysical location. Foreign policy working at the territorial borders of the country constitutes a special case, not its generalized condition. The apparent homology between foreign policy and territorial borders should be seen as an element in the self-representation of foreign policy, not its actual practice.

It is important to note also that border games do not exhaust the stock of foreign policy's territorializing practices. The most vivid example of these performances in the Indian case might be the daily flag-hoisting parade that takes place at Wagah, on the border with Pakistan, a performance so exaggerated and stylized, even parodic, that it has now become a tourist spectacle.[74] These performances are designed to produce the "illusion," what Timothy Mitchell calls a state "effect," that there is something essential to the state called foreign policy.[75] The "performance" of foreign policy seeks above all to show that there is a stable and fixed boundary between the domestic and the foreign, through the tireless repetition of these performances.[76] Boundaries between home and abroad are produced through a myriad of modest and wide-ranging actions from the official Indian stamp on world maps that "wrongly depict the official boundaries of the state" to the rules that determine the size of the photograph to be submitted as a part of the application for a voter ID card. These latter actions may be less noteworthy; however, it is their very ubiquity and repetition that makes them powerful links in the chain of performances that go to confirming the "truth" that there is a domestic space, marked by loyal citizens moving about their daily lives in conditions of physical and emotional safety, a zone that is ontologically different from "foreign" spaces inhabited by aliens and characterized by danger and treason.

Boundaries produce powerful hierarchies of distinction between places and people.[77] The most common form of geopolitical hierarchy is the relation of center/heartland/core to periphery/rimland/margin. Very different political weights are ascribed to each pole of these binaries. The heartland is represented as the foundation of normative political space and is hence the most valuable of interior spaces, while the rimland or margin is associated with danger and threat to that core. Yet, due to shifts in the meanings of nation and state, the locations of heartland and periphery are not permanently fixed. When the eastern Indian province of Bengal was partitioned in 1905 for administrative reasons, the huge public outcry in reaction led to its reversal a few years later, a shocking outcome for a powerful colonial state that faced scant public accountability. Yet when Burma was separated from British India in 1931, there was little outcry, in spite of the grave difficulties faced by people of Indian origin, mostly Bengali, Telugu, and Tamil.

What distinguished Bengal in 1905 from Burma in 1931 was the meaning of these territories for the nascent Indian nation. Geographically peripheral (to New Delhi), Bengal was deemed a "heartland" of the nation in 1905, while Burma in 1931 little more than a periphery whose partition was not construed in terms of national loss, even if many nationals lost everything they owned.

An entirely different set of meanings was produced when Pakistan was created in 1947, leading again to the partition of Bengal along boundaries little different than in 1905, amid horrendous violence. East Pakistan was now defined as a Muslim majority region in official discourse, a classification that soon showed its limits. Islam notwithstanding, East Pakistan soon dissolved into a struggle for the affirmation of Bengali language and culture against a dominant Punjabi nationalism and Urdu language dominance. When Bangladesh was created in 1971, Pakistan survived the loss of a region containing more than half its population. A region of Bengal once affirmed to be a national heartland, later defined as a Muslim country, had now become a new state defined around a Bengali identity with a majority Muslim population. This exclusive definition of national identity was in turn contested by Bangladesh's minority populations, Hindu and non–Bengali-speaking, as well as by those who sought to define the country primarily as a Muslim state. (West) Bengalis in India today might look to the east in terms of nostalgia, but irredentism is not on the political agenda. Few Bangladeshis today would see the restoration of historical Bengal as a national project worth a second's thought. The territorial map of the nation, no less than state territory, is not fixed or absolute when seen in historical terms. At any specific moment in time, however, the boundaries of national territory inscribe a political value that is construed in terms of absolute permanence making its loss appear to be equivalent to the loss of state power.

Boundary practices produce hierarchies among people in the form of insiders and outsiders, citizens and aliens. Distinctions between people may be produced around any number of politicized categories, including religion, language, place of birth, culture, civilization, ethnicity, and, gender, producing the "super-sign" of liberal political societies, namely, majority/insider and minority/outsider.[78] Insider-outsider boundaries can be drawn anywhere in political space, as the boundary in question is not primarily geospatial but conceptual and political. Boundary practices are concerned with policing these distinctions to ensure that insiders and outsiders are kept in their respective places. When these boundaries are transgressed, when insiders are identified "outside" the national body, and outsiders found "within," immanent contradictions of the nation-state become apparent. In a postcolonial world where borders were inscribed willy-nilly across continents and communities, outsiders may be found anywhere at "home." When, as is often the case, marks of outsiderness are identified with the majority community of a neighboring country, outsiders become a potential fifth column. Furthermore, when outsiders occupy the geospatial margins of the country, they bring together two kinds of political distinction, the conceptual-political, as well as the geospatial.[79] This juxtaposition marks the borderlander, a figure who is found at the limits of domestic territorial space. As we shall see in more detail in a later chapter, borderlanders come to represent a particularly fraught political danger for the modern state, for they threaten the stability of the vital inside/outside hierarchy while also being located on the threatening edge of national territorial space.

This chapter has argued that what we mean by territory is neither fixed nor stable, and, rather than territory, practices of territorialization should be the focus of our attention. These practices establish how and where territorial boundaries are drawn and, in the process, how the categories of inside(r) and outside(r) get established; in short, how territory is produced. The boundaries created by these practices are not cartographic; rather they establish moral boundaries that police distinctions between inside and outside, within and without. Foreign policy is a territorializing practice that institutes, polices, enacts, and performs state boundaries. However, it must be asserted, this is not a simple or benign process. As Lefèbvre reminds us, "Every state is born of violence and state power endures only by virtue of violence directed towards a space."[80] The violence of foreign policy state making is played out in spaces well beyond familiar representations of the national body. To drive home this crucial point, the final section of this chapter analyzes a tragic moment in India's transition from colony to postcolony to show how women's bodies became a vital site of territorialization. Establishing control over women's bodies was a crucial step in establishing the identities of and hence difference between India and Pakistan, two new postcolonial states.[81]

Territorializing Gender: Abducted Women during India's Partition

Following the creation of the United Nations, members of the international community convened an international conference for the purpose of creating a regime for the protection and management of refugees.[82] While the League of Nations had earlier created both a legal order for the protection of refugees as well as a high commissioner for refugees to act in the name of the international community, it was clear that post–World War II conditions produced challenges beyond the scope of the earlier regime. The League of Nations was primarily concerned with European refugees displaced and left without legal protection or excluded by the formation of new nation-states after World War I. The situation after 1945 was a far more serious and urgent matter in terms of numbers, with those affected by the war now found across the world, joined also by human migrations due to ideological differences with new political regimes.

India and Pakistan faced among the most serious refugee challenges encountered anywhere in the world. Even before the partition of British India and the creation of two new successor states, as many as ten million people began to move between the two states across what would become international borders drawn through the provinces of Bengal and Punjab.[83] Given the poor state of physical infrastructure and the lack of resources, it is not surprising that both states turned at once to the United Nations in the expectation that the international community would recognize and assist with the immense problems originating from these population movements. To their surprise, Indian and Pakistani diplomats seeking assistance received little support. Their delegates to various UN drafting committees found the refugee issue at once trapped in Cold War politics. The humanitarian problem of providing relief was not the primary concern of the Great Powers, especially the United States, who sought to restrict the definition of refugees to persons directly affected by World War II, unless they were thought to be escaping from Communism.

India and Pakistan took a far more expansive view of the refugee issue, seeing it foremost as a humanitarian problem, with aid and assistance to those affected by forced displacement overriding the problem of definition and eligibility.[84] Moreover, the established idea of the refugee as a temporary condition, meaning that the international community's responsibility to refugees would end when conditions in the former country of residence improved, clearly could not be applied either to India or Pakistan. These "refugees" had crossed the border knowing that they would never again return to their place of origin. Under these circumstances, neither India nor Pakistan agreed to sign the UN Refugee Convention of 1951, the principal international legal instrument governing the care of refugees and detailing corresponding international responsibilities. Nevertheless, as Pia Oberoi points out, convention holdouts India and Pakistan have adhered to the spirit of this convention far more faithfully than many actual signatories, in spite of having had "in excess of 30 million" persons seek refuge in their countries since independence and lacking the resources available to many more developed countries.[85]

India's unquestionably progressive and humanitarian response to refugees in general, however, must be set against the country's deeply conflicted response to one particular category of people who had been forcibly displaced. This is the category of displaced persons known collectively known as "abducted women." During the chaos and violence of the months leading up to and following the formal separation of the two new countries, hundreds of Hindu and Sikh women were removed forcibly from their homes and families by Muslim men, while Muslim women were, likewise, abducted by Hindu and Sikh men. Abducted women were victims of the violence and traumas of partition in a double sense. They were violently separated from their homes and families and, if not killed, had been forced to live with men from "another community" either as wives or chattel. It was a problem that took place on both sides of the border. In response, the new government of India took it on itself to "recover" Hindu and Sikh women in the interests of preserving national honor.

In their seminal account of this episode, Ritu Menon and Kamla Bhasin explore the multiple contradictions surrounding the recovery of abducted women.[86] In 1949, the Indian government passed the Abducted Persons (Recovery and Restoration) Bill. This act empowered the police with extensive powers to recover women suspected of having been abducted (as well as male children under the age of sixteen), without warrants of any kind. These women and children were to be placed in camps until returned to Pakistan. Abducted women found in India were assumed to be Muslim; all Muslim abducted women had to be "returned" to Pakistan, their proper place. At the same time, India sent female social workers to Pakistan to organize rehabilitation shelters to collect abducted Hindu and Sikh women. While the law required Hindu and Sikh women to be repatriated to India, their children, presumably born of Muslim fathers, had to remain in Pakistan.

To their surprise, Indian social workers in Pakistan found that some abducted women, in spite of having been removed forcibly from their natal families, preferred to remain in Pakistan in their new conjugal state. Some feared the consequences of coming to India in a "dishonored" condition; others had built lives for themselves and could not bear to be parted from their children. However, these women's choices did not matter. If they were found to be Hindu, they had to be sent back to India. Similarly, some

Muslim women in India also desired to remain there. Their wishes too had no place in the law, though they were permitted to "return" to Pakistan with their children. Once "recovered," not all Hindu and Sikh women were able to be "restored" successfully to their families. Some committed suicide, while others were rejected by their birth families for the public shame that they represented. The Indian government was forced to set up hostels for abducted women who had no other place to turn, where they sadly lived out the rest of their lives.

"Recovery and restoration" in this context comes to mean the following. It was impossible for Indian authorities to believe that women could willingly want to stay with their abductors; their "false consciousness" could be attributed to their gender, but, in any case, such a choice could not be countenanced. The loss of national patriarchal honor was at stake. Women would be recovered whether they wanted it or not. As one legislator argued, making an explicit equation between two very different kinds of territorial loss, "If you are prepared to go to war over a few inches of land in Kashmir, why not over the honour of our women? It is more important and is [more] likely to affect our political prestige."[87] Both women and land were the state's territory, and when it came to the prestige of a state, women's (read "men's") "honour" easily exceeded "a few inches of land." The slide between women's bodies and land is not an innocent juxtaposition. The "loss" of women due to abduction by Muslims and the "loss" of Indian territory embodied by the creation of Pakistan bear a close and mutually supportive relation to each other. In both cases, something essential to the nation had been forcibly removed, and it was incumbent on the state to recover it to restore patriarchal order and congruent national honor. Honor is a deeply gendered trope that recurs in the account of abducted women, a masculine quality played out on the—territorialized—bodies of women.[88]

This tragic episode brings into focus a number of issues that speak to the boundary-making functions of foreign policy, or foreign policy as a territorializing process. The account of abducted women, "hovering on the edges of history," does not appear in any account of Indian foreign relations, yet it is clear that there is no better way of describing the years-long process of recovering the bodies of "lost" Hindu and Sikh women. Recovering abducted women was a way of restoring to the national body what had been taken away, even if the women in question didn't want to be returned and even if there was nowhere to put them once restored. The protection of women who had been abducted was not the issue: their status as representatives of national-religious communities exceeded any subjectivity they might have possessed. Although India would proudly define itself as a secular state, the government's actions belied this claim. Hindu and Sikh women alone were the targets of the extensive measures taken to recover abducted women. Muslim women, likewise, had no choice but to be repatriated to Pakistan, even though they had never lived there and may have expressed a preference for staying on in India.

Among the first acts of independent and secular India's "foreign policy" was territorializing gender, drawing religious, national, and sexual boundaries on and through women's bodies. Women's bodies represented both the inner core of patriarchy—couched in the language of honor and prestige—as well as marking the boundaries of social and national reproduction. As Menon and Bhasin put it, "Our discussion on the recovery of Hindu and Muslim women . . . and the role of the Indian state in both reinforcing ethnic difference and reaffirming the necessity of regulating women's sexuality in the interests of national honour, underline[s] the significance of women as reproducers of ethnic and national boundaries."[89]

Gender, as much as land borders and maritime boundaries, can become the focus of territorializing practices aimed at establishing a clear and dividing line between "us" and "them." But, as with all boundary-making practices, the process is never easy and always incomplete. Boundaries do not just divide; they also separate. Moreover, they also create hierarchies of value. Although India opened its doors to millions of refugees seeking safety and relief, it found that some bodies were missing and had to be recovered. At the same moment, other bodies that were present in India had to be excluded for the successful restoration of national order. Seen from its point of view, Indian foreign policy had no choice but to decide whose bodies mattered (more than others), regardless of the desires of the women involved. This account of recovering abducted women offers troubling insight into the meaning of both nation and state. The privileging of Hindu and Sikh female bodies over Muslim ones to restore national honor tells us which bodies were deemed the most authentic representatives of the ostensibly secular nation. The need to "recover" women at all reaffirms the core arguments of this chapter. First, territorializing practices produce moral hierarchies that separate the valuable from the unwanted. Second, states do not establish boundaries as a result of—following—their command of territory. Boundary making is required for the state to claim it has a legitimate control over territory. The violence attendant on boundary making works to obscure the order of political control and demonstrates that the legitimacy of the state is a product of successfully establishing boundaries, not its progenitor.

Conclusion

This chapter constitutes the first of a two-part discussion of India's encounter with the world. Trying to understand why countries find it so difficult to extricate themselves from protracted territorial disputes and, relatedly, why territorial loss is seen as such a great challenge to the state, this chapter returns to first principles to enquire what is meant by *territory*. In contrast to views that define *territory* in fixed and ahistorical terms, whether in terms of land or terrain, or as an exclusive space dominated by a single sovereign, this chapter follows recent scholarship from human geography to argue that what we mean by *territory* is the product of a particular set of state territorial practices. Moreover, territory thus produced is socially divided, unevenly valued, and politically ranked. Some territories matter more than others; other territories are valued for some time and then decline in importance; some territories are feared rather than valued positively. All in all, the meanings of territory are far from fixed; rather, variability is the only constant.

The stark difference between a conception of territory as a singular and homogenous space and territory as the uneven product of historical and political power forces our attention to the practices that produce territory. This chapter highlights one particular practice, foreign policy. In general, the object of foreign policy is to produce security for the nation-state by separating and bounding zones of threat from zones of safety. Given this imperative, foreign policy does not have the luxury of merely maintaining boundaries at the state's geophysical borders; it must identify and root out sites of national insecurity wherever they may be. In the process of distinguishing between home and abroad, safe and unsafe, citizen and alien, boundaries are drawn though lands, representations, communities, and bodies. Foreign policy's objective is to produce a homogenous unified nation congruent with its territorial homeland, the state's geobody. Although state borders may not shift appreciably over time, national boundaries are much more unstable. The work of foreign policy, in other words, is never complete.

The larger purpose of foreign policy, like all state territorial practices, is to ensure that the seams joining state, nation, and territory are as invisible as possible. State territorial practices work to produce the appearance of a permanent and timeless conjunction of political forces so as to preclude any question of the legitimacy of the prevailing political order. Marxist theorists of the state have long argued that state legitimacy depends on the appearance of neutrality between classes or opposed social formations. As a result, the state will often act with "relative autonomy"; namely, it may even act against the short-term interests of the most powerful classes of a society to serve the long-term interests of capital and social stability.[90] Such a view had a powerful influence on an earlier generation of analyses of the state in the developing and postcolonial world, especially to explain how a number of states took on leading roles both as regulator and actor in economic affairs, and why some dirigiste states even picked "winners and losers" among sectors of capital.[91] Neutrality between classes or social groups was not merely a tactic to permit the state to act as arbiter in case of social conflict; it was also strategically necessary to engender the popular consent that lies at the heart of sustainable hegemony. Hegemony required that the state also become a site for popular identification and representation.

In the general Marxist schema, the origins of the modern state are so far removed in time that state hegemony and legitimacy are reinforced, not produced for the first time, through its relatively autonomous behavior. Such a luxury is not available for the postcolonial state. Postcolonial state legitimacy depends on creating new bases for popular representation and identification (ideally, overnight) without being able to take advantage of the amnesias of a hoary past. Across the developing world there remains even today an entire (if aging) generation whose active memories explicitly include the historic political transition from the colonial to the postcolonial eras. Moreover, the terms of that transition are very much an active and ongoing item of debate among intellectual and political classes. Under these conditions, the postcolonial state's claims to popular representation and neutrality between classes come up directly against memories of a repressive colonial state apparatus and nationalist anticolonial movements that claimed to be agents of progressive change. The nonrevolutionary state has to come to terms with the multiple legacies of its colonial predecessor while also claiming postcolonial difference: it typically does so through multiple acts of socialization and economic development, glossed as "nation" and "state" building respectively.

But for the postcolonial state, producing the conditions for domestic legitimacy is only one side of the story. External legitimacy, the recognition of the newly created state as a legitimate international presence and representative of a meaningful domestic political order by other states in the international sphere, was equally important and necessary. The first generation of postcolonial states could not count on automatic recognition as legitimate international actors. Their very presence in the postwar international system signified a standing repudiation of the exclusionary practices and rules of international order that had prevailed for the last two centuries. On what terms were they going to be included? To what extent could the international order change to accommodate these new states without overturning the old order entirely? It was all too obvious that once all former colonial territories became independent, the Great Powers would lose, at the very least, the numbers game. Under these conditions, could existing international hierarchies be sustained?

If these were the anxieties circulating in London, Washington, and Paris, an equally fraught set of concerns dominated minds in Peking, New Delhi, Baghdad, Addis Ababa, Istanbul, Damascus, Cairo, Teheran, Beirut, and Manila.[92] Did their newly arrived states meet the unwritten standards of international statehood? Would they be admitted to the international system as full international actors? Was this international system going to reproduce the imperial order of the past, or were their demands for a new world order going to be taken seriously? The next chapter turns to address these questions, examining the question of decolonization from the point of view of its impact on the international system. Territorial possession, we find, would be the first precondition for international recognition, but the price paid for achieving external legitimacy would be not be small.

2

A Brief International History of the Nation-State

This chapter begins from the historical moment when the territorially sovereign nation-state became identified as the most legitimate international form of collective political organization and tracks its far-reaching consequences for the prospects and meanings of decolonization. The historian Eric Hobsbawm reminds us that this outcome—the territorial nation-state as a global norm—was far from predetermined:

> If there was a moment when the nineteenth century "principle of nationality" triumphed, it was at the end of World War One, even though this was neither predictable not the intent of the future victors. In fact, it was the result of two unintended developments: the collapse of the great multinational empires of central and eastern Europe and the Russian Revolution which made it desirable for the Allies to play the Wilson card against the Bolshevik card.[1]

The Communists had, over intense debates during the course of the first two decades of the twentieth century, come to realize the proximity and potential of "national and colonial" questions. Sanjay Seth argues convincingly that Lenin's critique of imperialism was the bridge between earlier Marxist positions that treated Western and Asian developments as spatially and historically independent of each other and a later, more integrated, global perspective that saw the anti-imperial potential in movements for national liberation.[2] Supporting national movements for colonial independence became a source of strategic and moral strength for the international communist movement for the next many decades.

The Western Great Powers had to find a way of managing the aftermath of the defeated Austro-Hungarian and Ottoman political systems while also coming to terms with the physical devastation of World War I and the effects it had had on their far-flung empires. London and Paris did not have radical political change on their minds, but matters were forced to a head when one of their own would acknowledge the legitimacy of the "right" to national self-determination as a way of resolving Europe's political uncertainties. U.S. President Woodrow Wilson's Fourteen Points speech, made to the U.S. Congress just weeks before the inauguration of the Paris Peace Conference, was not intended to become the clarion call in support of anticolonial movements around the world that it would become. Nevertheless, and notwithstanding the diverse roots of and internal divisions among both the West and the Communists on the question of national self-determination, seemingly overnight the territorial nation-state had become the publicly acknowledged hegemonic form of modern political architecture.

By the time of the Paris Peace Conference, belonging to a nation-state had taken root as the dominant aspirational goal for all subjugated peoples who sought political sovereignty. Struggles against colonialism and imperialism and for political independence now came to be defined in terms of this discrete political objective. However, the apparent clarity of the ascribed political goal was shadowed by a number of unresolved questions. This chapter will focus on two related issues that assailed the imaginations of anticolonial nationalists seeking political freedom. The first was the conceptual and material opacity over the definition of national self-determination: Was there an unambiguous meaning for the master terms of *nation* and national *homeland*? What did it mean if the social and territorial boundaries of a particular political struggle did not appear to correspond to these privileged terms? Would that then mean the withdrawal of the right to political freedoms? The second issue addresses the practical conditions surrounding the implementation of this norm, built around the doubled meaning of national sovereignty. If the community of already existing states (read "victorious empires") could proclaim the terms by which new sovereign entities could come into being, this international "society" also retained the power to deny recognition to those states that did not meet their loosely defined standard of national self-determination. This was no hypothetical consideration, as the travails of the early Soviet state made only too clear, reinforced by contemporary knowledge of the history of humiliations faced by the Ottomans, Siam, Persia, China, and other partially recognized states.[3] Internal sovereignty was clearly incomplete without external recognition and entry into the society of independent states, but on what terms would this be granted? This chapter argues that these two problems, attaining recognition as a complete international person and the terms on which India's internal political architecture could meet the standard of a "national homeland," could only be resolved by foregrounding territorial control and defining India as above all a territorial entity.

This chapter thus takes on the task of showing how, in this novel international context, territory came to be a defining characteristic for new nation-states. It begins with a discussion of the 1919 Paris Peace Conference from two contrasting perspectives on the problem of partial sovereignty. By contrasting the government of India's prevailing status as an incomplete international person with the worries of Indian nationalists that the diversity of India prevented it from meeting the new standards of nation and homeland, two practical concerns emerge that shaped the struggle for Indian independence, defined in terms of attaining external sovereignty. The anxieties of nationalists in meeting the standard of national self-determination without the division of India into a number of smaller entities was conceptually finessed by dispensing with the idea of the nation-state in favor of a territorially defined federal state, understood as the latest innovation of modern political architecture. International personhood was achieved through control over a territorial expanse inherited from and defined by colonial administrative boundaries. Territorial sovereignty thus became the grounds both for identifying India as a legitimate modern nation-state while also claiming to meet the indeterminate standards of international recognition. Actually attaining full external recognition as a sovereign state was another matter. External recognition produced multiple binds: although it was essential to achieving full international personhood, it also meant meeting ill-defined and exclusive standards of civilization that had long been used to deny the legitimacy of states and political entities outside the European core. Gaining acceptance into the "family of nations" would also turn out to require giving up India's long-standing interests in the well-being of its overseas nationals. Becoming independent meant, in other words, reterritorializing India to exclude the diaspora. Finally, external recognition also meant conforming to international norms established by imperial powers. What would this do to India's expressed desire to decolonize and reform the international system?[4] There were no easy solutions to these dilemmas.

Paris and National Self-Determination

For most scholars, the Paris Peace Conference is ultimately about Germany and the future of Europe.[5] This event can, however, also be conceptualized as the meeting of two international scales to explore, thematically, questions of national self-determination and international recognition. In the introductory chapter, I sketched the outlines of an international space composed of scales that overlapped with but were not identical to the international realm of diplomacy and interstate interactions. Paris was a moment when two scales met: the first, an insurgent, dynamic, modern, people-centric, future-oriented transnational space, driven by the forces of political and technological change; the other, a conservative, traditional, backward-looking, state-centric space, seeking to contain and restrain these vectors of change. Neither scale remained uncontaminated in the encounter. Nonstate actors began to speak like and identify with the modern state, while state actors found their concerns echoed and amplified across extrastate spaces. The first tendency dominated the second, confirming the language and concerns of the state as the dominant voice of international space, but the second tendency, although subordinate, would remain a fixture shaping transnational scales for decades to come. Paris is also, in other words, a moment when the boundaries between interstate and transnational scales becomes less well defined and states began to claim the right and responsibility for regulating all extradomestic space.

In a recent study, Erez Manela examines the global impact of Wilson's Fourteen Points speech, delivered in the U.S. Congress on January 8, 1918.[6] With the majority of the world's people living under some form of colonial rule, the speech's preamble, which invoked "all the peoples of the world"; its fifth point, which called for "the interests of [subjugated] populations" to have "equal weight" with their rulers; and its closing demand for the "principle of justice [to be applied] to all peoples and nationalities, and their right to live on equal terms of liberty and safety with one another, whether they be strong or weak" raised enormous hopes that the United States would put its considerable weight behind the cause of ending colonial and imperial rule. This turned out to be wishful thinking. Wilson, like the Japanese with respect to their racial equality proposal (see the following discussion), did not realize that his proposals would have far greater consequences than he had intended. He assumed, as did most of his staff, that European problems were the primary problems of world peace. It came as a shock for him to realize that he had been responsible for a global "tragedy of disappointment" in the wake of his Fourteen Points proclamation.[7] Manela argues that the Paris Conference, due to its lack of interest in altering in any substantial way the subordinated political condition of the majority of the world, had a significant impact on the politics of international relations. He concludes that as disillusion over the failings of the conference set in, anticolonial struggles would take a far more radical turn in Korea, China, Egypt, and India than in the past. After raising hopes appreciably, the failure to address the problems of the colonial world markedly sharpened the contradictions of colonial rule and made it clear to nationalist movements that they could not count on international benevolence to remove their political fetters.

Wilson had unwittingly set up the encounter between interstate and transnational spaces through his call for national self-determination for all subjugated peoples. His advocacy of the "right" to national self-determination helped reshape the international arena fundamentally, even as it created enormous confusion in practical terms. For the first time, and in a world still dominated by racially divided empires, colonies, territories, and dependencies, a leading power of the international community had affirmed the right of people to be free, along with a political formula for attaining political freedom. Wilson identified the foundational political unit of future international society as a sovereign state that represented the intersection of a culturally defined "people" with a historic homeland.[8] Yet it was soon clear that a deep ambiguity structured this new norm. Even as Wilson proclaimed the arrival of liberal freedoms around the world, he found himself unable to specify unambiguously what defined a "people" and how their national "homeland" should be identified.

The Fourteen Points speech did not address the colonial world directly. Its central focus was the future of Europeans once subject to the defeated German, Austro-Hungarian, and Ottoman empires. Speaking of the political changes soon to come to Europe, Wilson's speech begins on a strong note. He refers to the Belgian "nation," to "clearly recognizable lines of nationality" in reference to Italy, and to "indisputably Polish populations." We are led to believe that, after Paris, the political problem of national self-determination is resolved: "Indisputable" and "clearly recognizable" people would have the right to live in their own homelands and to enjoy political independence. But as the speech goes on, its language falters and betrays a curious hesitation. Other states and peoples are less easy to pin down, especially in Eastern and Southern Europe. The speech refers twice to "several Balkan states" without identifying them, while tacitly acknowledging that their territorial boundaries were not as clear as would be desired. When it came to the aftermath of the Ottoman Empire, Wilson found it easy to acknowledge the Turks as a people but was far less sure what to do with the political futures of "other nationalities which are now under Turkish rule." Serbia, Montenegro, and Rumania are mentioned, but Albanians, Croatians, Slovenians, Slovaks, and scores of other putative national communities do not get a hearing. It is not clear whether these "nationalities" were entitled to their own state(s) or whether Wilson hoped only for guarantees of "undoubted security of life and an absolute opportunity of an autonomous development" for them as protected minorities living under the rule of another state.

The difficulties Wilson faced in being clearer than he was are now much better understood. The conceptual, political, spatial, and historical problems that haunt the concepts of nation and nationalism are fraught with violence, myth, and contradiction.[9] But, in the aftermath of his speech, it became evident that the conditions for meeting the uncertain norm of national self-determination became a problem for the *colonized* to work out for themselves, not for those Great Powers who would sit in judgment as to whether standards for joining the international community had been adequately met. These immanent contradictions of the norm of self-determination would haunt nationalist thought and those who would use it to claim sovereignty for decades to come.

Although the path to sovereign independence now appeared to be clearly and universally specified, the practical meaning of that norm was still unclear. At the same time, the prevailing international community was determined to make sure that the ensuing transformation of the international system would take place in an orderly and stabilizing way. Given the inherent messiness of defining a people unambiguously, what would turn out to be far more congenial for international adjudication was defining territorial boundaries, not national ones. Drawing lines on maps, after all, was a familiar imperial practice, as Siba Grovogui has shown in his classic study of Africa and the infamous Berlin Conference of 1885.[10] Although it was impossible to identify "indisputable" nations, it was much easier to define new national territories. Wherever possible, national borders would be inscribed over existing imperial boundaries to reduce the likely disorder of the transition from empire to nation-state. The practical consequences of the new norm had serious implications for the many communities historically resident in what was soon to be redefined as a singular national homeland. Within those new national borders, one political community would be granted the "right" of national self-determination: the new state would be created in their image. All other political communities lying within that national territory would be subordinate to this majority nation's state.

The slide from the identification of a national people to the privileging of a national territory as the practical outcome of the norm of self-determination would also coproduce the national minority, a political category that became a structural feature of the postimperial nation-state. Minorities are a people living with, but different from, the allegedly original occupants of the land. They are a "national" community fated to be permanently unequal in political terms. Their unequal condition was produced by the proclaimed inviolability of existing territorial boundaries as the dominant international norm. With the objective of imperial cartography being the separation of empires for reasons of mutual security, even if it came at the cost of dividing a community from itself, more often than not this minority would find itself physically separated from conationals lying on the other side of a new "international" border. National self-determination produced minorities; at the same instant it also produced a profound insecurity on the part of the majority population. "Majority" nation-state insecurity based on the fear of minority irredentism thus also became a consequence of the norm of national self-determination, due to the prevailing practice of territorial overinscription. "Cartographic anxieties" joined the insecurities of minorities as a lesser population within a new nation-state dominated by a majority ethnicity with the insecurities of new nation-states conceived as a majority population facing an internal threat that could potentially always call on foreign support.[11] The structural problem of territorially defined majorities and minorities, as we shall see in the following section, would shape postcolonial Asian foreign relations in significant ways.

Official India in Paris

There were two Indias present in Paris: one, the partially recognized political entity and member of the British Empire, the government of India; the other, Indian nationalists, representing the interests of the politically subordinated populations of that country. Both lacked complete sovereignty and faced distinct problems achieving it.

Arguing that the dominions' significant contributions to the war effort demanded their presence (and thereby also ensuring additional votes in support of its imperial interests), Great Britain overcame French resistance to the presence of Australia, Canada, New Zealand, South Africa, and India as official, if in practice unequal, delegates to the Paris Peace Conference.[12] Indian soldiers and resources were a major factor in the British victory. According to the Commonwealth War Graves Commission, 74,187 British Indian nationals died in combat during World War I.[13] This was a causality figure larger than suffered by any of the self-governing dominions of the British Empire and second only to the number of British war dead.[14] Naoko Shimazu calculates that the overall "Indian contribution was numerically larger than all Dominions combined, totaling one million men and over 146 million pounds sterling."[15] However, the government of India's official presence at arguably the most important international conference of the twentieth century did not mean that India was now a fully recognized and equal member of the international system. Indeed, in 1919, India was a political entity very difficult to define unambiguously.[16] Victoria was crowned empress of India during her Diamond Jubilee celebration, making India nominally the "crown jewel" as well as strategic linchpin of the British Empire. But India was unlike Britain's other colonies and dominions. In recognition of its singular importance, India had a dedicated member of cabinet, the secretary of state for India, looking after its affairs. Its substantial financial and military contributions to the British Empire made the secretary of state both a representative of Indian interests in London as well as the last word on imperial interests. At the same time, India controlled its own extensive "informal" empire of territories and protectorates, ranging from Aden to Singapore to Zanzibar.[17] Decisions regarding this empire were, practically speaking, entirely under the purview of its Calcutta-based (from 1911, Delhi-based) viceroy. It had considerable political independence in foreign affairs, a condition that was also a function of the relatively slow pace of international communication during the nineteenth century. From the point of view of the state, if not the Indian people, India was partially sovereign and partially subordinate, simultaneously empire and colony: truly, an "anomalous international person" in one scholar's view.[18]

In the historical recounting of the conference proceedings, official India's actions in Paris have been long and rightly dismissed as entirely inconsequential. Its two Indian delegates were a senior civil servant representing British India, Sir (later Lord) S. P. Sinha, then under secretary of state for India, and the Maharaja of Bikaner, representing the Native States. The latter, albeit a "splendid figure of a man" according to the awestruck *New York Times* correspondent, appeared to do little of consequence beyond throwing "nice dinners."[19] Nonetheless, India's official presence at the conference had significance beyond its gustatory contributions to world peace. Lord Montagu, secretary of state for India, appeared to be the first to realize that colonial India's inclusion as an official delegate had created a problem with serious political implications. By virtue of giving India tacit recognition as an entity with an international legal presence, the British government had put "India insofar as international affairs are concerned on a basis wholly inconsistent with the position of a subordinate country." As Erez Manela points out, "Montagu was concerned that India's achievement of 'external' . . . recognition as an international actor, would eventually compel Britain to grant it 'internal' self-determination, or the right to choose its own rulers."[20] Montagu's fears seem overstated, as legal ambiguities had for long plagued liberal imperial policies and were unlikely to determine the final outcome of the anticolonial struggle for independence.[21] Regardless, the official intimation of India's ambiguous position in international affairs highlights the gap between India's international presence and its lack of full sovereignty, a condition that would become increasingly pronounced over the next few decades, especially at the League of Nations.[22]

Very little has been written on India at the Paris Conference.[23] However, one way of assessing the substantial content of India's ambiguous international presence is by examining its behavior. How did the official Indian delegation respond to issues that bore directly on its own interests? As already noted, of the many issues discussed at the months-long conference, more scholarly attention has been paid to the question of German reparations than any other. On this deeply contentious issue, the Great Powers would find themselves tied up in knots. British Prime Minister Lloyd George would eventually bow to political pressure and, against the advice of John Maynard Keynes and his treasury, demand from Germany far more than they could conceivably pay.[24] On war reparations, in spite of their considerable contribution to the war effort, the opinion of lesser powers and British dominions would count for little. Powerful elite Indian opinion had proposed that India be permitted to take over the German colonies in East Africa as a mandate, but that did not happen.[25] Indian Muslims were deeply concerned with the fate of the Turkish caliph, whom they saw as the leader of the world's Islamic community, and sent a delegation to Paris to plead their case, to little avail. Perhaps the most obvious case for assessing official India's extent of autonomy, however, can be found in the delegation's response to the Japanese proposal for a Racial Equality Clause.

The proposal for racial equality was a demand that all countries accord "equal and just treatment in every respect making no distinction, either in law or in fact, on account of [the] race or nationality [of alien nationals who were states members of the League of Nations]."[26] The widespread support for such a proposal, well beyond Japan, speaks directly to the prevailing international context when institutionalized racial differences between Europeans and the "coloured races" were too prominent to be ignored. The first time the chief Japanese delegate, Baron Makino, raised this issue, no decision was taken. When Makino raised it again, nearly two months later, he found more support. Against the wishes of Woodrow Wilson, the chairman of the Covenant Committee, a vote was taken that showed majority support for the proposal. Seeing this, Wilson changed the committee rules. Overriding protests from the French and Japanese, he argued that on such a contentious issue, unanimity, not a simple majority, was needed. Great

Britain and the dominions, which had led the opposition, quietly abstained from voting. Although Hugh Purcell notes that Sinha "said bravely that if there would be a chance in the Plenary Conference to vote, then he would vote with the Japanese," this opportunity never arose.[27] On a proposal that directly affected the interests of millions of Indians, the official Indian delegation was silent.

There has long been debate over the intent and significance of the Japanese proposal. Was the proposal for racial equality a realpolitik stratagem to ensure Japanese control over German colonies in Asia, was it put forward in response to the restrictions imposed on Japanese immigration overseas, or was it an effort to consolidate Japanese Great Power status with an official acknowledgment of universal racial equality? Naoko Shimazu explains the origins of this proposal through a detailed analysis of domestic politics and bureaucratic politics in Japan. She argues that the prime minister favored it to get public opinion behind his internationalist approach, while the Foreign Affairs Ministry favored it to deal with the immigration problem. At the same time, Shimazu makes it clear that the Japanese had no intention of elevating this proposal into a universal principle of international intercourse. The proposal was initially directed to raise the status of Japanese nationals alone. It was only after the—especially hostile—public reaction to their proposal that the Japanese realized the larger significance of the proposal. Shimazu also shows clearly the divisions within the British Empire delegation. Eventually, it was the overwhelming pressure applied by Australian Premier Billy Hughes to preserve "White Australia" that led to the British Empire's rejection of this proposal, although London was keenly aware of the impact this would have on Indian, and world, public opinion.[28] Hence, while leading the opposition on behalf of its white settler colonies, Britain would discreetly abstain from putting its hostility to this proposal on official record.

Indian nationals were as—if not more—likely as Japanese migrants to face discriminatory treatment in the Anglo-Saxon world. By the end of the war, Indians had been seeking legal residence in Canada, South Africa, and Australia, as well as the United States, for two decades with little success. As subjects of the British Empire, Indian entry into other British dominions could not be legally denied. However, Canada, South Africa, New Zealand, and Australia understood Indian immigration in existential terms: allowing Asian bodies to enter the white settler dominions would lead to a demographic, economic, and sexual crisis.[29] In a seminal article, Radhika Mongia has shown how Canada first sought to justify the exclusion of Indians on the basis of an "unsuitable" climate. It would then seek to use financial rules and quotas to block the official entry of Asians and, finally, based on carefully collated intelligence, introduce a policy specifically designed to block the entry of Indians into western Canada. This policy took shape in the form of an infamous condition that permitted immigration only on the basis of a "continuous journey" from the immigrant's point of origin to Canada. Matters would come to a head with the arrival in Vancouver harbor of *Komagata Maru*, a ship that had been leased by Indian Sikhs to carry them to Canada, in 1914. Eventually, Mongia argues, this would lead to the creation of the "passport." She defines the passport as a novel governmental technology placing, for the first time, the burden of controlling international mobility on the sending state.[30] London was keenly aware of the contradictions involved in dominion policies but agreed with British Indian officials that as long as a way could be found to deny Indians entry without naming them (or other Asian nationals) directly as unwanted aliens, the dominions could continue to adopt their racially exclusionary policies.[31] With the breakdown of the Canadian approach, the British Empire's white dominions would turn to adopt South Africa's "Natal formula," which used obscure language tests to deny Asian immigration.[32] The importance of keeping the racial order in place would override Indian contributions to the war effort and its importance to British economic and strategic dominance.

The turmoil greeting the racial equality proposal offers up a number of insights into the contemporary state of the international system and India's place in it. The gap between the Covenant Committee's majority vote and the sordid outcome of the Japanese proposal makes clear both the contours of world opinion and the limits of possible change in the postwar international system. When an acknowledged Great Power, Japan, was unable to get the other leaders of the international system to accept fully its standing as an equal in every respect, it demonstrates the continuing presence of racial difference as a key marker of international order. Racial fault lines within the Empire, notably between the white settler dominions and India, Britain's largest colony, and London's selective response to their respective interests demonstrate the continuing contradictions of a liberal imperial order still subject to the "rule of colonial difference."[33] Australia, although like India only partially sovereign, was able to block the racial equality proposal by appealing to the importance of preserving the existing global racial order. Racial divides would continue to shape interunit relations within the Empire and its successor body, the British Commonwealth, eventually reaching a crisis over South Africa's unapologetic policy of racial apartheid. Notwithstanding unremitting international pressure over apartheid's immorality, it would take Britain decades to distance itself from its former colony.

Given the high stakes over overseas immigration and the strong views that were repeatedly expressed in influential public opinion in India, official India's silence on the racial equality proposal can only be read as a reflection of their lack of meaningful autonomy. For all the geopolitical significance of its "informal empire," Paris shows clearly that official India was an "incomplete" international person. Away from the glare of official international conferences, however, and within intraimperial councils, India was still able to exert some influence. The continued exclusion of Indians from imperial settler colonies in particular would not be treated passively (see the following discussion). The cause of overseas Indian labor would be of particular concern. British Indian officials in Delhi would continue to press London for better treatment of Indians working in overseas plantations and as indentured labor. This pressure would finally lead to colonial India's first explicit foreign policy successes. New Delhi would be permitted to appoint official British Indian representatives to different African countries, including South Africa, to monitor and report back on the well-being of the overseas Indian community.[34] India may have been less than sovereign abroad, but it was clearly not without some influence within the British Empire, reinforcing again its condition as an anomalous international person.

The "Other" India in Paris

Petitions from around the world making a case for national self-determination poured into the diplomatic boxes of the Great Powers assembled at the Paris Peace Conference in 1919. Most, indeed the majority, of such memoranda received no response at all. Among them were petitions from nationalists representing the Irish cause, Sean T. O'Cealloigh and George Gavan Duffy, and from the Indian Home Rule League in London.[35] Indian nationalist leader Bal Gangadhar "Lokamanya" Tilak had hoped to be in Paris to present this petition in person to U.S. President Woodrow Wilson and French Premier Georges Clemenceau, but, unable to procure an official visa, he was forced to send the document by post. In essence, both petitions made the same case to the Great Powers: Ireland and India, suffering under the boot of British imperial rule, deserved to be free.[36]

Both petitions drew directly on the theme of national self-determination articulated by Woodrow Wilson in his Fourteen Points speech to explain why they should be allowed to govern themselves and why the international community should grant them this right. Both petitions explained eloquently and angrily that British rule had been deeply detrimental to the development of their countries. India had become nothing more than "mart and mint" for British interests, the Indian Home Rule petition argued, while Ireland was said to have suffered the "perversion of justice" and "corruption of the rule of law." Illegitimate British control over their countries was, in the words of the Irish petition, "at all times and . . . conspicuously at the present time, an outrage to the conscience of the world."[37] Both petitions rejected any effort to delay granting them freedom. "We cannot have liberty step by step . . . The chains of slavery cannot be struck off link by link . . . Liberty must be given at once and at one stroke and then progress will follow," proclaimed the Indian petition.[38] Foreseeing a response that called for some "breathing room" while these important demands be considered, the Irish insisted that such delay would be treated "as deceptive and dangerous. [The Irish] are thoroughly capable of taking immediate charge of their national and international affairs, not less capable than any of the new states which have been recognised since the beginning of the war, or which are about to be recognised."[39] Rhetorically striking an important chord in the context of an international peace conference called to bring a permanent end to war, both petitions emphasized the link that Wilson had made between national self-expression and global peace. They argued that the self-determination of nations was entirely consistent with the self-interest of individual states, for as long as justice was denied nations suffering under alien rule, there could be no peace in the international system.

Undoubtedly already prepared to be denied an opportunity to make their case directly to the Great Powers, both petitions prominently included rebuttals to likely British arguments seeking to continue the status quo. The Irish expected the British to repeat their long-standing argument that their rule had in fact been beneficial to Irish interests. This claim their petition rejected out of hand, offering numerous examples to show that British rule in Ireland had been "an outrage to the conscience of the world." The Irish petition also expected that the British would claim, as they had before, that they needed to control Ireland for strategic and commercial reasons, namely maritime defense and the protection of British commercial fleets. Their response was that such a claim, if generalized into a principle of international relations, could only lead to an indefinite perpetuation of war: "Ireland protests that the interests of one country, be they what they may, cannot be allowed to annul the natural rights of another country. If [the British] claim be admitted, then there is an end to national rights, and all the world must prepare to submit to armed interests or to make war against them."⁴⁰

Like the Irish, Indian rebuttals were equally vehement on the question of the alleged benefits of British rule. The best proof was the historical evidence provided by their rule over India. The British Empire in Asia, the petition reminded its readers, was "built by British merchants," and, in case the point was not clear, "British merchants are not philanthropists."⁴¹ British control over Indian wealth, moreover, had created new international tensions, as other imperial nations were now casting covetous eyes on her prize colony. However, if left to govern itself, India would be transformed. "In 150 years of British rule the progress in India is less than the progress in Germany and Japan in 50 years. Indians have as much intelligence and capacity as the Germans or the Japanese . . . [Yet] India, with her unrivalled resources is still in industrial swaddling clothes."⁴² The petition left no doubt that British rule had not been in Indian economic interests.

For all their similarities, the two petitions diverged tellingly on one issue. The Irish were able confidently to begin their petition saying, "For over a thousand years Ireland possessed, and fully exercised, Sovereign Independence, and was recognised through Europe as a distinct Sovereign State."⁴³ For Irish nationalists, it was self-evident that for Ireland the political question was the *recovery* of sovereignty, not a demand for a novel state of political independence. Not so for their Indian counterparts. The Indian rebuttal had a very different concern to address, an issue that was quite independent of the costs of British misrule. This was the issue of whether India even qualified to take advantage of the new international norm of national self-determination. Was India in fact a nation at all?

A major section of the Indian petition was devoted to rebutting the view that India was either "a congeries of nations" or a "continent," arguments that in Indian eyes served only to "obscure the truth and delude the ignorant."⁴⁴ The length of this rebuttal, however, makes it clear that the ontic status of the Indian nation was not a trivial issue at all, whether for the international community or for Indians themselves. India as well as the international community had to be convinced it was a nation like others in the international system. Read against the grain, this rebuttal also provides us with a contemporary statement of how the constitution of a "genuine" nation was imagined in the new international context.

The Indian nations described in the Indian Home League petition would have been all too familiar to one of the first theorists of modern nationalism, the French Middle East expert Ernest Renan.⁴⁵ Bengalis, Punjabis, Rajputs, and Mahrattas, the petition averred, were no different from English, French, and Poles. These people were "ethnologically . . . descended from the same race"; they had the "same blood, the same language, the same civilization, literature, customs, and traditions."[46] Together, there were twelve such nations in India, the petition noted (without specifying which these were). Individually, they were just as much nations as their European counterparts. Together, they constituted the "United States of India." Putative unity, however, had to be set against the most distinctive (at least as seen from abroad)—and, in this case, divisive—elements of Indian society, namely caste and religion.[47] Did caste not divide this potential nation? No more than class divided the English nation, was the reply. What about religion? If England was home to "hundreds" of antagonistic sects of Christianity and yet could claim to be a viable country, why could not India? It had only five religions (again not specified) to deal with, covering 95 percent of the country. In any case, India, the petition argued, was more than the sum of these nations: "India is said to be the epitome of the world; but there is unity in diversity."[48] Ethnologically, the Indian race was descended from the Aryans, that is, was racially unified; India was "Hinduized long before Alexander invaded India in 315 BC," the petition claimed.[49] Moreover, Hinduism was not only a religion, it was a culture, based on "ancient traditions, impulses, and sentiments" and tied together by Sanskrit, from which "three fourths" of Indian languages emanated. The petition firmly concluded, "India therefore possesses all the elements of nationality—viz., same blood, same culture, same traditions, and same faith."[50] And India was unified in other ways as well. Its unique geography marked it out as a singular entity. Quoting approvingly a series of foreign, and hence presumably objective, observers the petition noted: "Encircled by seas and mountains, [it] is indisputably a geographical unit . . . Beneath the manifold diversities . . . there can still be discerned a certain underlying uniformity of life from the Himalayas to Cape Comorin."[51]

At this moment, the petition turns on itself, as if it fears even geography added to the affirmed uniformities of culture was not enough to satisfy the skeptics of Indian national unity. These familiar criteria were, the petition goes on to say, only the "popular sense" of what made a nation. What follows drops history, geography, and culture altogether in favor of an altogether new authority, the scientific knowledge of politics. "It is midsummer madness," the petition notes, to imagine that the diversity that was India could be collapsed into the Wilsonian definition of a nation, that is, one people, one religion, and one language. Under India's special conditions, these normative strictures would lead to nothing less than "tyranny." For India's claim to be seen as a modern nation-state to be understood, the petition noted that recent innovations in political thought would need to be added to the weight of historical and geographic evidence. The first was federalism, a gift to the world from the American people, "the last of the political principles, but the richest in promises of peace and freedom."[52] Federalism in India would allow these twelve nations to live together harmoniously, preserving their individual customs under one government. But, also, the latest scholarship showed that nations were no longer defined as they once were, namely by common ancestors or religion, but rather were best understood as "moral and political being[s]" created by political action. This elusive creature, the nation, was the product of the state's power over society, not the other way around. Quoting Lord Acton (with more than a hint of Hegel) approvingly, the petition stated: "A State may in the course of time produce a nationality, but that a nationality should constitute a State is contrary to the nature of modern civilization."[53] Following Acton and federalism, the political embodiment of India's twelve constituent nations would be a unified Indian state. "Modern civilization" demanded that the true object of India's demand for international recognition was a sovereign Indian state, regardless of how many nations this state represented.

With this shift, the Indian petition entirely contradicted the new Wilsonian measure of nationality, while in the same breath appealing to self-determination to allow India to be free. Wilson's idea of self-determination applied uncritically to the Indian case would lead British India to devolve into twelve independent nations, an outcome that was so unacceptable as to be unmentionable. To accommodate Indian diversity, national self-determination had to mean the freedom of the Indian *state*, which could only be defined in territorial terms. Nothing else would allow the "underlying uniformity of life from the Himalayas to Cape Comorin" to remain a single political unit. Geography, even before history or culture, would assure India's unity and fix India's boundaries. What remained unsaid was that the limits of territorial sovereignty would be defined by the boundaries of the predecessor colonial state of British India.

Demands for national self-determination set into motion by the Paris peace conference led to intense efforts to accommodate the diversity of existing political entities to the normative strictures of one nation, one territory, one people. This standard was impossible to achieve, not only for India but also for the scores of colonized communities around the world that had been subsumed by imperial cartography, military invasion, and extradiplomatic negotiation. The only possible solution to their lack of obvious nationhood that Indian nationalists were able to imagine was to separate national identity from territorial sovereignty and to make territorial sovereignty the prime measure of their international presence. As we will see, this was the same condition that had come to be a prerequisite for recognition by the existing international community of states.

Recognition in International Law

The nineteenth century consolidated a shift underway from the natural (international) law espoused by Hugo Grotius and Francisco de Vitoria to what is now called positive international law. The significance of this shift lies in two related domains. First, it points to two very different modes of conducting international life before and after the nineteenth century. Second, once positivist international law became hegemonic, the membership criteria for joining the international "community" changed radically. The following section develops these arguments through a discussion of how the practical meaning of recognition shifted in international law over the nineteenth and twentieth centuries.

Grotius's initial claim to fame, it must be remembered, came from his brief for the Dutch East India Company (VOC).[54] In his lengthy treatise arguing for the freedom of the seas while seeking to justify the seizure of a Portuguese vessel by a VOC privateer, *Mare Liberum*, he argued that the Catholic pope had no right to award the Indian Ocean to the Portuguese as if it were his sovereign property. Moreover, and following Vitoria, Grotius would argue that the rights of the local people, even if "infidels," could not be dismissed under the standing precepts of natural law.[55] In support of this claim, he acknowledged that the East Indians, as Grotius refers to the people of the Indian Ocean, were "free men and *sui juris*" possessing full civil and social rights. Before we start reading Grotius as an early proponent of cultural relativism, Edward Keene offers a salutary reminder that the same Grotius would also provide the legal justification for the forcible appropriation of native territories not being used for productive ends, as Europeans saw it, through the doctrine of divisible sovereignty.[56] Like any good lawyer, his brief determined his views.

The legal historian C. A. Alexandrowicz has provided rich details of the nature and quality of interactions between Europeans and Asians from the seventeenth century onward.[57] Alexandrowicz recounts a history of trade and political relations to show not only that legal ties between Asian rulers and European traders were extensive, but also that treaty relations were conducted on the basis of prevailing *Asian* codes and rules. Grotius's *Mare Liberum* was in fact a codification of Asian ways of conducting international affairs. Siba Grovogui affirms in addition that these "legal systems and commercial rules were founded on distinct ethical norms different from those of contemporary Europeans."[58] Treaties between European trading companies and Asian rulers were signed on the basis of mutual, if unequal, recognition, tacitly acknowledging what Grovogui calls a "cultural parity" between the major regions of the world.[59]

Things began to change in the nineteenth century. By this time, mutually established trading relations between Asians and Europeans were giving way to outright colonial possession across much of Asia. David Strand calculates that "in the hundred years between 1790 and 1880, new colonies were formed at the rate of five a decade. Between 1880 and 1910, new colonies were formed at four times this rate, or twenty per decade. The pace of colonial formation declined after 1910," not because of an imperial change of heart, but rather because "the number of candidates for colonial imperialism declined."[60] With the writings of the Swiss lawyer Emer de Vattel leading the way, the rise of so-called positive international law in the nineteenth century, Anthony Anghie compellingly argues, would alter entirely the prevailing rules of international relations.[61]

Colonialism was of course the original instance of what David Harvey would, much later, come to call "accumulation by dispossession." It was the antithesis of liberal norms, based as it was, in the first instance, on the violent alienation of land and suppression of local customs and rules. A host of European international lawyers, from Grotius to Vattel, would provide strong justifications for the legitimacy of these patently illegal and immoral actions. With time, colonial rule would also come to presuppose an ineradicable difference between colonized and colonialist. The "standard of civilization," as Gerrit Gong has pointed out, became a key term in institutionalizing culture and race as a foundational mark of difference:[62] "Non-Westerners were viewed as failing to comprehend the requirements of Western international law and as constitutionally unable to appeal to it."[63] John Stuart Mill would put it unambiguously,

> To suppose that the same international customs, and the same international rules of international morality, can obtain between one civilized nation and another, and between civilized nations and barbarians is grave error ... to characterize any conduct whatever towards a barbarous people as a violation of the law of nations, only shows that he who so speaks has never considered the subject.[64]

The positivist tradition in international law played no small part in justifying the extraordinary political transformation that created a world unequally divided between the established Euro-American Great Powers and a subordinated "colored" majority. In Anghie's terse summary, "Positivists were engaged in an ongoing struggle to define, subordinate, and exclude the native."[65] The world was now divided into two discrete spheres: "[Positivist jurists] postulated a gap, understood principally in terms of cultural differences, between the civilized European and uncivilized non-European world: having established this gap, they then proceeded to devise a series of techniques for bridging this gap, of civilizing the uncivilized."[66] The civilizing mission, justified in terms of the sophistication of material attainment, was spatially contained to the colonies.[67] Responding to the transformation of international space by the movement of unrecognized entities and people, the difference of civilized and uncivilized became a means of controlling and limiting the boundaries of international society.

Anghie's argument is twofold. Not only did positive international law seek to justify colonialism, in the process erasing a centuries-old history of mutual correspondence and exchange between Europeans and others, but what is today meant by state sovereignty was also fundamentally shaped in this process.[68] He argues that sovereignty was not invented via the Treaty of Westphalia or through the process of interstate intercourse on the European landmass, as affirmed by the foundational narrative of International Relations; rather, the colonial encounter was "constitutive" of modern sovereignty.[69] He spells out the steps by which positivists undertook to reshape global hierarchies to exclude non-Western nations. The positivists critiqued natural law for not distinguishing between civilized and uncivilized political entities and also for not privileging states as the only sources of public law. In their view, law could only be made by civilized entities, and only states possessing such qualities could be admitted into international society. Some societies were dismissed because they did not have a legal system at all, at least not one that was recognizable to European eyes. Others, who did have a codified legal system, were rejected because their systems were so alien that no "proper legal relations" could be imagined between them and Europeans. As Oppenheim's standard reference on international law would affirm, "There are numerous states outside the international community . . . international law [should not be] regarded as containing rules concerning relations with such states."[70] These arguments were sustained even when there was prior historical evidence of Europeans signing treaties with indigenous rulers, as Alexandrowicz has shown. With the positivists, the threshold question became marked by the intertwined concepts of race and civilization.[71] International society was now "limited to the civilized and Christian people or to those of European origin."[72] Non-European states, for all their prior participation in international intercourse for four centuries, were now deemed to be beyond public law because they lacked the prior enabling condition of civilization. This condition brings into focus the liminal condition of states including Turkey, Siam, Japan, and Persia, who had an "anomalous" status in the international system.[73] These were countries that were clearly sovereign and boasted of long civilizational histories but were neither European nor colonized. European states recognized their independence, and even signed treaties with them, but stopped far short of including them as members of international society. The dividing line was race, and the racial hierarchy of states was made most visible through the doctrine of extraterritoriality. Turkey, Siam, Persia, and Japan were deemed to conform to minimal standards of recognition as long as European nationals living in and trading with these states were granted the right of not being subordinated to municipal law. To be recognized by European states, in other words, required the loss of local judicial sovereignty. Full sovereignty was the privilege of the European nations alone.

A fundamental question for positivists was whether non-Western states could be deemed sovereign. This issue was of great concern as the possession of sovereignty was considered a minimal condition for making law. Anghie notes that "[t]he general answer [held by positivists] was that sovereignty implied control over territory."[74] This immediately excluded from consideration political formations that were nomadic or itinerant, or whose control over territory followed modes other than the prevailing organicist metaphor of territory as the state's body.[75] However, a number of non-Western states did meet this criterion. How then could they be excluded from international society? In a remarkable feat of legal and logical legerdemain, positivist doctrine would split sovereignty from society. The standard of civilization was now applied to exclude states that in all "other" respects were sovereign territorial entities ruled by laws. To have territorial sovereignty was no longer sufficient as a criterion for entering international society: states had to be civilized as well. By adding this new condition, "Positivist jurists [were] able to overcome the historical fact that non-European states had previously been regarded as sovereign" and need no longer be considered worthy of full recognition.[76] The logic now went as follows: Rather than defining territorial sovereignty as the most vital measure by which states could be included in international society, membership of international society was restricted to those who were deemed civilized.[77] Those who were admittedly civilized in some respects need not be admitted into the inner circle of international society. Recognition by other civilized states was now a prerequisite for establishing full sovereignty. By this circular (il)logic, non-Western states that in all other respects were civilized, territorial, and well governed were now excluded from international society because they were not recognized by Western states as sovereign. This maneuver consolidated the binary opposition of civilized and sovereign, uncivilized and unsovereign. The threshold of international society was now marked by the conjoined super-sign civilized/sovereign.[78]

In brief summary, Asian states and European trading companies and states once engaged in commercial and political relations with each other, in mutual if unequal recognition of each other as legitimate international persons. In the nineteenth century, the nature of relations between the West and Asia changed: now, European states and empires increasingly controlled the entire globe. Asian states and rulers suffering under colonial rule were no longer considered legitimate international persons, even as their legal identity was established through legally binding treaties. By applying the standard of "civilization" under the formulations of positive international law, non-European states once considered sovereign were no longer granted that standing. The international system was redefined as a two-tier world: a set of sovereign and civilized Euro-American countries that recognized each other, and other political entities that lacked civilization and/or sovereignty and hence international recognition.

The exclusion of non-European states from international society produced an entirely new meaning for the term recognition. The positivist jurist William Hall would propose that recognition required states being "brought by increasing [levels of] civilization within the realm of law."[79] A system of partial recognition built around incomplete sovereignty emerged. As the prominent nineteenth-century positivist John Westlake would bluntly state, "Our international society exercises the right of admitting outside states to parts of its international law without necessarily admitting them to the whole of it."[80] Partial recognition was functionally practical for the colonial enterprise. To fend off the claims of other European powers, it was expedient to acknowledge the legitimacy of treaties and other documents signed by local native chieftains and others. Keene notes (presumably referring only to Asia) that

> ...non-European rulers were very seldom denied sovereignty altogether, but they were usually permitted to retain only those prerogatives which they were deemed

competent to exercise, and certain specific prerogatives were nearly always vested with a European government ... in order to ensure the promotion of commerce, technology and good government, as well as the establishment and protection of individuals' rights, especially to property; civilization in other words.[81]

Anghie is more blunt: natives were granted legal personality only in order to "be bound."[82]

Over time, a hierarchy of civilizational achievement came into being. Asian states with some claim to civilization in European eyes could be acknowledged as having the right to "transfer sovereignty" to Europeans but not Africans, who were deemed not yet to have reached this pinnacle of human achievement.[83] African lands could be alienated even without papering over the means of exclusion. Such views formed the backdrop for the infamous Berlin Conference of 1884–1885, the "scramble" for Africa. The expediency of the colonial-legal enterprise meant also that the scale of civilizational achievement was applied in ambiguous and contradictory ways. With no possible legitimate adjudicator of the standard of civilization, individual European states would make these assessments for themselves and in their own interests. As a result, and bearing in mind the erasure of the long history of international intercourse that preceded this moment, recognition doctrine became, in Anghie's words, less about "ascertaining or establishing the legal status of the entity under scrutiny" and more about "affirming the power of the European states to ... reinforce their authority to make such determinations and, consequently, to make sovereignty a possession that they could then proceed to dispense, deny, create, or partially grant."[84] This system of graduated international standing would come to be institutionalized through the Mandate system that flourished during the interwar period.[85]

For "new" states emerging from centuries of colonialism, the positivist doctrine of international recognition would prove a daunting and uncertain threshold to cross. Sovereignty was now critically dependent not only on territorial control but on the level of civilizational status achieved by the state seeking recognition. The difficulty of meeting this standard is easy to see: civilizational standing would be assessed by European states that had justified their colonial empires and "civilizing mission" precisely on the absence of such conditions.[86] In effect, the necessary condition of external recognition as a means to full sovereignty had become a set of rules that applied only to "new"—non-Western and nonwhite—states seeking international legal personality and thereby entry into international society.

Civilization and Territory

In response to the Western discourse of civilizational supremacy from the nineteenth century onward, Asian philosophers and thinkers had responded, very broadly speaking, in two ways. They initiated programs of social reform seeking to remove what they saw—or what had been identified—as debilitating and regressive tendencies within their cultures, even as they began to produce, at the same time, a counternarrative of Asian difference. Conceptions of Asian civilizational distance from the West, built around a shared cosmopolitan ethos, took root across the region and were most famously articulated by Rabindranath Tagore in India, Zhang Binglin in China, and Okakura Tenshin in Japan.[87] Drawing variously on strands of Buddhist and Advaita (Hindu) philosophies, the common thread of these discourses combined claims regarding the mutual respect that Asian societies held for each other along with cultural difference. Asian philosophical traditions, they argued, privileged the social quest for spiritual achievement over material success. All agreed, moreover, that, due to the depredations of the West, Asian societies had slumped into a collective stupor, making national rejuvenation the order of the day.[88]

This counternarrative was all too visible in the historic Asian Relations Conference, held in Delhi's Purana Qila (Old Fort) in March and April 1947, a few months before India became independent. The conference was a semiofficial affair, with the organizational lead taken by the newly formed Indian Council for World Affairs. Held in order to reestablish the bonds between Asian countries that had been severed by colonial rule, invitations were issued to twenty-eight Asian delegations ranging from Armenia, Georgia, and Azerbaijan in the West to Korea, Tibet, and Nationalist China in the East. Opening speeches by the representatives of different Asian countries repeatedly stressed the same themes that marked the lofty presidential address by the Indian poet and nationalist Sarojini Naidu. This was a meeting to celebrate an Asia that was being reborn, a continent marked by spiritual development rather than material power, joined by the common elements of mutual tolerance that made Asia entirely different from prevailing Western norms of domination and subjection.

To quote Sarojini Naidu's address:

> What has Asia always stood for? ... there is one thing—it is the most authentic feature of this great continent—that beckons every nation of Asia to come and partake of the common ideal of peace ... the peace, militant, dynamic, creative, of the human spirit that exalts.... And what will Asia do with her renaissance? Will she arm herself

for new battles to conquer, annex, and exploit, or rather will she forge new weapons and refashion her armoury in accordance with ancient ideals, as soldiers of peace and missionaries of love.... Not through bitterness and hate, not through anger and strife, but through compassion, love and forgiveness shall the world be redeemed.[89]

For all the high-minded principles expressed in the opening speeches, however, discussions in the roundtable sessions proved that conference delegates were hardly oblivious to the political difficulties of achieving independence and then maintaining it, once achieved. A number of speeches and questions made clear that Asians were less than confident that European states had reconciled themselves to the eventual loss of their colonial empires. The Indonesians and the Vietnamese appealed for help to remove Dutch and French troops, respectively, from their lands, while also asking for collective support for their membership in the United Nations. But practical concerns were not only directed at revanchist Western powers. Postcolonial Asian countries also identified each other as objects of political anxiety. The Burmese asked whether India would continue to play the role of a military proxy of the British empire, given the long history of use of Indian troops to put down rebellion and establish order across Asia. The Nationalist Chinese (KMT) delegates were asked if they could guarantee the loyalties of overseas Chinese long resident in Burma, Thailand, Malaya, and Indonesia. In multiple sessions and roundtables, the "problems" raised by national minorities, namely, overseas Indians and Chinese, would be raised.[90] While the Chinese would prevaricate, Indian delegates including Jawaharlal Nehru would declare that Indian diasporas were no longer of any interest to an independent India seeking to restore its Asian roots. Overseas Indians had no claim on the protection of the Indian state due to their long sojourns abroad: in effect, they were no longer authentically "Indian."[91]

Reading between the lines of the speeches and impassioned discussion, the following findings are all too clear. The first is the absolute acceptance of the nation-state model by all the delegates present at the Asian Relations Conference. The Asian political entities soon to be free were uniformly represented as states composed of national majorities joined by ethnic or cultural minorities. Independent Burma, for instance, would be a state with a Burman majority and Indian and Chinese (and many other) minorities; likewise, Malaya was to be a state defined by its Malay majority, Ceylon by its Sinhala majority, and so on. Communities marked by difference from these national majorities were being recast as aliens and outsiders, notwithstanding their long residence in these countries. For all the high-minded sentiments expressing Asian spiritual difference during the introductory speeches, not a single delegate questioned the right of the majority community to define singularly the new nation-state, and none remarked on the syncretic cultures that had come to prevail across Asia due to the long interactions of different social groups. At best, the presence of minorities was attributed to the economic and political machinations of colonial empires, making their presence beyond the control of any present political force. Under these circumstances, all that could be hoped for was goodwill on the part of majority communities leading to legal and constitutional protections for these "new" minorities. The Asian Relations Conference made it clear that political independence for Asia would mean a state dominated by a nation defined in terms of an autochthonous majority community.

The other implication is the simultaneous reterritorialization of Asian states, a consequence of the dominance of the nation-state model. Consider India's volte-face with respect to its overseas populations. As discussed earlier, for all its lack of sovereignty, for decades the "official" Indian response to the discrimination and problems faced by its overseas residents was to push back against the racially exclusionary policies of the British Empire and dominions. The vulnerability of India's diaspora had led to an active foreign policy of protection and concern, driven by domestic public pressure and led by British Indian officials. Overnight, this policy had changed. An independent India led by Indians finally unconstrained from defining its own national interests was now publicly distancing itself from its long-standing concerns over the condition of its diaspora. Faced with the anxieties expressed by delegates to the Asian Relations Conference and seeking to establish friendly ties with them, India would reterritorialize itself unambiguously. By turning away from its diaspora, India's national boundaries were being redrawn to exclude any Indians who did not already live within its new territorial borders. Territorial identity now emphatically trumped national identity.

Conclusion

How else could it have been? What complicates the explication of territory to sovereignty is, for India, its overdetermination. First, as we have seen, a territorial definition of India became the means by which a multinational India finessed the impossible conditions of meeting the standards of Wilsonian self-determination. Second, positive international law also required territorial sovereignty as the first condition for external recognition. Third, India's response to the problem of its overseas populations would be to reterritorialize the nation-state, replacing a dispersed nation with a fixed territorial identity. This overdetermination of territoriality was further reinforced by the material and cultural traumas of independence. Political freedom for India was a territorial as much as a temporal transition. India's founding as an independent state was coterminous with the creation of the state of Pakistan, two states physically carved out of the space of British India. Although Pakistan's official national myth may have seen its creation as the unlikely fulfillment of a once-faint dream, a homeland for the Muslims of South Asia, the corresponding account for India was construed as a nightmare.

Midnight's Child, once stretching from Peshawar to Kohima, was truncated, dismembered, lopped off, divided: in a word, *partitioned*. Independent India, which claimed to be the natural legatee of British India, had been created through territorial "loss." Little wonder that territory was now the ontic condition of both India and Pakistan, one construed in the idiom of loss, the other claimed in the form of gain. When perceived incompleteness was the outcome of the transition from unfree to free, not surprisingly, the phantom limb of territorial nostalgia would become a trope running through Indian literatures and foreign policies for decades to come. Loss brought with it demands for recovery but, more critically, produced an imperative for complete control and mastery of what remained. Seeking to overcome conditions of incomplete sovereignty construed in multiple idioms across multiple registers, India would turn repeatedly to a territorial response. The stakes over territory, in this context, could never permit anything short of territoriality: complete political control over the physical limits of the state's (new) body in the ongoing effort to represent Indian state space as a legitimate national territory.

Territory may have been overdetermined, but postcolonial India still faced considerable uncertainty over the territorial stability of the new country. It was not alone in this anxiety. A number of postcolonial countries that became independent soon after World War II also faced unsettled domestic boundaries within the borders of claimed state territory. Although, in general, it can be seen that the administrative boundaries of the prior state, whether a colonial possession or a quasi-independent entity, have almost always become the claimed territorial borders of the future postcolonial state, territory remains a highly contested object within many Asian countries. As this chapter has argued, the need to reduce uncertainties over the likelihood of external recognition forced newly independent states to forego other possibilities of political organization in favor of the safer, more inertial, option of claiming the territorial legacy of the prior state. This outcome has often been taken to mean there exists an international norm expressing a collective preference for not adjusting existing interstate territorial borders. However, the relative lack of change of interstate borders must be set against considerable domestic territorial instabilities. Indeterminate domestic territorial borders could be found across Asia, where civil war, secession, and efforts to recolonize lost territories would, in some cases, take decades to resolve. Even after the creation of Pakistan, ostensibly Indian territory was riddled with political enclaves under extraterritorial jurisdictions, most visibly French and Portuguese colonies, not to mention the 500-odd semi-sovereign principalities that were almost all eventually coerced into joining India. The landlocked Hyderabad monarchy would even appeal, unsuccessfully, to the United Nations to hear its case for sovereign independence before being subsumed into India by military force.

Pakistan itself is a case in point, as the creation of Bangladesh from the former East Pakistan makes all too clear. Indonesia is another good example. Nationalists led by Sukarno declared independence in 1945 but for the next four years had to fight a war with the Dutch, who seemed unable to realize that their days as colonial masters were over. Even when this realization was forced on them by international pressure and military defeat, the Dutch held on to West Papua/Irian Jaya, which the Indonesians claimed as an inalienable part of their new country. Yet Irian Jaya has never fully accepted its incorporation into the Indonesian state and remains a contested space. East Timor would remain under Portuguese rule until annexed by Indonesia in 1975. It is now, decades later, an independent country. Non-Burman majorities in the northern hills of Burma assumed that Burmese independence would mean their own freedom only to find that the Burman-dominated lowland state did not see things that way. From independence in 1948, the Burman majority has been willing to use military force to maintain the territorial status quo of British Burma. Burmese hill tribes and minorities are still contesting this, as they see it, illegitimate territorial annexation. More than a half-century after decolonization began, the gap between international territorial stability and domestic territorial uncertainty has yet to close entirely. As the conclusion to this book will argue, although the *origins* of interstate territorial disputes begin from territorial possession as the prime index of the national identity and external legitimacy of the post-colonial state, their *persistence* is a function of the gap between seemingly "settled" international borders and unstable domestic territories.

3

Diaspora as Foreign Policy

Diasporas have long been conceptualized in relation to the idea of return. Return harks back to the search for a national homeland, a characteristic considered typical of the "classic" diasporas of the globally scattered Jewish and Armenian peoples.[1] After 1919 and the creation of the new international norm of national self-determination, the idea of diaspora took on new meanings. If the meaning of diaspora had once been dominated by the idea of an original dispersal, now diaspora began from a condition of spatial separation. "National self-determination" had led to the suturing of the nation and a territorial homeland, limiting the idea of the nation to a territorially bound community. Once these new meanings of nation and homeland came to shape political imaginaries, postimperial regions of the world took shape as entirely anomalous spaces. Across Central and Eastern Europe and adjoining West Asia, once the lands of the Austro-Hungarian and Ottoman empires, the putative national homeland of one nation was found to be populated by large numbers of people identified with other national communities. Other national communities could be found well beyond the claimed boundaries of their homeland, scattered across what was once a unified imperial space. Urban concentrations, major ports, and imperial capitals that were inevitably home to people from across the former empire and beyond often found that no single community, however dominant, could claim to be in a numerical majority. The results of what were now perceived to be serious political dislocations could be tragic.

The forced "exchange" of Orthodox Greeks and Muslim Turks between the new nation-states of Greece and Turkey in 1923 was one of the great humanitarian tragedies of its time.[2] Cities whose majority population now constituted a national minority, typified by the German-Polish city of Danzig/Gdansk, became the object of competing irredentist claims. What we would now call "ethnic cleansing" led the thriving port city of Trieste, claimed by Italy after the dissolution of the Austro-Hungarian Empire, to lose its Slovenian- and German-speaking minorities as well as access to its economic hinterland.[3] New hybrid multiethnic states were created, such as

Czechoslovakia and Yugoslavia, while cosmopolitan, polyglot, and multicultural cities such as Salonika found their days numbered.[4] Adding to the original meaning of a people *without* a homeland, diaspora now also meant a people living outside the borders of a defined national homeland.[5] The common feature of old and new diasporas is the idea of a national *absence*: in the first case, a homeland; in the latter, a people.

The meaning attributed to diaspora after 1919 is a postimperial definition. It presupposes the norm of a people living in a homeland and a state that represents and embodies both: a territorial nation-state. For colonial peoples, diaspora as a political condition would not take hold until the post–World War I arrival of the nation-state as a political fact. In 1919, Indians were to be found across the globe, especially within the borders of the British Empire, but were not a diaspora in the modern sense. Theirs was a globally dispersed nonterritorially defined national formation. Indians were long resident in some places, such as the Caribbean, and recently arrived or short-term residents of other locations, such as Japan and Germany. These sojourners identified with India to a lesser or greater extent, in various ways including the nostalgic, political, and religio-cultural, but would be uniformly identified as "Indians" outside India as a result of the ethnoracial codes prevalent across the world during this period.[6] Only in 1947, when India became politically sovereign, would what was once a globally dispersed nation be formally differentiated into citizens of the territorial Indian state and an "overseas" diaspora with little claim on the protections of the Indian state. In the 1990s, the relation of India to its diaspora, and overseas Indians to their "homeland," would change again. Now, the global diaspora would be welcomed back into the national family, deterritorializing the idea of India. Shifting territorial boundaries first sought to separate and later to join members of the Indian nation-state and their overseas compatriots, now known variously as "non-resident Indians," "overseas citizens of India," and "people of Indian origin."[7]

This chapter addresses the foreign policy practices that first created and then revised territorial boundaries within the global Indian nation over the last century. The process of territorializing India to *exclude* the diaspora at the moment of independence is enormously significant—and was quite unexpected—for a number of reasons. First of all, the struggle for Indian independence was a struggle fought not only within territorial India but across the globe, wherever Indians were to be found. The miserable condition of Indians living overseas was high among the issues that shaped anticolonial actions, both directly, in the form of political outrage in British India at the treatment of overseas Indians, and indirectly, as the political tactics of Mohandas Gandhi first honed in South Africa and further refined in British India would show.[8] Overseas Indians participated actively in the struggle to free India from British rule; yet, when success in the project of Indian freedom came, it was coterminous with the exclusion of the diaspora from politically sovereign India. Second, "India" was far from the geopolitically fixed space that it would become after 1947. Not only were the borders of "India" indeterminate in relation to an Indian "nation," but the boundary between India's geobody and its overseas populations was fluid enough that prominent Indians (including the nationalist leader and poet, Sarojini Naidu) could unproblematically demand former German colonies in East Africa as sites for Indian settlement as reparation for sacrifices made during World War I.[9] In the 1920s, in other words, the idea of India was flexible enough to include a noncontiguous overseas homeland. The boundaries of the Indian nation and the borders of the new state remained far from settled when India became independent in 1947, as the wars, "police actions," and annexations of the following years would show. Turning away from the diaspora, in other words, was part of a larger process by which India's borders were "hardened" to conform to the norm of the territorially bound nation-state.

That this practice of bracketing the diaspora from territorial India defined foreign policy between 1947 and 1990 is most clearly indicated by India's response to the political and humanitarian crisis that erupted in Uganda in 1972. On August 4, 1972, Ugandan president Idi Amin announced the expulsion of 40,000 "Asians" from the country where they had been resident for generations, giving them ninety days to settle their affairs and leave. These Asians were almost entirely of Indian and Pakistani origin. Most Ugandan Asians were British overseas subjects, a category that, although offering some protections, did not give them the right to settle in the United Kingdom. Eventually, the majority would leave Uganda for England, Canada, and Australia. No more than 5,000 "returned" to India. The Indian government's reaction to this expulsion, which led to global condemnation of the Ugandan regime, was unsympathetic in the extreme. Faced with the grave humanitarian crisis and appeals for refuge from displaced Ugandan Asians, the government's first reaction was to create a visa regime to ensure that India did not become a "dumping ground" for people of Indian origin living in Africa. Part of the reason for this callous response, Aniruddha Gupta argues, is attributable to India's hostility to newly passed British citizenship laws and, more important, its unwillingness potentially to alienate fellow nonaligned African states by appearing to interfere in their internal matters.¹⁰ But also, it is worth considering the stereotypes held in New Delhi of Uganda's "Asians," as they were termed. The prevailing Indian impression of their national compatriots in East Africa was that they exploited Africans and were racially prejudiced against them, as exhibited by their unwillingness to assimilate into local society.¹¹ Indians living in Africa in turn complained that Indian diplomatic representatives did little to aid and protect them and their property, other than to lecture them to integrate more.¹² The net result was that India sat back and waited for the British to resolve "their" problem of Asian expulsion from Uganda. The same country that had absorbed millions of refugees during the Partition in spite of extremely limited resources would loudly proclaim that these displaced overseas Indians had no right of return. A political vision that had once prevailed of a global nation struggling toward the same end, namely freedom and sovereignty for India, no longer held. Indians overseas were now something else.

By contrast, two decades later, on August 19, 2000, the Indian Ministry of External Affairs constituted a high-level committee headed by a distinguished lawyer and former High Commissioner to the United Kingdom, L. M. Singhvi. The committee's mandate was to "review the status" of persons of Indian origin and non-resident Indians with an eye to the contributions they might make in the future economic, social, and technological development of the country.¹³ The hope that overseas Indians might be encouraged to share their skills and resources with their country of origin was repeated more than once in the committee's mission statement. This reference indicated that India was hoping to replicate China's experience from the 1980s, when funds from overseas Chinese poured into southeast China, catalyzing an economic boom that has yet to diminish.¹⁴ The decision to turn to the Indian diaspora by calling on their latent patriotism, however, was a radical departure for the government of India. If China had long held the view that Chinese nationality was something essential that could never be lost regardless of time spent away from the homeland, the prevailing Indian approach to its overseas nationals, as the Ugandan story highlights, was quite different.¹⁵ Given the sharp break with their overseas populations at the moment of independence, the creation of a committee designed to review the status of overseas Indians marked a major foreign policy shift. A new, far more inclusive, boundary was being drawn between India and its diaspora.

At first glance, political reasons are dominant in explaining the drawing of the initial boundary between India and its diaspora, while economic factors explain its later revision. In 1947, independent India sought to assuage the fears of, especially, Southeast Asian countries with large Indian minorities by disavowing any formal connections between India and its overseas nationals. By denying them any right of return, India was making a promise not to interfere in the internal affairs of other countries under the guise of protecting its diaspora. These were not abstract fears. Burmese and Malay elites would repeatedly express their anxieties in this regard long before either country became independent. In similar vein, the state of relations between India and Ceylon, now Sri Lanka, could effectively be measured by the extent of India's willingness to repatriate "Estate Tamils," former indentured workers from southern India, back to their "homeland." Interstate politics, in the form of promoting good relations with other countries, could be taken to explain India's repudiation of its diaspora in 1947.

The subsequent revision of the territorial boundary between India and its overseas populations from the 1990s onwards can be explained by the need to respond to the demands of neoliberal globalization. Following on the heels of the worst balance of payments crisis in its history, India turned its back on its state-led developmental model and began to liberalize its economy. "Opening up" its economy was a process of softening India's boundaries with the world outside, including with its diaspora. In appointing the Singhvi Committee, India explicitly sought to emulate China's experience, postliberalization, by taking advantage of the financial resources of its overseas residents. In other words, this revision can be explained as a policy shift driven by the hope of (and need for) material economic benefit. But there is more to these rewritings of territorial boundaries than either politics or economics in a narrow sense. By setting these two boundary-making moments against each other, it becomes possible to see this turnaround in Indian foreign policy in entirely different terms.

This chapter will argue that these major policy shifts need also to be framed against the potent intersection of nation, caste, and class. At independence, the Indian nation was defined by territorializing itself against its overseas nationals, assumed to be of lower-caste and working-class origins. In the 1990s, the Indian nation was redefined in nonterritorial terms in order to achieve the same outcome: to keep intact its dominant caste–class hierarchy.

Underwriting the transformation of India's diaspora policy was an entirely different representation of the overseas Indian. Earlier representations of the overseas Indian as a poor and lower-caste economic migrant were replaced, in the 1990s, by the image of the overseas Indian as an educated male, middle-class, and upper-caste person: the normative Indian citizen.[16] This chapter will argue that notwithstanding the genuine political outrage at the treatment of overseas indentured labor during the colonial period, these workers were not identified as genuine national subjects. Their social profile—presumed to be lower-caste, working-class subjects who had left the country for economic reasons—made it possible for Indian elites to turn their backs on them and insist that they continue to make their homes abroad. An entirely different narrative greeted the overseas Indian in the 1990s. This revision of India's diaspora foreign policy was initiated by decades of domestic social upheaval that had led to greater political participation by formerly excluded social groups. The politics of numbers opposing socially sanctioned discrimination was overturning entrenched caste hierarchies, bringing into question the normative structure of the Indian nation. The widening and deepening of Indian democracy, buttressed by affirmative action policies, was tacitly identified as the reason behind the overseas flight of educated male middle-class and upper-caste Indians from the 1960s onward. The desire to restore the natural order of caste and, by extension, nation, underwrote the revision of Indian diaspora policy. Upper-caste non-resident Indians' successful overseas sojourns could be taken as proof that their talents were inherent rather than the product of inherited privilege, making it possible to reinscribe national social hierarchies by inviting them to return home. This desire was the starting point for the revision of India's diaspora policy, leading to a new boundary being drawn within a now deterritorialized Indian nation.[17] Diaspora is foreign policy as a class-caste boundary.

Indians Overseas

Although people of Indian origin had traveled overseas for centuries, the period that is most important for this study begins in the 1830s, when Indians were recruited as indentured labor to work on plantations across the British Empire.[18] The shortage of labor caused by the British ban on slavery using British vessels provided the impetus for a "new system of slavery," the title of Hugh Tinker's classic study of this topic.[19] British planters, facing financial ruin with the impending end of their superexploitation of slave labor, utilized their considerable influence in the British Parliament to allow labor migration from India to take the place of freed slaves. Millions of Indians, mostly from Bihar, Bengal, and Tamil Nadu, were recruited using a variety of methods to work under contract (*girmit*) for a period of (usually) five years in plantation colonies including Mauritius and Réunion in the Indian Ocean; Natal province in South Africa; Trinidad, Guyana, and Jamaica in the Caribbean; and Burma, Sri Lanka, Malaysia, and Fiji in the Asia-Pacific region.[20] Although the Indian government attempted to ensure that migrants had freely chosen to emigrate and sought to regulate the conditions under which they would work, official rules were often flouted in practice, leading to backbreaking work under the most primitive and harsh conditions imaginable. Charles Anderson, member of a committee to look into the conditions of indentured labor in Mauritius in 1839, would write to the colonial secretary: "With few exceptions [coolies] are treated with great and unjust severity, by overwork and by personal chastisement; their lodging accommodation is either too confined and disgustingly filthy or none is provided for them; and in cases of sickness [there is] the most culpable neglect."[21] Indian emigration differed in one important respect from Chinese migration to many of the same locations during the same period. Unlike Chinese flows, Indian indenture was regulated by officials of the East India Company acting under a legal regime created by the British Parliament.[22]

Radhika Mongia points to the unusual circumstances shaping the regulations that governed Indian labor emigration.[23] There was no precedent, she argues, for a liberal state to regulate the movement of free individuals. Planters in Mauritius who were keen to encourage emigration from India wrote to the colonial secretary pointing out the novelty of these regulations and questioning their legitimacy. It could be understood, they proposed, if a sovereign government prevented the departure of their subjects, but there was no justification for the same government preventing the entry of a subject into *another* territory. Such prohibition struck at the heart of basic freedoms: of movement, most obviously, but also of choice. Mongia argues that more than simple economic interests shaped this exchange. Regulating human mobility between territorial possessions was an entirely new state technique, and, although it was perhaps understandable under the special circumstances of coolie labor, it raised concerns that the precedent could be extended to British subjects as yet "unmarked" by race. The colonial state's response included a number of key qualifications that remind us how colonial law always distinguished between racialized colonial and unmarked metropolitan subjects (the rule of colonial difference) and between subjects on the basis of their class.[24] Controls over emigration were targeted at the poorest Indians seeking to work abroad. Although even among indentured laborers there were upper-caste emigrants, especially from Bihar and Bengal, their primary reason for traveling away from their place of residence was economic hardship and, for the women among them, social exclusion.[25] Merchants and well-to-do classes of Indians traveling abroad did not face restrictions on their movement until the white settler dominions and the United States sought to prevent Indians from entering their territories.[26] Class, this chapter shows, continues to shape practices affecting and perceptions of overseas Indians well into the present.

Indians traveling overseas were not all drawn from the lower end of the economic spectrum. Another class of migrants was far less encumbered economically. These were members and representatives of "vernacular capitalists," to borrow Ritu Birla's term, namely transnational business families and networks, both Muslim and Hindu, and most famously Rajasthani Marwari, Tamil Chettiar, Gujarati, and Sindhi trading communities.[27] Long-distance trading communities were concentrated in entrepôt ports such as Malacca, Surat, Canton (Guangzhou), and Basra until the control of the Indian Ocean was ceded to European trading companies, after which they tended to concentrate in ports and trading cities dominated by the East India Companies.[28] By the end of the nineteenth century, closely linked networks of merchant capitalists could be found across the British Empire and its colonies, including South and East Africa, Singapore, and Hong Kong, as well as across British India. Merchants did not, however, confine themselves solely to empire's boundaries. Historian K. N. Chauduri notes that "Gujarati *bania* merchants [could be found] in Mocha [western Saudi Arabia], Gambroon [Bandar Abbas], Constantinople, and even Moscow."[29]

If indentured labor and transnational merchant communities mark the lower and upper bounds of the Indian diaspora, respectively, there were varieties of overseas Indians falling between these economic limits. Some circulated between India and the world; others settled abroad. G. Balachandran has shown how Indian sailors (lascars) had long been recruited to serve on European vessels trading with India, and, by the late eighteenth century, "were a common sight" in London.[30] Some sailors had been abandoned by their shipowners, while others jumped ship or were prevented from traveling on due to sickness and other misfortunes. By the beginning of the twentieth century, he notes, Indian sailors settled in England by choice, "to take advantage of employment and other opportunities."[31] Sugata Bose has drawn our attention to another kind of movement of Indians, namely the hundreds of thousands who served overseas in the Indian Army. The Indian Army, notwithstanding its name, was one of the most powerful instruments in the employ of British imperialism. Especially after 1857 and the formal incorporation of India into the British imperial system, the Indian

Army would scale up its mission from primarily being a means of extending and maintaining British power in territorial India to serving global British needs and interests.³² Like many other sojourners, the subalterns who fought and died in colonial and imperial wars from Afghanistan to Sudan to Gallipoli developed what Bose calls "diasporic patriotism": a novel sentiment that could not be contained by a stark choice between "the global British Empire and the territorial Indian nation with rigid borders."³³

As well as sailors, soldiers, businessmen, and coolies, overseas Indians included students and revolutionaries in exile.³⁴ These latter groups enter the historical record from the beginning of the twentieth century. As Harald Fischer-Tiné points out, this was a function of numbers more than anything else, aided in particular by new communications technologies and the increasing ease of long-distance travel. In 1903, there were a mere fifteen Indian students in Japan; by 1910, there were over a hundred.³⁵ Not surprisingly, students and exiles constituted the most explicitly politicized groups of Indians abroad and as a result, drew the most attention from colonial intelligence officers. Groups of Indian exiles could be found in continental Europe, especially Germany and France, the United States, Canada, and Japan, as well as in England. The Ghadar Party was active in San Francisco, while Berlin was the headquarters of the Indian National Party. "India Houses" emerged in London, Tokyo, and New York as important meeting points where plans were hatched, students radicalized, associations formed, transnational solidarities forged, and journals published and circulated. The *Indian Sociologist*, under the editorship of Shyamji Krishnavarma, started in 1905, was a particularly important example of such an effort.³⁶ As a result, nationalists, radicals, anarchists, and communists like V. D. Sarvarkar, Madame Cama, Mahendra Pratap, Barkatullah, Taraknath Das, Har Dayal, and M. N. Roy soon became well known, not only to British counterintelligence officials but also among the political youth and colonial intelligentsia in India. It was in this fervid context of transnational political activity that the Gujarati lawyer Mohandas Karamchand Gandhi emerged as a leader of South African Indians in the early twentieth century.³⁷

The End of World War I and Nationalist Reactions

The debate over indenture and the maltreatment of Indian labor overseas would spark multiple divisions within and across the British Empire: conservative planters versus liberal progressives, the dominions versus India, the government of India versus its subject populations.³⁸ Gandhi stands out among those entirely opposed to indenture in any form. But he was not alone. What we would now call nongovernmental organizations, such as the British Anti-Slavery Society and the Aborigine Protection Society, were consistent in condemning the system for its manifold abuses from as early as the middle of the nineteenth century.[39] They were resisted by the planter elite for obvious reasons but received support from English missionaries who had seen firsthand what the system really looked like. By the end of the nineteenth century, Indian organizations such as Gopal Krishna Gokhale's Servants of India Society had also taken up the cause of abolishing indenture and were pressing the Indian government to end this practice permanently. Lord Curzon, viceroy of India from 1900 to 1905, was not unsympathetic to this position, especially in relation to Indians in Natal, but stopped well short of ending indenture altogether. Matters first came to a head in 1912, when Gokhale introduced a motion in the Indian Legislative Council to end the practice of indenture permanently. After a heated debate with strong counterarguments offered by the government, the vote broke down on racial and official lines. All twenty-two Indians on the council voted for the resolution, and all thirty-three British officials voted against.[40] The motion did not pass.

In 1915, C. F. Andrews and W. W. Pearson, supporters of the Congress and associates of Gandhi, returned from a fact-finding mission to Fiji and wrote a devastating account of the conditions faced there by Indian laborers. In response, "civil society" organizations sprang up in opposition to indenture across the country. Meetings were held by, among others, the Home Rule League, Bengal Provincial Congress, UP (United Provinces) Congress, League for the Abolition of Indentured Emigration, and the Anti-Indenture League of Madras.[41] The Indian government took stock of the intensity of the feeling against indenture and wondered whether it might be time to make an official determination of the condition of Indian laborers and what steps to take in response. Their motives were less humanitarian than political, as Tinker points out. Viceroy Lord Hardinge would write to the Secretary of State: "[Indenture] arouses more bitterness [among Indians] than any other outstanding question" and should be abolished in the interests of "imperial unity and progress."[42] It is noteworthy that Hardinge spoke explicitly of Indian interests as distinct from imperial ones, showing that Indian views were not synonymous with imperial opinion on this issue. He would end his letter to London sharply pointing out: "It is not the duty of the Government of India to provide coolies for the colonies."[43]

The need to respond to Indian public opinion on this issue would continue to distance the government of India from the empire. It would eventually lead to Indian officials taking up residence in other parts of the empire to intervene in the treatment of overseas Indians, one of the first material signs of a foreign policy not subordinated to imperial needs and demands.[44] This novel extraterritorial extension of sovereignty by a colonial state was a direct outcome of the complex balance of power between the Empire, India, and its diaspora.

Some Congress leaders maintained great hope that the Paris Peace Conference would raise support from world opinion for Indian freedom. At the Delhi session of the Indian National Congress (1919), Madan Mohan Malaviya would describe Wilson as nothing less than "the great American who has evidently been appointed by God to be the master mason in building the new temple of international justice."[45] Bal Gangadhar Tilak would be nominated by the Congress to represent India's case at the Paris Peace Conference, hoping to draw the attention of the Great Powers to India's contemporary state of unfreedom.[46] However, Tilak was prevented from leaving London for Paris by the British government, who denied him the papers he needed for travel, forcing him to follow the conference proceedings from across the Channel. He would write to French President Clemenceau as well as to U.S. President Wilson, explaining why self-determination would apply to India, even though it was not a classic nation in the European sense.[47] He got a response only from Wilson, who assured him that India's case would be considered in "due time by the proper authorities."[48] Tilak tried to strengthen India's case by affirming that an independent India would be an active agent of peace and security in the region, continuing to defend British imperial interests, to little avail. The decline of faith with the international community and the growing distance between moderates and nationalists within the Indian National Congress would lead to demands for an autonomous foreign policy more closely aligned with Indian interests and needs.

Tilak's affirmation that Indian self-determination would not seek to break up the British Empire was a position increasingly at odds with postwar trends in nationalist opinion. Motilal Nehru's presidential address to the Congress in Amritsar (1920) makes clear that Indian nationalists had lost faith in the good offices of the Great Powers of the international community, notwithstanding Wilson's advocacy of national self-determination: "The pledges made by statesmen have proved but empty words . . . is it any wonder that the peace has aroused no enthusiasm and the vast majority of the people of India have refused to participate in the peace celebrations?"[49] With Gandhi's enormous success in leading the resistance to the Rowlatt

Act extending wartime emergency provisions, and amid rising industrial unrest in Bombay, Bengal, and Gujarat, the Congress Party would come to take a more forthright position on Indian independence, moving from "home rule" under British tutelage towards a call for *swarajya*, or self-rule.[50] The Congress announced a "noncooperation" policy, leading students to boycott their classes in droves: by the end of 1921, there were 20,000 nationalists in jails.[51]

The end of World War I led to an increasing public awareness of the importance of the international sphere and the need to formulate political positions on a variety of international issues beyond those important to elite Indian public opinion. Gandhi would write in his magazine *Young India*, "Indeed, while we are maturing our plans for *swaraj* (self rule), we are bound to consider and define our foreign policy."[52] Prompted by a request from the Central Khilafat Committee to "formulate a clear and definite foreign policy for India," the Congress tasked its Working Committee and Gandhi to take the first steps in formulating an independent foreign policy during its 1921 annual conference, held in Bombay.[53] The draft policy made clear that the Congress disassociated itself from British Indian foreign policy, notably with regard to its Asian neighbors, and affirmed that an independent India would behave very differently. Gandhi would turn his back on his own support for the British cause during the war and now announce that it was a "crime" to join the imperial armed forces.[54] On Burma, he would write, "I have never been able to take pride in the fact that Burma has been made part of British India. It never was and never should be."[55] Bimla Prasad, writing on the colonial-era foreign policy of the Congress, also notes how, from the early 1920s onwards, the Congress's annual reports would refer sympathetically to the situation in China and demand the withdrawal of Indian troops from the British contingent. Prasad also points to the early attraction of a pan-Asian federation among some of the Congress leaders, such as Chittranjan Das, a view supported by the Khilafat leader Maulana Mohammed Ali.[56]

The Khilafat movement was a direct outcome of the Paris Peace Conference.[57] Indian Muslims were aghast at the Great Powers' dismemberment of the Ottoman Empire and, especially, the removal of the Turkish caliph, custodian of the holy places of Mecca and Medina, in spite of promises made earlier. They first sent a delegation to London and Paris to plead their case and, when that failed, responded by calling for a national agitation. Mohammed Ali, one of the key Khilafat leaders, called on all Muslims serving in the British Army to resign. Gandhi supported the movement wholeheartedly, much to the dismay of Hindu-identified leaders such as Tilak and Malaviya, who saw this movement as confirmation that the political sensibilities of Indian Muslims were driven primarily by transnational confessional concerns, making them unreliable allies in the nationalist cause.[58] Lala Lajpat Rai, while also disturbed by this association with a Muslim cause, would address the international dimension differently. Recently returned from exile in the United States, Lajpat Rai was unsurprised by the British betrayal of the pledge to Indian Muslims to preserve the Ottoman sultan. Such was, he felt, imperialism at work. He would say in his address to the Congress in 1920 that "there is no such thing as a League of Nations. Great Britain and France are the League."[59] The Khilafat movement would eventually collapse with the arrest and jailing of the main leaders, including Gandhi and the Ali brothers. In hindsight, as Richard Gordon argues, it is possible to see this period as the apogee of political unity of Hindus, Muslims, and Sikhs in the anticolonial movement.[60]

Foreign Policy in Colonial India

There is no doubt that the international arena mattered significantly for "domestic" politics.[61] Major international events, from the Japanese military victory over Russia in 1905 to the Paris Peace Conference in 1919, altered the thinking of elites troubled in differing degrees by British rule in India. The dismal end to the optimism generated by the Paris Peace Conference in particular marked a turning point in Indian nationalist thinking.[62] The failure of Western powers to take seriously the injustices of colonialism marginalized Indian political figures unable to think beyond the "moderate" call for a greater degree of self-rule under a reformed colonial government.[63] Over the first two decades of the twentieth century, nationalists based in India would strengthen ties with Indian nationals agitating abroad for self-determination for India, as well as develop ties with other anticolonial and anti-imperial activists operating through transnational networks. Important meetings where Indians met with other revolutionaries and anticolonial nationalists included the Universal Races Conference, London, 1911; the Communist-led Baku Congress of Peoples of the East, held in 1920; the Bierville Peace Conference of 1926; and in particular the historic anti-imperial congress held in Brussels in 1927, which brought together 180 delegates from thirty-four countries. Indian National Congress delegate Jawaharlal Nehru was appointed to the Presidium of the Congress and would deliver one of the opening speeches. Along with Albert Einstein, Madame Sun Yat Sen, writer Romain Rolland, and British Labour Party leader George Lansbury, Nehru would also be elected to the Executive Committee of the newly formed and Berlin-based League Against Imperialism and for National Independence.[64]

During the 1920s, the intensity of anticolonial views grew among the Indian diaspora, especially students and exiles, who worked across Europe, America, and Asia to raise consciousness and support for the cause of Indian independence. Tactics learned and honed in one location could be deployed successfully in another one, as Gandhi showed most effectively. International issues with no apparent connection to India (for instance, the end of the Ottoman Caliphate) would have serious domestic implications. Most important, public opinion in India was deeply exercised by the cause of indentured Indians working in horrifying conditions in British plantation colonies. The well-being of Indian nationals living far from the territorial homeland was a matter of grave concern to a range of Indian opinion, beyond the Servants of India Society and the Indian National Congress. The condition of Indians in South Africa was a particular problem, made especially visible by Gandhi's long struggle for racial justice in that country. The pressure applied by public opinion on this issue would force the colonial Indian government to distance itself both from the white settler dominions as well as from the imperial government in London, taking, in effect, the first steps in the making of an independent Indian foreign policy. Increasingly exclusionary and restrictive legislation against Indians would lead to the appointment of an agent-general of the government of India to South Africa in 1927, in spite of the active resistance of the South African government, to monitor the treatment of Indians and to report back directly to the Imperial Legislative Council. This de facto diplomatic representative of India was tacit recognition of the inadequacy of the imperial system to protect the interests of Indian subjects and, simultaneously, the power of India, albeit less than fully sovereign, to insist on a separate channel of representation that was not subordinate to white dominion interests.

The need to respond sympathetically to Indian public opinion on the question of indenture strengthened a tendency toward relative state autonomy in colonial foreign policy already underway. As already noted, the viceroy in Delhi was the de facto sovereign of an extensive "informal empire" that stretched from the Gulf of Aden to Singapore.[65] Decisions to be made regarding this enormous sphere of influence rarely waited for permission from London. Moreover, the need to conform to London's onerous dictates was often seen as inconsistent with Indian interests. From the late nineteenth century onwards, the demands placed by the imperial center on Indian finances and military staffing had increasingly raised the ire of successive viceroys.[66] The liberal government of India had long balked at having to pay for the use of Indian army for imperial pacification due to the financial demands it implied, demands met largely through increased domestic taxation. As John Gallagher and Anil Seal note, "Expenditure on field armies in France . . . Mesopotamia . . . Damascus . . . Persia and South Russia might be in the interests of larger imperial interests but they had little to do with Indian interests more narrowly construed. London knew this; Delhi knew this; and so did Indian politicians."[67]

During World War I the British government allowed duties to be placed on English exports to India for the first time. Lancashire textiles were slapped with a 7.5 percent tariff, giving the government of India a new source of revenue to turn to when finances were strained. With the war also permitting Indian industry to flourish due to the unavailability of British imports, domestic industrialists sought to build on that momentum and called for greater protection through tariffs with some success, a remarkable policy change for what was once an avowedly laissez faire colonial state.[68] With the end of the war, which left India with a 370 million pound sterling debt, domestic political reforms led to Indians having a relatively greater say in fiscal decision making, making the task of extracting new revenues from India more difficult. Indian officials were now able to put even more pressure on London to reduce the use of the "sword arm of the empire,"[69] now over 40 percent of Delhi's annual budget expenditures.[70] If imperial and Indian interests had never been identical, this combination of international events and domestic political and economic pressures would force even an unrepresentative government of India to begin to privilege the interests of some of its more vocal and powerful domestic publics over its formal sovereign.

Signs of foreign policy independence, albeit less active ones, would not be restricted only to overseas Indians and fiscal relations with London. Indian high commissioners for trade would be accredited in London, Zanzibar, Alexandria, and Hamburg in the 1920s. In September 1930, India would sign a commercial treaty with Turkey, an independent state outside the British Empire.[71] India would be an active member of the League of Nations, join the International Labour Organisation (ILO), ratify the creation of a Permanent Court of International Justice, and become a founder-member of the United Nations organization, all before being recognized as a full international "person." In 1941, an Indian agent general would be appointed in Washington, D.C. In 1947, when India became a sovereign state, the country was already a party to no less than "627 treaties, conventions, agreements, etc., and a member of fifty one international organizations."[72] By any account, we can agree with T. T. Poulose, who calls India between 1919 and 1947 an "anomalous international person."[73]

"Old Friends Long Parted": Relations between Asia and India

If World War I and its aftermath marked a turning point in India and Indians' relationship to the international arena, World War II only strengthened these tendencies. During the 1914–1918 war, even nationalists like Gandhi were willing to help the imperial cause in the expectation that the end of the Great War would bring substantial benefits to India. The dashing of those hopes shaped India's response to World War II in important ways. For one, there was little possibility that Indians could now be voluntarily encouraged to join the war effort en masse. British military humiliations in Southeast Asia, particularly the loss of Singapore, and the rapid movement of Japanese armies to the edge of British India made it clear that the British were no longer the dominant military force they once were. The celebrated exploits of Subhas Chandra Bose and his Indian National Army raised from Japanese prisoners of war and overseas Indians in Malaya and Burma divided public opinion on the means to national independence.[74] Nationalist leaders took advantage of the relative weakness of the British to push their cause for full sovereignty even further through massive campaigns of mobilization with an unequivocal message: Quit India. By the end of the war, it was clear that Indian independence was imminent. Although there was still little clarity on the shape of the new state to be, there was no doubt that independence would come, and soon. With sovereignty on the horizon, Jawaharlal Nehru, prime minister in the interim government of 1946–1947, would begin to consider India's international responsibilities and overseas commitments more explicitly.

In his close attention to Indian relations with other Asian countries, Nehru was following in the tradition of the Indian National Congress since the early 1920s. The Congress had repeatedly mentioned their concern about the use of Indian soldiers in imperial military actions in other Asian countries, including China, and had identified with nationalist movements in Burma and Ceylon. A Vietnamese delegate had attended the 1928 session of the Indian National Congress, and both Indochina and Indonesia had sent delegations to India soon after World War II seeking support for their nationalist movements. The Indonesian cause in particular found ready support in Delhi; somewhat less so the appeal from the Viet Minh. Nehru would reject Sarat Chandra Bose's proposal to create an Indian-led pan-Asian auxiliary force—"Indian Lafayettes"—who would fight with the Vietnamese against the French. Nehru's reaction to this proposal, Sardesai convincingly argues, showed his growing concern over the power of Communist forces across much of Asia.[75] Indonesia was led by nationalists who had already proven their anti-Communist credentials and would go on to crush the Communist rebellion in 1948; Indochina showed a much more complicated configuration of anticolonial forces, making it far more difficult to know which nationalist side to back. In general, however, Nehru's approach to Asia was shaped by imprint of colonial geopolitical thinking (see Chapter 4), the strong desire to resist efforts by European powers to recover their colonial possessions lost during the war, and what might be called a sense of diplomatic noblesse oblige, that a large state like India bore no small responsibility in assisting the less fortunate people of the region.

Soon after taking office, he would say in a radio broadcast, "We are of Asia and the peoples of Asia are nearer and closer to us than others. India is so situated that she is the pivot of Western, Southern, and South-East Asia."[76] The centrality of Asia to Indian thinking about the world would take active shape in the form of the Asian Relations Conference, held in March and April 1947, a few months before India became independent.[77] The Asian Relations Conference was the first international conference organized in a colonial state that brought together delegates of the leading nationalist movements in Asian countries still under colonial rule. Among the delegations were Palestine (represented by the Hebrew University of Jerusalem), Tibet, the Soviet Central Asian countries, Egypt, and Soviet Georgia. Indian ambivalence over whom to back in Indochina was reflected in the decision to invite both the Democratic Republic of Vietnam, led by Ho Chi Minh, and the French-supported regime in Cochin-China. The largest delegations were from India, Indonesia, Burma, Ceylon, and Malaya.[78]

The intent of the Asian Relations Conference was to allow Asian countries, long isolated from each other by colonial rule but soon to become sovereign states, to get to know and understand each other better. As Nehru would put it in his opening statement:

> This Conference is significant as an expression of the deeper urge of the mind and spirit of Asia which has persisted in spite of the isolationism which grew up during the years of European domination. As that domination goes, the walls that surrounded us fall down and we look at each other again and meet as old friends long parted.[79]

Almost all the opening speeches of national delegations took up this high-minded rhetoric, especially dwelling on essentialized civilizational differences between Asia and Europe and celebrating the likelihood that a free Asia would inaugurate a new, less belligerent, mode of international discourse.[80]

However, once the round table discussions on Racial Problems and Asian Migration (Group B) began, inter-Asian differences, rather than civilizational unity, would take over the discussion.[81] The question that dominated the Group B roundtable discussion was the issue of racial—particularly Chinese and Indian—minorities. It was agreed by all the delegates that sovereignty brought with it the right to control who would enter their territories. The problem was how to address the conjoined historical legacies of colonial rule and international capital's need for labor. This politico-economic conjuncture had led to the presence across Asia of linguistically and culturally distinct communities who were long-standing residents of one country but had emigrated there from somewhere else. Delegates from a number of Asian countries saw the presence of nonindigenous ethnically distinct communities—minorities—as among their most pressing political problem, once sovereignty was achieved.

The discussion revolved around two related questions. To whom did overseas Indians and Chinese owe their primary loyalty: Was it to their former homelands (as most delegates suspected), or was it to their current countries of residence, as these ethnic communities claimed? Moreover, would the largest countries of Asia, India and China, become the new hegemons in the region, using these overseas nationals as a fifth column? A Burmese delegate stated this fear bluntly: "[While] it was terrible to be ruled by a Western power, . . . it was even more so to be ruled by an Asian power."[82] Moreover, the problem was not a static one, he argued. What made the issue even more pressing was that while Indian and Chinese birth rates were steadily rising, "The death rate among Burmese was mounting."[83] If these trends continued, Burmese could look forward to becoming the demographic minority in their own country, he feared. The demographic pressure on local populations was repeated by a number of delegates. A Malayan delegate bemoaned that only 40 percent of his country's residents were indigenous; the rest, he claimed, were Indians and Chinese.[84] Another delegate cast the issue in explicitly political terms. Citizenship could be granted only to those who "regarded Malaya as the [sole] object of their loyalty." Indians and Chinese living in Malaya should "make a vital and final choice" about which country they owed allegiance to. The "Chinese in Malaya," he said bluntly, "cannot have their bodies there and their minds in China."[85] Some delegates identified the paradox produced by emigrant ethnic communities. Granting them citizenship and permanent residence would "go against the [interests of] indigenous races," one Burmese delegate noted: at the same time, it was "unfair" to send emigrants back to homelands they had long since abandoned. Representatives from Ceylon (Sri Lanka) pointed to complications in identifying who was or was not a legitimate resident of the country, notwithstanding an immigrant past. Tamils in Ceylon were of two kinds, he noted, the relatively recently arrived "Estate Tamils," who were nothing more than an "itinerant alien labour population," and the long-resident "Jaffna Tamils," who had lived in Ceylon "for generations." He insisted that only the former should be asked to return to their places of origin.[86]

As the discussion went on, concerns generated by ethnic loyalties and lengths of overseas residence were supplemented by other markers of difference. Responding to a Chinese delegate's accusation of communal violence against Chinese living in Indonesia as well as legislation targeting the interests of the Chinese community, Indonesians reacted strongly. The problem was both historical and cultural, they responded. The Dutch colonial regime had "enriched the Chinese at the expense of the Indonesians" and used them as "agents provocateurs." But more important, the Chinese were "narrow minded" and quite unassimilated despite "three centuries of stay." The Republican Chinese chairman of the session, Dr. Wen Yuan-ning, agreed to some extent with these comments, noting the "exclusiveness" of the Chinese community and acknowledging that their wealth tended not to be spent for the benefit of the country they lived in but sent elsewhere. An Indian delegate tried to explain the dilemma faced by emigrant communities. He argued that funds were sent elsewhere because of the insecurities faced by overseas Indian and Chinese communities. Precisely because their legal status was uncertain, they had little choice but to protect themselves by sending money overseas as a hedge against being expelled. This repatriation of funds then created a vicious circle where local communities resented emigrant businessmen for not investing in their country of residence.[87] Exacerbating these concerns was the emerging geopolitical map of Asia, namely smaller Asian countries' fear of militarily powerful India and China. As one delegate put it: "The problem was not so much of racial dislike as a suspicion . . . of India and China . . . [smaller countries] might get mixed up with these big countries through their immigrant communities."[88] Chinese responses to these charges ranged from the conciliatory to the aggressive. They pointed out that overseas Chinese were not politically active; they were primarily a commercial community and hence no threat to their country of residence. If they were "economically functionless," as one delegate put it, they could be sent away, and the Nationalist Chinese government would find ways of absorbing them back.

These responses did little to assuage stated fears. Chinese delegates went on to argue that Nationalist China did not encourage emigration and that consular officials had told the Chinese residents of Malaya explicitly that they had to make a choice between local and Chinese citizenship. While stating that Chinese law did not permit dual citizenship, they also acknowledged that reacquiring Chinese citizenship was not at all difficult. Seeking to explain why Chinese continued to retain their citizenship in spite of long stays overseas, a delegate noted, "Citizenship [is] a personal affair." It might be held as "a matter of sentiment." An ominous note was struck when one Chinese delegate reminded the roundtable that if immigrants were asked to "naturalize within a short time or get repatriated" there was a good chance that violent conflict might break out.[89]

By contrast to the Chinese, Indian delegates at the roundtable appeared to identify far less with their overseas compatriots. In spite of the overwhelming and valuable support of the Indian diaspora for the freedom of India, the Indian National Congress had begun "sounding" like a state from as early as the 1920s. Conference delegates reaffirmed their distance from the diaspora and expressed little concern about cutting ties with their overseas compatriots permanently. Indian delegates began by stressing that inter-Asian migration had come about through "no fault" of the sending or receiving countries. The problem faced by soon-to-be independent countries was a legacy of imperial power over which they had had little say or control. But when it came to the condition of the migrants themselves, Indians were quick to question whether they were really "Indian" any more. Speaking of Indians in Ceylon, delegates noted that they "had lost touch with India" and were thus "not in a position to get help from [India]." India had enough problems of its own to deal with and "did not have space enough to take them back." Nevertheless, "Their case demanded human justice all the same." Overall, the Indian response to the problem of ethnic emigrant communities was clear: "Countries like India and China should not encourage emigrants to look for help to their home country, . . . emigrants permanently settling in a foreign country should be advised to identify themselves with that country."[90] The conference proceedings show clearly that, first, an independent India was going to reaffirm the Indian

National Congress's position that, notwithstanding their sacrifices and support for the cause of independence, overseas Indians should not expect to be able to return to a free India. They were encouraged to continue to make their homes overseas and to make whatever local political compromises they needed to in order to ensure their own safety. Second, Asian countries on the brink of independence had no doubt that independence from colonial rule would lead to the inauguration of sovereign nation-states defined as territorially bounded entities ruled by a majority nation. However, as in a newly redrawn Europe, postcolonial sovereignty would have to grapple with the permanent ethnic minority as a "foreign" element integral to the new Asian nation-state.

Ethnic Minorities and Indigenous People

In his biography of the American geographer Isiah Bowman, a key advisor to Woodrow Wilson in Paris, Neil Smith notes, "More than religious differences, military considerations, resources, and economics, ethnicity was the fulcrum of territorial conflicts and settlements at [the Paris Peace Conference]."[91] After Paris, ethnicity meant much more than a singular combination of racial, linguistic, and cultural traits. It had now become the sine qua non of political identity. The new norm of national self-determination meant that ethnic groups were now nascent political communities, provided they could successfully claim a homeland, the first and indispensable step toward international recognition as an independent state. Put another way, having a political presence presupposed an ethnic community with long-standing claims to a place in the world.

Underlying the expressed anxieties of Burmese, Malayan, Indonesian, and Ceylonese delegates to the Asian Relations Conference was an implicit clarity over the character of the political entity that would come into being at the end of colonial rule. As the previous section has shown, it was widely agreed that postcolonial Asia would be inhabited by territorially bound nation-states, as the Wilsonian norm of self-determination appeared to stipulate. Asian Relations Conference delegates' expressions of concern over the loyalties of Indian and Chinese emigrant communities was paralleled by a confidence that the character of the new states would be defined by the norms of the "original" inhabitants of these countries. Newly independent states would "belong" to the ethnic majorities of these countries, of whose identity there was no doubt. Yet it is impossible not to be struck by the extreme contrast between this new and confidently articulated vision and the lived historical experience of the Asia-Pacific region.

"Asia before Europe" was a multiracial, multiethnic, polyglot space of circulation.[92] Even small trading ports like Hoi An in eastern Vietnam would see "ships from Japan . . . Chinese merchants . . . Portuguese and Dutch" during their four-month trading fair, and "the Vietnamese welcomed [them] all."[93] In the mid-fifteenth century, one-quarter of the 400,000 residents of Ayutthaya in central Thailand were alleged to be foreign born. André Gunder Frank quotes the Portuguese traveler Tome Pires that trading vessels could be seen leaving the Thai city for "China, Ainam, Lequois, Cambodia, Champa, Sunda, Palembang . . . Cochin China, and Burma and [Chiangmai]. From the Tenasserim [western] side Siam also traded with Pase, Pedir, Kedah, Pegu, Bengal and [Gujarat]."[94] Historian K. N. Chaudhuri tells us of the "millionaire bankers of Surat [who] financed trade to Delhi, Agra, Bijapur, Golconda, Mocha, Hormuz, and Bandar Abbas."[95] Even the urban topography of Asian cities spoke of faraway places: "The skylines of Canton [Guangzhou] and Hugli were pierced by buildings of totally dissimilar architectural forms and idioms. The soaring roof of the Chinese pavilioned-style houses symbolized the Celestial Empire as much as the Indo-Islamic architecture of power with its arched gateways, domes, cupolas, minarets and latticed balconies."[96] The most famous of all ports was of course Malacca (Melaka), founded in the thirteenth century, with thousands of foreign traders in long-term residence, including Gujaratis, Turks, Armenians, Arabs, Persians, and people from the African continent.

This cosmopolitan trading space was not all of Asia, by any means. Rural Asia was still very much in the grip of rulers who brooked little resistance to their absolute rule. However, majority ethnicity and hard territorial boundaries did not define precolonial Asian states. As James Scott notes, speaking of Southeast Asia, "Unambiguous unitary sovereignty, of the kind that is normative for the 20th century nation-state, was rare outside a handful of substantial rice-growing cores, whose states were, themselves, prone to collapse. Beyond such zones, sovereignty was ambiguous, plural, shifting, and often void altogether. Cultural, linguistic and ethnic affiliations were likewise, ambiguous, plural, and shifting."[97] It took the European conquest of this region to reconfigure political space such that a state infrastructure emerged that was consistent with, and sought to institute, territorial norms of sovereignty. It was colonization that actively produced the ethnic realignments that made ideas of majorities and minorities a vernacular common sense.[98]

The effect of postcolonial sovereignty was to erase these multiple histories of the region, conflate indigenous and ethnic categories into a national majority, and render it all into a national myth. To produce this national myth, ethnic history was collapsed into territorial possession and became static and timeless.[99] By the middle of the twentieth century, Malays, Burmans, Javanese, and Sinhalese could identify themselves as the indigenous nation that would inherit their soon-to-be independent states, and, in the same breath, dismiss the rights of other communities, whether Chinese, Shan, Toraja, or Tamil, as nothing more than the special pleadings of "ethnic minorities." The claims of aboriginal communities, from Malaya's *orang asli* to Ceylon's Veddas, were not even worthy of mention. The political logic of nation-territory-state led to two hierarchies: on the one hand, majorities versus minorities, imagined on the basis of demographic size and migration histories; on the other hand, modern/civilized versus primitive/backward, a distinction between populations who had entered and accepted the norms of modern Western civilization and their uncivilized counterparts, the indigenous people. The newly unmarked national center would produce two corresponding margins: the ethnic minority, who were too new to be politically entitled; and the indigenous people, who were too old. Let us now look back to the Asian Relations Conference.

The Asian Relations Conference began with speeches that sought, above all else, to rewrite the hierarchy of world civilizations. Establishing Asia as a distinct cultural space marked by norms of tolerance, openness, and enlightened pacifism was a means of discursively claiming the right of Asia to be politically free.[100] But "civilization" was more than a rhetorical device to be used and dropped when circumstances changed. The deep logic of civilizational thinking had sunk deep into the minds of Asian elites, as is most clearly demonstrated in the discussion of Asia's own civilizational Others, namely "backward" and "indigenous" peoples. Reporting on discussions in Group B, the conference proceedings note:

> The Group finally discussed the problem of *indigenous* and *backward* populations ... Some backward tribes had already been assimilated into the local communities, others were in the process of assimilation, and some still remained *untouched by civilization*. A scientific study of these people was advocated with a view to finding out how and why the aboriginal tribes had remained primitive in the midst of civilization. International cooperation seemed to be called for in handling the problem of backward and tribal people.[101]

Discussing this aspect of the report in the group plenary, the chair of the session, well-known Indian official, writer, and diplomat K. M. Pannikkar (who will reappear in the next chapter in another guise), would point out that "these people," were "distinct from the rest of the population" not due to "political development, nor to administrative arrangements" but "owing to their age-old cultural and racial isolation. Their assimilation to the standards of advanced civilization was by no means easy and could not be left to chance."[102] The irony of discussing, in words that could have been taken directly from the mouths of much-reviled European colonial administrators referring to Asia, the "problem of indigenous and backward populations" seems to have been completely missed by the conference delegates. Castigating European arrogance in one session, and turning around and using the same language when speaking of "these people . . . untouched by civilization" in another, demonstrates vividly how deeply ideas of racial and civilizational superiority had become a part of the Asian elite worldview.

This slippage should not come as a surprise. Colonial Asian elites had long been steeped in the knowledge-systems of Europe; indeed, such expertise was a condition of having political voice and being taken seriously within colonial societies. Hence, that Asian elites would adopt and internalize the explicit conditions of distinction embedded in dominant social and political institutions is to be expected. Asian articulations of their own difference worked by inverting the familiar hierarchy but were not able to transcend it. This new articulation did little more than relocate Asian civilization in global hierarchies, seeking to make it preeminent rather than subordinate; it did not go further and offer a critical appraisal of the *idea* of civilization. The limits of such thinking, epitomized by the low esteem indigenous people were held in, show that Asian elites were not able to think outside the categories of race and civilization as a way of identifying and marking their social and cultural boundaries. Even as they sought to go beyond colonial categories, we find Asian elites had internalized entirely the racial logics through which the world was seen and its various divisions naturalized, a practice that would have important implications for foreign policy decision making, as the next chapter shows.

The Identities of Overseas Indians

Speaking in the Constituent Assembly some months after the Asian Relations Conference, Nehru would acknowledge the insecurities generated by overseas Indians in their countries of residence. He would frame it as a "romance" gone tragic. On the one hand, Indians had gone overseas to seek their fortunes and through sheer dint of hard work "gradually worked their way up . . . [because] India is a country which in spite of everything has abounding vitality and spreads abroad." However, "That [vitality] naturally frightens others who may not have that vitality in them, and they want to protect themselves against it." He would go on to say that in spite of India's obvious concern with protecting the "legitimate" interests of Indians abroad, the government would not "injure the cause of the country they are in."[103] The cause of Indians overseas would forever be subordinate to bilateral relations between India and their countries of residence.

Hanging in the balance was the question of whether overseas Indians were really Indians at all. A few months later, in another legislative debate, Nehru would ask, "These Indians abroad—what are they . . . If they are not [Indians], our interest in them becomes cultural and humanitarian, not political."[104] Nehru would make it clear that the only option for overseas Indians if they were to have any political rights and entitlements was to become citizens of the countries they lived in. For those who insisted on retaining Indian nationality, the Indian government could, at best, seek "most favoured" treatment given to resident aliens in those countries. Overseas Indians could expect little more because their long residence abroad had made them something other than entirely Indian. Speaking a decade later, his position had hardened further:

> There are the other [people of Indian origin] who have been in countries like Ceylon for 30, 40, 50, or 60 years, whatever the period may be, whom we do not consider our nationals. They have settled down in these countries and many of them have been born there. So far as we are concerned, strictly, legally and constitutionally, it is none of our problem. They are not our nationals.[105]

Referring to Indians living in South Africa (and in spite of intense diplomatic efforts by India in the United Nations and the Commonwealth to condemn the apartheid system from 1946 onwards), Nehru would say, "[They] are not Indian nationals . . . they are [only] people of Indian descent."[106] Such a distancing of overseas Indians from "real" Indians reached its apogee, as already mentioned, with the Ugandan crisis in 1972.

The first sign of change in independent India's diaspora policy emerged in 1987 when the Fijian military overthrew the elected Indian-dominated government of Dr. Timoci Bavadra. Fiji, like Guyana, was a former plantation colony where emigrant Indians had since become a demographic majority. Ethnic tensions between Indo-Fijians, the majority population, and native Fijians, who were now numerically a minority, were long-standing. Relations were particularly strained over the control of the economy. Fijians of Indian origin dominated much of the small business and commerce in the country, while ethnic Fijians controlled almost all of the land. When the military coup took place in Fiji, Indian diplomacy responded quite differently when compared with the Ugandan crisis a decade before. While contemporary commentators saw India's reaction charting a middle ground, between "intrusive interest and complete indifference," in fact, to show any interest in the fate of overseas Indians was in itself a remarkable change of policy.[107] Prime Minister Rajiv Gandhi sought to impose Commonwealth sanctions on Fiji, to little avail. He then turned to regional powers, Australia and New Zealand, to find a solution that would protect the condition of Indo-Fijians. India's reaction to the plight of overseas Indians was far more aggressive than in the past but, given its lack of resources and reach, could amount to very little in real terms. However, that there was a reaction at all is worth noting. Although it would not be incorrect to see India's reaction to the Fiji crisis as another symptom of its efforts to assert itself as a regional power under Rajiv Gandhi, it is worth noting the novel object of those efforts, namely, a far-flung diaspora that India had shown little interest in for decades.[108] In retrospect, India's response to the Fiji crisis can also be seen as a very early first step in shaping a new policy toward overseas Indians.

India's approach to its diaspora, from the brink of independence until the end of the twentieth century, can be summed up simply. India would privilege state-to-state relations with the governments of the countries in which Indians lived, rather than extend to the diaspora the help and support they often requested and needed. The official position of the government of India was that Indians who were longstanding residents of foreign countries had given up their rights of protection from the Indian state, even when they continued to hold Indian passports. India would continue to have a "cultural and humanitarian" interest in overseas Indians, but, if they wanted political voice, their best recourse was to become citizens of the countries they lived in. With the arrival of political independence, what was once a globally dispersed Indian nation struggling for the right of national self-determination and a partially sovereign Indian state that saw the protection of Indians anywhere in the world as an issue of state concern had undergone radical change. The meaning of Indian nationality had been territorialized to include only those resident within the Indian geobody.

Diaspora, Territory, and Hierarchy

This chapter has argued that the political imperative of developing good relations with its Asian neighbors was the most direct reason for India's repudiation of its diaspora after independence, notwithstanding the close and mutually supportive relations between India and its overseas residents during the colonial period. Underlying this turnaround in 1947 was the global political transformation initiated by the new international norm of national self-determination. India, as we have seen in an earlier chapter, was an unlikely candidate for sovereignty and international recognition, based on a narrow reading of the self-determination norm. India's partial recognition as a member of the international system was at best an imperfect guarantee that it would be recognized as a sovereign state when the British withdrew. India's long-standing uncertainty over the terms of its international recognition was exacerbated by the geopolitical truncation of what was once the British Indian state. With the simultaneous creation of Pakistan, it could not even claim unambiguously to be the sole successor state of British India. In response, India moved swiftly to reconfirm its territorial sovereignty in all possible ways. It speeded up the process of absorbing semisovereign territories—princely states—lying within its newly defined political territories and militarized its borders to the extent it was able, including sending its armed forces to prevent the accession of Kashmir to Pakistan.[109]

Under these circumstances, to promote ties with a globally dispersed Indian nation that far exceeded its new territorial borders was a struggle beyond its capacity to sustain. India could not afford to have a global diaspora making claims on its nationality at the moment when it was one of the first postcolonial states seeking recognition as a new nation-state. To enable the imperative of external recognition to be as uncomplicated as possible, Indian foreign policy drew a closed territorial border within the global Indian nation, corresponding to the limits of the land physically occupied and militarily controlled by the successor state. Adding to the pragmatic diplomatic reasons for dividing the global nation, the new nation-state sought to contain the contradictions inherent in its claims to be recognized as sovereign by bounding India territorially.

Starting in the late 1970s, India's understanding of the value of its overseas residents underwent important shifts. The first change was the enormous growth in financial remittances generated by Indian migrant workers in Saudi Arabia, Iraq, Kuwait, and Persian Gulf sheikhdoms such as Dubai, Muscat, and Oman.[110] Following the oil shocks of the 1970s, the huge economic revenues that poured into the coffers of the Arabian members of OPEC had created an enormous local demand for modern infrastructure, technology, goods, and services on a scale unimaginable a few years before. South Asian men, especially Indians, Pakistanis, and Bangladeshis, began to migrate in large numbers to the Gulf to participate in this economic frenzy.

Indians were concentrated at the lower end of the economic ladder, especially in the hardest and most demeaning activities, including construction, sanitation, retail, and household services.[111] In spite of the relatively low wages, racial and religious discrimination, and harsh working conditions, the sheer number of Indians workers working in the Gulf led to substantial financial remittances returning to India from the 1980s onwards. No serious economic policy maker could deny that India's historically weak balance of payments calculus was now eased in no small measure because of the contribution of Indians coming from the lower end of economic and social scales.[112] For all that, and in marked contrast to the evolving policies of countries such as the Philippines who also derived considerable returns from remittances, it would take the government of India decades to appreciate the economic value of these working-class migrants and to begin targeted diplomatic activities directed at protecting their rights. In the eyes of Indian diplomats and domestic middle classes, the Gulf workers were direct descendents of the *girmitiyas*, an uncouth and embarrassing national burden that was willy-nilly representing India abroad. The situation was made all the worse by the remittances this working class sent home to a country suffering the lack of foreign exchange.

By the 1980s, the number of middle-class, upper-caste Indians living overseas had also become quite substantial.[113] Beginning especially with changes in U.S. immigration laws in 1965, Indians coming from the upper echelons of society had taken advantage of professional skills acquired in India at highly subsidized cost to emigrate abroad. Canada, the United States, Singapore, the United Kingdom, and Australia now had sizable Indian communities concentrated in business and high-value service sectors such as banking and information technology as well as professional areas such as higher education, medicine, and engineering. It was to these overseas Indians in particular that the Diaspora Report of 2001 was addressed. The report proposed that Indians living in North America (United States and Canada), Europe, Australia, New Zealand, and Singapore (Thailand and Malaysia are also mentioned elsewhere in the report) be granted dual citizenship. "Non-resident" Indians (NRIs) who lived in these countries were a special case because these were "highly developed countries," and the Indians in question had emigrated after India became independent. The report found that NRIs living in advanced countries were coming under pressure to give up their Indian citizenship for practical reasons, while retaining great affection for their homeland. Dual citizenship was their solution to the problem. Earlier waves of Indian emigrants to the Caribbean,

Pacific, and Africa were noticeably not included as potential candidates for dual citizenship.¹¹⁴ Nor was any mention made of the need to make more effort to protect the rights of working-class Indians living in the Gulf states, from whom the bulk of overseas remittances were received. These groups were classed as economic migrants. The reasons for their departure, it was implied, were quite unlike the conditions that had led to the exodus of the upper-caste middle-class migrants to the West.

Also noted in the report is a chapter on "security considerations." This turns out to refer to the danger that ineligible candidates could sneak through a newly liberalized citizenship regime. Betraying a deep anxiety over who constituted a "real" Indian, the chapter dismisses unidentified fears that these new provisions could lead to an influx of Muslims living in neighboring regions that were once part of territorial India. The report was confident that existing governmental machinery would ensure that only "worthy" candidates would be admitted to dual nationality status. There need be no fear that Muslim Pakistanis and Bangladeshis who might fall under the provisions of the law would be awarded this status, it assured its readers, as Article 7 of the Constitution had already withdrawn Indian citizenship from those who had left the country by March 1, 1947.

The report is clear in its purpose in proposing the creation of a system of dual citizenship. It argued that restricting the special status of dual citizens to overseas Indians living in developed countries was entirely justified. This would not create a new "social divide" in the country, in the opinion of the committee, as the existing "social divide [at home] in terms of economic disparities is already sharp." In other words, adding a few more thousands to that existing divide would not make much difference! New rules would allow those Indians who had left the country after independence, that is, the majority of whom were presumably upper-caste and middle-class Hindus, to regain Indian nationality, while at the same time preventing religious others from taking advantage of these new rules. There was no question about including working-class Indians or the descendents of working-class Indians who had left India generations before.

Latha Varadarajan offers a compelling set of arguments explaining why India recast the boundary that divided the global Indian nation into territorial and overseas Indians. Her explanation draws on the political economy of the Indian state, in particular the "neoliberal restructuring of the state" that required a "rearticulation of bourgeois hegemony."¹¹⁵ Varadarajan argues that the economic crisis of the early 1990s that began with a severe balance of payments problem marked the effective end of the postcolonial development model. Moreover, the crisis was preceded by a split within the bloc of Indian capital as new, more transnationally oriented capitalist sectors sought to supplant the old "large business houses" that had long dominated the Federation of Indian Chambers of Commerce. After decades of a relatively inward-looking and carefully regulated economic model during which the international sphere had been treated with more than a little suspicion by state bureaucrats and dominant sectors of domestic capital, a full-blown crisis of legitimacy was now underway. In this context, the need to adapt to the changes required for neoliberal restructuring produced an ideological challenge for the maintenance of bourgeois hegemony: "What was needed was a subject who could plausibly embody national aspirations [demonstrating] the potential of India to succeed in the global economy. . . . The rearticulation of bourgeois hegemony made essential a diasporic reimagining of the nation [. . . producing] the new subject, 'the global Indian.'"[116] This novel political economy–based argument makes an important contribution to our understanding of the rearticulation of the Indian nation in the last decade of the twentieth century. The contradictions of class and caste embedded in this intricate formulation can, however, be extended still further.

Underlying this inscription of a new boundary between home and abroad was an entirely new conception of the Indian diaspora. As we have seen, postcolonial Indian elites had long dismissed the category of overseas Indians by reducing it to the colonial-era movement of poor, low-caste Indians to faraway, relatively underdeveloped locations, including the Caribbean islands, Fiji, and Mauritius. India did not want to encourage a return of the descendants of the original *girmitiyas*. They were an embarrassing reminder of a time when India was weak and colonized. Moreover, living in countries even less developed than India, they had little to offer a country embarking on a new phase of neoliberal development and international visibility. The Diaspora Report replaced the tarnished image of the *girmitiya* as the emblematic overseas Indian with an entirely new sign, the NRI, or non-resident Indian. NRIs were invited to return to the Indian state as the exemplary representatives of a now globally prominent and internationally recognized Indian nation. Their success and presence in the most advanced countries of the world was symbolically important in providing a new image for India and Indians in the world. In addition, their numbers and resources in the United States in particular gave India a new diplomatic edge, as was evidenced by furious Indian-American lobbying in the aftermath of the India–U.S. nuclear agreement of 2005.[117] As

Varadarajan notes, the global Indian national was now subsumed under the sign of globalization, transforming the NRI into a representative of the most advanced forms of ethnic capitalism. The return of the global Indian nation was a product of the transformation of the image of the normative diasporic subject.

The starting point for the NRI as global Indian—a well-educated, well-paid, middle-class and upper-caste Hindu subject—foregrounds a patriotic citizen unfairly forced to go abroad due to the mistaken social policies of earlier Indian governments.[118] The narrative goes as follows: Under the socially progressive legislation that had shaped postcolonial India's social contract, special provisions termed "reservations" had been created for communities and groups long underrepresented in India's elite educational institutions, enabling them to obtain stable and prestigious government employment. Members of Backward and Scheduled Caste communities, Dalits, and Scheduled Tribes were given privileged access to education and jobs to compensate for their historic exclusion from a social system that had valorized and justified an economic and social hierarchy based on the accident of birth. With increasing numbers of formerly underprivileged groups now taking advantage of their legal rights and economic entitlements, upper-caste elites found themselves increasingly squeezed out of traditional occupations and unable to take full advantage of a system that had once catered entirely to their needs. The political turning point was the decision by the V. P. Singh–led government to implement the pro-reservation recommendations of the Mandal Commission in 1990.[119] Violent street demonstrations broke out across northern India, including a number of highly publicized self-immolations, accompanied by a public and reactionary upper-caste discourse of "merit."

Merit (or to be more precise, the decline of merit), was a politically loaded term that suggested that unworthy and incompetent lower castes were taking over positions for which they were unqualified, purely on the basis of the advantages conferred to them by the misfortune of their birth. By this view, the policy of reservations had gone too far and was now threatening the stability of the social order. Rather than acknowledge that their own elite privilege did not reflect pure merit but had been conferred on them by the fortune of their birth, large numbers of highly trained professional middle-class Indians had, since the 1960s, turned to the exit option. Their eventual economic success in their new homelands, seemingly without the benefit of prior privilege, was taken as objective evidence of their inherent talents. Such an outcome could also be turned into proof that it was impossible for India's best and brightest to reach their full potential in a socialistically inclined, overdemocratic India. The lessons were clear to those who could read them. Socialism had to be replaced by a market economy; Indian upper castes could now be brought home having proved that their success had nothing to do with inherited advantage. Success in a faraway and undiscriminating market economy had become proof of the inherent superiority—merit—of the upper-caste, middle-class Indian.

The political crisis accompanying the antireservation agitations reflected immanent contradictions in Hinduism as a cultural formation.[120] The 1990s were also the period when the Hindu majoritarian political party, the Bharatiya Janata Party (BJP), made its entry into national politics. A party dominated by upper-caste politicians claiming to represent the Hindu community found itself on the horns of a complex dilemma. To mobilize all sectors of the Hindu population, the BJP could not avoid addressing the contradictions of caste injustice that had long divided this community from within. This, however, needed to be done by means short of engaging a critique of Hinduism as a system. To finesse this problem and to shore up the internal fissures of a stable Hindu identity, the BJP led a series of massive political mobilizations targeting religious "others," especially Muslims. This strategy to unify a Hindu community under their saffron banner would be successful in the short term, and the BJP would come to power twice during this decade.

The emergence of the NRI, in other words, came against a backdrop not only of economic crisis but a crisis of the nation more generally. The latent identity of India as a Hindu nation was being proclaimed explicitly by the BJP even as Hinduism was under attack from within for its normalization of a historically unjust and unequal social hierarchy. It is in this context that the NRI emerges, not only as representative of the global Indian, as Varadarajan correctly points out, but also as a means of resolving domestic political tensions that began from the deep intertwining of caste and class. Even as the political landscape of India was becoming increasingly heterogeneous, the NRI could be represented as a site of social stability and traditional middle-class order for the reinstantiation of bourgeois hegemony. NRIs were "people like us," albeit living abroad. Having become financially successful and increasingly prominent in their adopted countries of residence without the benefit of ascribed social and economic privileges, upper-caste NRIs could now argue that their high ritual status was a reflection of their endemic talents, not merely an outcome of their birth.

The successful NRI was evidence that reservations were an unnecessary handicap in the quest for excellence as well as proof that the hierarchy of the Hindu system was based on an internal logic that was universally applicable.

The counterpoint to the postcolonial successes of overseas Indians in the developed West was the condition of working-class Indians in the oil-rich principalities of the Persian Gulf and Arabian peninsula. The millions of Indians who worked in the Gulf were not classed as NRIs. They represented the contemporary version of the original Indian emigrant *girmitiya*, poor, unskilled, lower caste, often Muslim, unquestionably subjects who left India as economic refugees.[121] Marginal figures at home and abroad, many existed only at the edges of the financial boom of the Persian Gulf, working long hours under brutal and unfree conditions to send home small sums of money to keep their families afloat.[122] Although the net sum of financial remittances from the Gulf to India have long exceeded the contributions of NRIs in the developed West, the government of India was loath to acknowledge the importance of these workers for its continued financial well-being. It took the first Gulf War and the ensuing loss of income from remittances before elite opinion realized the value of the contributions of working-class Indians in the Gulf for India's balance of payments. Even then, the political importance of ensuring good relations with the Gulf emirates and Saudi Arabia, both to ensure that Indians continue to get access to jobs and also to maintain an uninterrupted flow of oil from this region, led the Indian government to downplay the harsh working conditions under which working class Indians existed. Just as India did to the globally dispersed descendents of indentured workers in 1947, interstate relations were privileged over the protection of overseas Indian nationals due to the social identities of these overseas subjects.

The recommendations of the Diaspora Report would lead, in 2003, to the creation of a new state celebration, Pravasi Bharatiya Divas, or Overseas Indian Day. At the inaugural meeting, the government would announce that Indians living in the United States, United Kingdom, Canada, and Australia would be permitted to acquire "dual" citizenship. A year later, a new ministry would be formed, dedicated to the cause of overseas Indians. Over time, the conditions for acquiring dual citizenship would become slightly more inclusive following protests by Indians living in less salubrious locations than the developed West. Eventually two categories of overseas Indians would be created, one for those who had emigrated from India long before independence and for the children and spouses of former Indian citizens, People of Indian Origin (PIO); the other for people who had once held Indian citizenship but had acquired foreign passports through naturalization, that is, Overseas Citizens of India (OCI).

The new territorial boundary dividing India and its global nation has shifted, but it is only partially more inclusive than the one imposed in 1947. Descendents of the original *girmitiyas* living in countries lower than India on a global developmental scale and working-class Indians living in the Gulf were not intended to be the beneficiaries of the newly defined scope of the Indian diaspora. The boundary between the Indian territorial state and the Indian global nation has been shifted selectively. Foreign policy built around new meanings of citizenship and national identification has reterritorialized the Indian nation to reinsert non-resident upper-caste, middle-class Indians back into the Indian nation but not the lower-caste, possibly Muslim, overseas residents of less developed countries or the Indian working class. Even as the global Indian nation is now imagined in terms familiar from the beginning of the twentieth century, namely a deterritoralized and dispersed community, class and caste distinctions constitute the new territorial boundaries that are applied to divide the Indian nation from itself. State foreign policy practices, as should come as no surprise, work to maintain and reinforce existing social and political hierarchies, not to overturn them.

4

Geopolitics as Foreign Policy

Geopolitics works most visibly at and beyond the border between the state and the world. As such, it appears to exemplify the traditional foreign policy imperative of inscribing a territorial border between home and abroad. It is, however, also a territorializing practice that, like diaspora, seeks to bind state and nation. While diaspora as a foreign policy practice produces the effect of a territorial boundary *within* the body of the nation, separating a cartographically bound and a globally dispersed national community, geopolitics as foreign policy practice engenders boundaries at the limit of the state's territorial reach. Diaspora comes into play when the nation-state becomes the paradigmatic form of global political organization, while geopolitics is a territorializing practice that draws on a much older history of imperial state formation. As an imperial practice, it is inherently expansionist and internally contradictory. In a never-ending cycle, geopolitics seeks to establish new territorial boundaries beyond the existing limits of state power in the name of reducing the insecurities that prior expansion engenders. Expansion is justified in terms of the organicity of the imperial state, namely its "natural" tendency to grow in order to survive.

As long as the imperial mode of state power is in place, expansion is justified in terms of enhancing military security. Once the nation-state becomes the prevailing mode of state power, however, geopolitical expansion leads to the realization that territorial growth has led to the incorporation of people of "other" nations into the body of the state. An entirely new form of insecurity is produced that foreign policy has to resolve. It does so by producing new territorial boundaries that seek to contain these other nations spatially. Geopolitics, in other words, is a state territorial practice that produces national "outsiders within" the state, as opposed to diaspora's effect of producing national "insiders without" the territorial state.

Geopolitics came to be naturalized in postcolonial Indian thinking primarily through British imperial influence, reinforced by views of territory emergent from various strands of nationalist and anticolonial intellectual thought. As the first chapter details, these nationalist tendencies included the powerful religio-cultural vision of Mother India and the mercantilist framing of the Indian economy. In addition, a virulent strain of Hindu nationalism produced a territorial imaginary that divided Indians on the basis of the origins of their religious identifications, while modern historians imagined a "Greater India" that followed from the premodern circulations of people, trade, religious practices, and cultural products, especially in Southeast Asia and East Asia. Given the range of these intellectual sources, a postcolonial Indian foreign policy based on geopolitical visions of the world comes as no surprise, as long as we adhere to the conventional meanings of the nation-state and its foreign policy. Once territory is identified as the contingent hyphen joining nation and state, however, geopolitics can no longer be understood simply in these terms.

The following archeology of Indian geopolitics traces the direct connections between postcolonial geopolitics and its colonial forebears.[1] Early Indian strategic planning was based on a vision of Indian territorial insecurities that was shaped under the imperial banner of the Raj. The influence of colonial geopolitics overwhelmed independent India's military planners even as the conditions facing a physically truncated independent India differed substantially from the imperatives that drove the British Indian Empire. Indeed, as this chapter shows, even the policy of nonalignment, India's most explicitly postcolonial contribution to international relations, was deeply shaped by the imprint of colonial geopolitics.[2] This discussion leads to the debate on the allegedly contrasting views of Jawaharlal Nehru and Sardar Vallabhai Patel, India's first prime minister and deputy prime minister respectively, with regard to Tibet and shows that their positions are far more similar than they are different. The chapter closes with an analysis of how geopolitical practices of territorially bounding the homeland from national outsiders has transformed one border region, India's Northeast, into a "space of exception." The violent geopolitics of bounding the Northeast has created, I argue, a normative territorial boundary for the conduct of everyday life in the rest of the country.

Imperial Geopolitics

Geopolitics is a form of knowledge dating from the apogee of imperial expansion, the end of the nineteenth century.[3] Halford Mackinder has long been identified as one of the founding fathers of geopolitics, based on his classic account of heartlands and rimlands,[4] although *geopolitics* is not a term that he cared for.[5] The modern geopolitical imaginary, Gearóid Ó Tuthail argues, emerged at the moment when "the last pockets of unclaimed and un-stated space were surrounded and enclosed within the colonizing projects of expansionist empires and territorializing states."[6] This moment of "closed space" arrives at the end of the nineteenth century when the world's landmass was entirely divided up into discrete political units. This closure brought into prominence a new way of thinking about the relationship of people, territory, and state power that we now call geopolitics. Geopolitics, from Mackinder's (and other imperialists') standpoint, was a panoptic vision of the world, an imperial gaze that observes the world in all its relations: centrally "implicated in the operation of this panoramic vision was . . . the impulse to *master.*"[7] Friedrich Ratzel, Mackinder's German contemporary, would supplement this desire to control with a neo-Lamarckian account of human evolution, seeking to normalize the imperial search for territory. Ó Tuthail summarizes Ratzel's views of the modern state: "As an organism in a competitive struggle for existence, every great state with a growing population need[s] space in order to sustain and nourish its civilization . . . *lebensraum.*"[8]

The imperial territorial imaginary drew heavily on prevailing ideas of natural philosophy that allowed imperial expansion to be discursively justified in terms of organic metaphors. As Hayden White has shown in relation to the structure and poetics of historical and philosophical writing in the nineteenth century, metaphoric language contains an "explanatory affect" that apparent transparency in expression and explanation conceals.[9] Metaphors drawn from nature were powerful instruments of imperial geopolitics as expansion conceived of in terms that explicitly drew on images, and "truths" coming from the natural world made the process of territorial aggrandizement seem natural and inevitable. Underlying such commonplace and allegedly scientific stock phrases such as "nature abhors a vacuum" lie a justification for military expansion by offering a natural gloss on what is nothing more than decision making based on perceived state interests.

Starting from their foothold in the immensely rich province of Bengal, the English East India Company first invaded Nepal (1814), followed by Assam and Burma (1826), then Sindh (1839), Afghanistan (1838), and the Sikh empire of the Punjab (1845).[10] Through the nineteenth century, the external boundaries of India remained fluid under the pressures of expanding the company's revenue and political holdings. By the time the British government took over the East India Company in 1858, the physical area under their control stretched from Nepal to Ceylon. In the coming heyday of interimperial competition, the frontiers of British rule would be extended beyond western Punjab and eastern Assam. At the dawn of the twentieth century, at the same time as Halford Mackinder was presenting his influential thesis of the geographical "pivot" at the Royal Geographical Society, George Curzon was putting into practice very similar ideas as viceroy of India.

Even before taking up his position as viceroy in Calcutta in 1896—an appointment he had lobbied strongly for—Curzon had developed a substantial reputation as a strategic thinker of the first rank through his writings on Persia and other parts of the enormous region he was eventually to rule.[11] Curzon, along with McKinley and Roosevelt on the other side of the Pacific Ocean, was among the first political executives to justify imperial expansion through the medium of geopolitical theories explaining the apparent necessity of their actions.[12] In his case, what was of overriding concern was to ensure the means for the long-term defense of the British Empire's largest and most valuable possession. Two related aspects of Curzon's geopolitical legacy are crucial to understanding later strategic thought and practice in India. The first is the identification of the primary political threat to the Indian heartland as deriving from the northern land borders of the country, rather than its southern marine approaches. The second is his explication of the "frontier" as a foundational geopolitical category and the territorializing policies that would follow from this thesis. Although the critical politico-military turning points of the three centuries preceding Curzon's viceroyalty had invariably begun with seaborne incursions into the Indian landmass, that history was erased in Curzon's vision of imperial geopolitics. In a self-aggrandizing Romanes Lecture, delivered at Oxford University in 1907 after he had stepped down as viceroy, Curzon described the gradual but "historically inevitable" process by which the British Indian Empire "pursued, and is still pursuing, its as yet unexhausted advance":[13]

> First [the Empire] surrounded its acquisitions with a belt of Native States with whom alliances were concluded and treaties made. The enemy to be feared a century ago was the Maratha host and against this danger the Rajput States and the Oude [Avadh] were maintained as a buffer. On the northwest frontier, Sind and the Punjab, then under independent rulers, warded off contact or collision with Baluchistan and Afghanistan, while the Sutlej States warded off contact with the Punjab. Gradually, one after another, these barriers disappeared as the forward movement began: some were annexed, others were engulfed in the advancing tide, remaining embedded like stumps of trees in an avalanche, or left with their heads above water like islands in a flood.[14]

What is most remarkable about this description is that the British Indian Empire is portrayed as a movement that starts from the heartland of the region and that moves inexorably to its rim. Two centuries of British presence in India, from their early and tenuous seaborne and port-based footholds to their entry into the hinterland and their simultaneous transformation from a trading community to a powerful political actor are entirely effaced. The British, in Curzon's telling, appear as the original inhabitants of the subcontinent. Their movement outward, engulfing the Native States, becomes the inevitable and naturally justified account of a stronger force against a weaker one. He goes on to say:

> When annexation of the Punjab had brought British power to the Indus, and of Sind, to the confines of Baluchistan; when the sale of Kashmir to a protected chief carried the strategical (sic) frontier into the heart of the Himalayas: when the successive absorption of different portions of Burma opened the way to Mandalay, a new Frontier problem faced the Indian Government, and a new ring of protectorates was formed.[15]

The "forward movement" Curzon describes draws directly on the images of a natural force—especially inertia, the continuing momentum of a moving mass—to show that imperial expansion was inevitable and followed quasi-natural laws. Human agency is nowhere to be seen. The British advance is akin to a raging flood that cannot be stopped. Annexation follows absorption in an endless process of conquest and takeover of weaker states with little to explain this tendency other than what Curzon elsewhere refers to as "centripetal tendencies." Imperialism is here stripped of older justifications, from civilizing missions or even commercial profit, and reduced to a primeval force that has no choice but to keep moving. There does not seem to be any human agent in charge of this ceaseless motion. Just as the tide, avalanche, and flood have no obvious author other than the force of Nature, understanding imperial expansion must look beyond the mundane world.[16] This expansionary process could not cease until one imperial power controlled the whole globe. By the same token, the moment of greatest danger to world order is when two or more Great Powers—each operating according to the primitive logic of natural domination of the stronger over the weaker force—come into contact with each other at the frontiers of their respective territorial holdings. Thus, frontiers become the "razor's edge on which hang suspended the modern issues of life and death ... Frontier policy ... the main source of diplomatic preoccupation ... and international danger ... has a more profound effect upon the peace or warfare of nations than any other factor, political or economic."[17]

Two disastrous Afghan campaigns and Anglo-Indian writers like Rudyard Kipling in *The Man Who Would Be King* (1888) had already helped create a fetish of the unruly inhabitants of the Hindu Kush mountain range, but it was Curzon's framing that brought the idea of the strategically vital mountain pass into political relief. Curzon offered up a vision of India at the center of an imperial theater of power. With the seas on three sides of the Indian peninsula controlled by the Royal Navy, the geopolitical eye seeking danger was drawn to the unguarded northern perimeter. Here, the forbiddingly high and long Himalayan mountain ranges appeared to create a natural defensive boundary to the Indian subcontinent, offering some comfort to the anxious military planner. What had to be monitored most carefully, however, were the gaps—"grooves" in Curzon's language—in this great natural defense, namely the passes through the Karakoram range, especially the Khyber and Bolan Passes, which joined Kandahar in the high plains of Afghanistan with Peshawar in the western extremities of British India. With no need for concern over the seaborne approaches to India, it seemed obvious that it was only through these openings that invaders—going back to Alexander the Great—had and would pass to attack the fertile and rich lands to the east. Nonepisodic and ongoing flows of travelers, traders, caravans, goods, scholars, and pilgrims would be entirely incidental—and irrelevant—to the geopolitical narrative of external danger and insecurity.

With the seas controlled by the Royal Navy, for Curzon the gravest threats to the security of the Indian subcontinent came from the north and northwest, where little stood between a rising Great Power and a much-coveted all weather "warm-water" port. The apparent inevitability of the Russian search for a warm-water port, and hence its "natural" interest in Persia and today's Pakistan, followed the same logic as the formation of the British Indian Empire.[18] One could look to immediate causes, such as the "rapid growth of population" or the "economic need for fresh outlets," to understand why Great Powers needed to expand, but, beyond those anodyne causes, the logic of expansion needed no explanation. The geopolitically determined drive for expansion to the warm waters of the Persian Gulf even made it possible to ignore the nature of the regime in Moscow. Whether representing the czars or the commissars, Russia would be driven to find an all-weather marine outlet by the geopolitical necessity of doing so. When Russian will was so determined, all that stood in the way of expansion was distance and terrain. The expansionist tendencies of Russia, the great heartland state lying to the north of India, whether in its royalist and Soviet incarnations, became an impeccable imperial alibi for the need to control the lands beyond the Himalayan mountain barrier.

A responsible imperial executive, according to Curzon, could not let the protective mountainous range do its work passively. Maximizing the defensive value of the natural frontier would lead to the pursuit of the "Scientific Frontier." This was a "frontier which unites natural and strategical (sic) strength, and by placing both the entrance and the exit of the passes in the hands of the defending Power, compels the enemy to conquer the approach before he can use the passage. It is this policy that has carried the Indian outposts to Lundi Khana, to Quetta, and to Chaman, all of them beyond the passes, whose outer extremities they guard."[19] The concept of placing military outposts beyond the weak spots in the administered frontier would come to be known as the "forward policy." The logic of the forward policy would later be adopted in toto by the independent Indian government to protect its imperial territorial inheritance from the danger of expansionist—in this case, Chinese—encroachment. Not only would this policy have profound effects on the course of Indian relations with China, it would also shape the political future of the Indian Northeast, as the concluding section of this chapter shows.[20]

The expansion of British India would eventually lead to an enormous "informal empire," as James Onley terms it, stretching at its height from Aden in the west to Singapore in the east.[21] The political and military incorporation of the kingdoms and regions identified above by Curzon would constitute British India's shifting land frontiers. To protect its "trade and communication" through the Persian Gulf, Britain "established spheres of influence in Persia and Ottoman Iraq," and, finally, to "protect its shipping routes through the Red Sea and Indian Ocean, British India annexed the port of Aden and established consulates and agencies in Western Arabia, Ottoman Egypt and Zanzibar."[22] In the east, Burma was a province of British India until 1937 when it became ambiguously "self-governing."[23] British India would consider Thailand a buffer state between itself and French Indochina and establish a consulate in Chiang Mai, while Singapore and the Straits Settlements of Malacca and Penang "with its Tamil stevedores, Sikh policemen, Chettiar moneylenders and Indian penal code . . . still bore the imprint of the Raj."[24] These latter territories were vital to protecting Britain's sea-lanes to the east and the route to China, while also offering considerable benefit to the empire as major trading ports of the region.

Although Curzon would claim, in 1903, that "to all intents and purposes, the state of [Muscat and Oman] is as much a Native State of the Indian

Empire as Lus Beyla or Kelat [in princely India] and far more so than Nepal or Afghanistan," the attachment of these "foreign" territories to territorial India was far less emotive in the nationalist imaginary.[25] When it would come to the dissolution of the empire, areas of the informal empire that were controlled from British India to protect sea-lanes were, for the most part, relatively easily detached from India, in spite of considerable capital investments and the large numbers of Indians living there. Curzon's imperial script had helped make the association of Indian national territory with contiguous lands far stronger than areas separated by the sea. With the safety of the seas guaranteed, threats to India could only be land-based invasions that would seek to enter the country through passes in the natural defensive belt of the high Himalayan ranges. Curzon's geopolitics was the most formal and explicit vision of a land-defined territory of India that saw its primary points of strategic vulnerability lying beyond its northern mountainous frontiers. His actions as viceroy consolidated that vision by creating a three-tiered political space arranged in the following hierarchy. First and most important was the directly ruled British Indian heartland that included the princely states. This space was in all respects superior to the second space, the indirectly ruled and uncivilized tribal borderlands of the eastern and western frontiers. Least valued from a civilizational standpoint but strategically critical to the defense of the British Indian heartland were the infrastructurally underdeveloped and physically challenging buffer states, most notably Tibet and Afghanistan. Within a remarkably short period of time and mediated through such figures as the colonial administrator, Olaf Caroe, these views would become institutionalized in territorial imaginaries and bureaucratic practices, not only in British India but also in its Indian and Pakistani successor states.[26]

Imperial thinking is central to understanding the form and practice of postcolonial Indian strategic planning and action. Imperial geopolitics had oriented the state's gaze northward to the Himalayan mountain range envisioned as a natural boundary and marginalized the importance of the seaborne approaches to India. Although incursions by sea had led to the most far-reaching political transformations of India over the last few centuries, this "fact" was largely forgotten in spite of the early writings of the well-known historian and administrator K. M. Panikkar.[27] The dominance of the Curzonian view led directly to the postcolonial imperative of defending the northern mountain frontiers through the logic of territorial expansion that required the political subordination of the sovereign states of the Himalayas and that saw the clash of empires as an inevitable outcome of this logic. This view derives no small part of its longevity from "scientific" metaphors that naturalize spatial relations tying together land and state power, making these relations appear inevitable and thereby producing territorially overdetermined ways of imagining and defending the Indian state.

Indian Geopolitics: *Hindutva* and Beyond

Among those calling for the end of British colonialism were nationalists whose vision of an independent India was the creation of an explicitly Hindu state. In and of itself, this was hardly a surprising development, given international pressures to conform to conventional definitions of the territorial nation-state and colonial discourse that defined India primarily as a Hindu civilization and saw the decline of Indic civilizations predominantly in terms of Islamic invasions. So widespread were these conjoined narratives that not a single Indian political leader of the colonial period, whether Hindu or Muslim, understood Indian history in any other way. Vinayak Damodar Sarvarkar, Keshav Baliwar Hegdewar, and Madhav Sadashiv Golwalkar, all *Chitpavan* brahmins from Maharashtra in western India, were the founders of modern Hindu nationalism.[28] The first two would found the extremist Hindu nationalist organization, the Rashtriya Swyamsevak Sangh (RSS) in 1925, ironically the same year that the Communist Party of India would come into being. The Hindu nationalist dilemma was to find a way of uniquely defining what constituted a modern Hindu subject. They would do so by turning to territory.

Hinduism, unlike the Semitic religions, has neither a central text nor a unified institutional structure; it does not recognize prophets, nor does it have a universal dogma. The practice and institutions of organized Hinduism in different parts of India look and sound quite different.[29] Very different gods, legends, myths, rituals, iconography, texts, and temples, all legitimately Hindu, can be found in close physical proximity. Indeed, it remains impossible to convert to Hinduism in a way that is uniformly recognized as legitimate by all the different sects and strains of the religion. Recognizing the enormous varieties of Hindu practices across the country and finding it impossible to identify a consistent unity underlying all these practices, Hindu nationalists would first celebrate this diversity through a critique of revealed religions.[30] How, they argued, was it possible to claim a single path to finding God? Hinduism's enormous variety was testament to the countless means through which the Supreme Being could be discovered.

This critique of the Abrahamic religions was only a first step toward cultural renewal and national self-respect. The next was to offer a positive conception of India as a Hindu state (*rashtra*) through the development of a novel territorial imaginary. Drawing on a selective reading of ancient texts and epics, India was reimagined as a holy land (*tapa-bhumi, punya-bhumi*) that stretched from the north of the Himalayas to the southern cape of Kanya Kumari, west to Afghanistan and perhaps even Iran, east to Burma and the Irrawaddy basin and sometimes even including Singapore. These distant points marked the territorial extent of the Hindu nation reimagined as a sacred space. As Hindu nationalist thought developed, Sarvarkar's concept of the nation as an omnipotent Fatherland would be transformed by Golwalkar into a Motherland, a place for regeneration, fecundity, and holiness, a view that resonated well with the far more widely held cultural image of Mother India. To address the range of Hindu practices, the votaries of *Hindutva* (Hindu-ness) would constantly resort to metaphors of unity in diversity. The most potent of these was the tree with many branches but with only one trunk: this central trunk had roots embedded deep in the soil of the Hindu homeland.

The cartographic imaginaries of India produced by exclusionary Hindu nationalists may have included Singapore as well as Afghanistan, but they failed to have the staying power of the visual representation of India produced by official state maps, as Sumathi Ramaswamy has pointed out.[31] Establishing external boundaries—the separation of India from the world—was not the primary thrust of these spatial visions. For Hindu nationalists, the central issue was the control of national domestic space. To be a legitimate member of the Hindu nation, in other words, a "proper" Indian, two conditions had to be met. The first was birth. Only those born within the boundaries of this holy land could be a part of the Hindu family. The second condition was religious affiliation. Both the origin of one's religion and its holiest places of pilgrimage had to lie within the sacred territorial boundaries of *punya-bhumi*, the Hindu homeland. This meant that millions of Christians and Muslims who may have been born within Indian territorial boundaries were not legitimate and rightful residents of India. The holy lands of their religions lay to the west, in modern-day Palestine and Saudi Arabia respectively. Their status, like other long-standing residents of India with "foreign" origins, notably Jews and Parsis (Zoroastrians), could only be that of guests, tolerated only due to the inherent generosity of the Hindu faith. Members of Indic-derived religions—Jains, Sikhs, and Buddhists in particular—were defined as Hindus who had left the orthodox fold. These individuals could be treated as legitimate Indian nationals as their religious identities all recognized the intrinsic holiness of India, and their holiest places all lay within the territorial limits of modern India. Although a latent irredentism was never far from the surface—in Golwalkar's words: "We shall only deaden our conscience by thinking and repeating that our present-day political borders represent our complete motherland. How humiliating it is to our manliness and how insulting to our intelligence!"— nevertheless, the primary territorial focus of Hindu nationalism was the production of India as a homogenously populated national space.

Another resonant, but less violent, territorial vision was produced by historians and intellectuals who foregrounded the premodern cultural transmission of Hindu religions, patterns of kingship, and intellectual, architectural, and aesthetic practices to Southeast Asia and beyond: Greater India. Not all these scholars were of Indian origin.[32] Western scholars were prominent among those who defined Southeast Asia as the product of the encounter of Indic and Sinic civilizations.[33] What uniquely distinguished flows of Hindu traditions to the east was summed up by French Orientalist Sylvain Lévi in 1926 (in what should perhaps be seen as a telling comment on the qualities of French colonialism): "India sent for many centuries many of her best men to carry far away her arts, her science, her philosophy, the magnificent productions of her creative genius; she brought nothing home as a compensation."[34] Unlike Western imperialism, this intellectual tendency alleges, Indian expansion overseas was not driven by the lure of political control or territorial gain; rather, local societies willingly adopted and adapted Indian civilization. The idea of Southeast Asia as a region framed primarily through the encounter of India and China would prove a resistant meme. As late as the 1960s, the Indian historian of Southeast Asia D. R. SarDesai would argue that:

> Southeast Asian kingdom (sic) preferred to adopt Indian ways, with the exception of Tonkin and Annam, which Sinicized their educational and administrative systems and adopted the Chinese calendar, court-system, civil service examination ... not so much to show their love for the Chinese as to equip themselves better to avoid if not to overthrow Chinese political domination. [By contrast] Laos and Cambodia came under Indian cultural influence, adopting Brahminism and later Hinhayana Buddhism, which came to them via Ceylon and Burma; ... the Indian centers of learning and culture at Nalanda, Taxila, Vallabhi, and Kanchipuram became the Hellas' of the Eastern world. Scholars from Funan ... Kambuja ... and Champa ... flocked to India ... The ruins of Angkor Vat and Angkor Thom in Cambodia and around Phanrang in Vietnam testify to the excellence of architecture and sculpture reached by the indigenous peoples, whose basic inspiration was Indian.[35]

The power of a geopolitical imaginary as an invisible frame shaping Indian conceptions of their place in the world was so pervasive that it led to an especially perverse outcome: geopolitical norms became so internalized that contemporary India has no established intellectual tradition of geopolitical writing.[36] Indian strategists rarely think in terms other than the geopolitical but never name it as such. The great exception to this assertion is the celebrated Indian historian, administrator, and diplomat K. M. Panikkar. Panikkar is the one Indian thinker spanning the colonial and postcolonial periods who was self-consciously geopolitical. Indeed, the intellectual event of 1953, by some noteworthy accounts, was the publication of K. M. Panikkar's *Asia and Western Dominance*.[37] The book is an account of the "Vasco da Gama epoch" in the history of the Asian region and offers a powerful reconstruction of how Asian political history had been transformed by the arrival of European trading companies from the sixteenth century onward. With so much of the book's historical content now enshrined as conventional wisdom, including in school textbooks, it is difficult today to appreciate the contemporary impact of the book. Apart from the unquestionable scale of its ambition, the volume's impact can also be discerned by its postcolonial subtext. For a generation of Asian students and intellectuals brought up to internalize the European point of view in all respects, the book would have shocked and exhilarated many readers for its effort to what we would now call, following Dipesh Chakrabarty, "provincialize" Europe.[38] This subtext is perhaps nowhere better captured than in Panikkar's succinct description of World War I as a "European Civil War."[39]

Panikkar's view was that the domination of the Indian Ocean by European trading companies and navies changed everything for nearly half a millennium. "It was an age of maritime power, of authority based on the control of the seas," he wrote. This epoch would only end when Asian "land masses . . . [shook] themselves free from the shackles of maritime mercantilism," and Asian history became its own again.[40] Panikkar was repeating, on a much larger canvas, views he had first expressed in a slim volume, *India and the Indian Ocean*, published in 1945. This book is the first modern geopolitical text published by an Indian and draws heavily on the work of geopolitical thinkers like Ratzel from Germany and the American Alfred Mahan, as is made obvious by its subtitle, *An Essay on the Influence of Seapower on Indian History*.[41] In the earlier book, Panikkar turns to *longue durée* history to argue that India was once a major maritime power with colonies around the Indian Ocean littoral. With the discovery of the sea route to India by the Europeans, India lost its hegemony over the ocean; at the same moment, it lost its sovereignty. The lesson was clear. India would need to return to its seafaring roots and develop naval power to ensure its freedom in the long run. In words that could have been taken directly from Mahan, he would write, "Her future is dependent on the freedom of that vast water surface. No industrial development, no commercial growth, no stable political structure is possible for her unless the Indian Ocean is free and her own shores fully protected. The Indian Ocean must therefore remain truly Indian."[42]

Although both Panikkar's early books adopt an explicitly geopolitical point of view built around the importance of the Indian Ocean, they differ in one crucial respect: they draw exactly the opposite conclusions. *Indian Ocean*, written in the awareness of an imminent Indian independence, begins with a quotation attributed to the Ottoman admiral Khaireddin Barbarosa, speaking to Suleiman the Magnificent: "He who rules on the sea will shortly rule on the land also." However, in *Western Dominance*, written some years after India had become an independent state, Panikkar affirms that, as a general historical rule, land empires always dominate sea-based powers.[43] The imperative of remaking the Indian Ocean into an Indian "lake" in 1945 was now reduced to supplementing the primary strategic problem, the control of land. This complete turnaround of perspective undermines the latent postcolonial thrust that contemporaries celebrated in *Western Dominance*.[44] Pannikar, who had once argued how important it was for India to see itself as a maritime power, now comes smartly into line with the conventional approach to Indian geopolitics that privileged land, especially the northern frontiers of the country, as the main focus of the geopolitical gaze. The power of the Himalayas had converted even the Malabar coast-born geopolitical theorist.

The strategic analyst C. Raja Mohan, in a well-received analysis of Indian foreign policy, has argued that geopolitics has now been "rediscovered" by the Indian strategic community. The "rediscovery" of geopolitics is associated with a group of "realist" scholars and thinkers who are critical of the "idealist" direction of Indian foreign policy associated with India's first prime minister, Jawaharlal Nehru. With Indian independence, Nehru is alleged to have turned his back on British geopolitical thought, making "no allowance for the essential nature of the international polity as a jungle where might confers right."[45] India's policy of nonalignment comes in for particular attack as it is seen to be a policy that privileged abstract principles of international behavior over—and at the cost of—the protection and defense of national interests. Bharat Karnad is prominent among those who consider Nehru an impoverished geopolitical thinker. The answer, he proposes, has to do with a myopic view of territory. Nehru—by contrast with

Curzon—saw territory merely as "pathways through which cultural influences and trade traveled, never invading armies."[46] Moreover, India's first prime minister was too much of a democrat. Citing Halford Mackinder, who preferred "organizers" to "democrats" when it came to geopolitics, Karnad dismisses Nehru's thinking as overly concerned with "principles, ideals, prejudices, or economic laws" rather than following the implacable terms of a world envisioned as a Hobbesian jungle.[47]

The inability to appreciate the extent of the connections between imperial and postcolonial views of territorial control is shared even by critical scholars, including the Marxist political scientist Achin Vanaik. Vanaik has argued that, during the Nehruvian period, Indian foreign policy had two "faces."[48] When it came to its smaller northern neighbors, independent India followed British colonial policy toward the Himalayan protectorates of Nepal, Sikkim, and Bhutan. As the first line of defense against invasion from the north, these countries would be allowed to remain nominally independent, but New Delhi would control their foreign and defense policies. Indian high commissioners would become de facto regents tasked with keeping their behavior in line with Indian needs.[49] With respect to the world beyond the region, however, Indian foreign policy behavior was strikingly different. Even before independence, India had called for an end to an international politics based on "power politics," especially nuclear arms races, and the need to structure international relations on the basis of mutual interdependence.[50] A formal expression of the superior norms it argued should govern international relations was contained in the landmark *Panchsheel* Agreement signed with China in 1954.[51] The five principles of the agreement established a new, nonhierarchical basis for international intercourse, including mutual respect for each other's territorial integrity and sovereignty, mutual nonaggression, mutual noninterference in each other's internal affairs, equality and mutual benefit, and peaceful coexistence. These five principles clearly do not apply to India's behavior vis-à-vis the Himalayan states, and Vanaik is quite correct to point to this inconsistency. What he fails to notice, however, is another kind of continuity between colonial and independent India's foreign policy, namely the salience of a geopolitical imaginary to the policy of nonalignment.

Although imperial "forward policy" is relatively well known as a source of Indian frontier behavior and even as a casus belli, there is also an explicit linkage between imperial geopolitics and postcolonial India's policy of nonalignment. At first glance, this connection seems far-fetched. The idea of nonalignment is traditionally represented as a conscious break with the power politics of the past, which in many ways it was. Nevertheless, the underlying logic of a bloc of states aligned with neither opposing side in the Cold War as a prophylactic against global conflict is very much a geopolitical vision, even if adorned with the universalist dressing of peaceful coexistence. At the heart of nonalignment is the idea of the nonaligned community as a *buffer*. It is this conception, built on the discursive power of scientific metaphors (drawing from the idea of friction in classical mechanics) that gives nonalignment its strength as a practical approach to world order.

In classical geopolitics, the perceived need to manage the deadly logic of imperial expansion produced the idea of a neutral, or, in some cases, neutralized territory, the buffer, a space whose liminality was defined by its larger and more powerful neighbors. The buffer "state" might or might not be an independent political entity; it mattered little. However engendered, Curzon would see the buffer's primary function as keeping apart those Great Powers "whose contact might provoke collision" from coming into direct contact with each other. The buffer's importance came from reducing the likelihood of major wars by standing between two empires.[52] Tibet and Afghanistan epitomized the buffer state. Weakly administered political entities occupying huge areas of land with little or no modern infrastructure, a harsh and physically bleak country inhabited by fierce and belligerent native peoples: these buffers helped to keep the riches of British India at a safe distance from rival Great Powers. Indeed, their lack of economic development was directly related to their value as buffers, in this view. Without the ability to move troops and equipment swiftly through these regions, any attack on India or its sphere of interest would be slow and ponderous, giving Indian military planners plenty of time to mobilize.

Just as the buffer state had theoretically helped reduce direct contact between imperial Great Powers in Asia, nonalignment would be conceived of as a means of reducing friction between two opposed blocs in the nuclear age. As Nehru would put it in the course of a long speech at the Bandung Conference:

> If all the world were to be divided up between these two big blocs what would be the result? The inevitable result would be war. Therefore every step that takes place in reducing that area of the world which may be called the "unaligned area" is a dangerous step and leads to war. It reduces that objective, that balance, that outlook which other countries without military might can perhaps exercise.[53]

Nonalignment argued that the likelihood of military conflict between the superpowers would increase in the absence of any mediating force between them. What was needed was a buffer that would reduce interbloc friction and allow for outcomes other than war. If every country in the world belonged to one or another bloc, the two opposing blocs would be in a constant state of military tension, as such a world would have too many points of possible contact and, hence, possible triggers to conflict. To prevent the Cold War from breaking out into a global military war, it was crucial that there remained some countries that remained outside the fray, unaligned with either side, precisely to provide that buffer zone within which interbloc friction could be dissipated. Of course, this was a buffer more conceptual than physical, a diplomatic strategy that sought to balance existing blocs from the "outside" while at the same time critiquing the reliance on power politics and force as a means to international order. Yet, at its core, the postcolonial policy of nonalignment was built around a long-standing principle of colonial geopolitical thought. It is no small irony that postcolonial India's most important contribution to international order was based, in part, on thinking that had first originated in empire's halls of power; more important, nonaligned policy shows clearly the continuity of the principles of geopolitical thought across the transfer of power from colonial to postcolonial India.

Competing Visions? Nehru and Patel's Geopolitics

Like others in the Indian strategic community, former Defense Minister Jaswant Singh is said to "bemoan the loss of the geostrategic perspective that had informed the British rulers of India."[54] By comparison, however, Singh adopts a more thoughtful response in his disagreement with Nehru's vision of territorial security.[55] Apart from offering his own account of Indian strategic culture, Singh argues that although Nehru might have lacked a proper understanding of geopolitical imperatives, Sardar Vallabhai Patel, the deputy prime minister until 1951, represented the continuation of this valuable strategic tradition. Based on the evidence of a series of letters exchanged between Nehru and Patel as Chinese troops entered Tibet in 1950, Singh suggests that if only Patel had lived longer and been able to force the issue, India would have realized far earlier than it did the real dangers posed by the Chinese Communist state.[56] Based on a careful reading of the available evidence, however, Singh's contention cannot be sustained. The following section shows that, although both Nehru and Patel were concerned with Chinese expansionist tendencies, their differences can be adduced to tactics rather than strategy. More important, both were in complete agreement about the nature of the dangers posed to and by the Indian Northeast, the region most threatened by Chinese expansion. Showing how imperial geopolitics shaped the thinking of postcolonial Indian elites is a necessary step in understanding how the territorializing practices of geopolitics has transformed one border region, the Northeast, into a "space of exception."

In his writing, Curzon acknowledged the practical difficulties of maintaining the "scientific frontier" across British imperial space. An important reason was, he felt, because it was a fundamentally European way of seeing space. "In Asia . . . there has always been a strong instinctive aversion to the idea of fixed boundaries" due to, he felt, the nomadic tendencies of its people. In Asia, he felt, the idea of a determinate border come up against the "dislike of precise arrangements that is typical of the Oriental mind." As a result, "in Asiatic countries it would be true to say that [spatial] demarcation has never taken place except under European pressure and by the intervention of European states."[57] The best proof of the Asian dislike of imperial "demarcation" came, in his view, from the experience of working with native surveyors, who, although operating in "a subordinate and advisory capacity" gave ample evidence of dislike for their work through an "exceptional measure of vacillation, obstruction, and every form of delay."[58]

Curzon was wrong. The allegedly "vacillat[ing] . . . obstruction[ist] . . . Oriental mind" had little trouble internalizing the importance of the Himalayas for India's national security. There is no question that the strategic privileging of India's northern frontiers resonated intimately with a cultural imaginary epitomized by images of Mother India that represented her with the Himalayas as her head and with her feet lapped by the Indian Ocean. This territorial vision was ably reinforced by Hindu nationalist sensibilities, historical writings, and early geopolitical thinking. In the postcolonial period, a strategic supplement came to join these mutually reinforcing tendencies. The event that crystallized the rift among independent India's foreign policy specialists was the Chinese annexation of Tibet in October 1950.[59] The official Indian reaction to the loss of its northern buffer was muted, though the secretary general of the External Affairs ministry privately described the likely removal of the Indian mission and trading posts in Lhasa, Gyantse, and Yatung as "humiliating." Sir Girija Shankar Bajpai wrote at once to Deputy Prime Minister Vallabhai Patel calling for a major defensive military response to secure the border—the McMahon Line—separating India from Tibet: "[T]he Peking government will, almost certainly, refuse to accept" the Line as a mutually recognized interstate boundary, "but it is a strategic necessity for us." Bajpai went on to wonder if Tibet's annexation would lead in turn to attacks on Nepal and Burma and proposed initiating talks with the two countries immediately.[60]

India had been among the first countries in the world to recognize the Communist government in Beijing. It had strongly advocated for immediate international recognition of the People's Republic and argued for its inclusion in the United Nations Organization (and in the Security Council as a permanent member) over Formosa, the rump Chinese state and U.S. ally. Most important, India had explicitly recognized Chinese indirect political authority—"suzerainty"—over Tibet in official correspondence with the new government.[61] This was a position wholly consistent with Curzon's own views.[62] Tibet, the viceroy would say, was "not a buffer state between Great Britain and Russia: the sequel of the recent [Younghusband] expedition has merely been to make it again [what it once was] . . . a Frontier Protectorate of the Chinese Empire."[63] Following the annexation, however, Nehru came to the decision that defending Tibet was not worth the costs, much to Bajpai's dismay.[64] India would not only not sponsor any appeal by Tibet to the international community for outside intervention but would prefer the United Nations not even to discuss such an appeal. The United Kingdom and United States would follow India's lead and advice and ignore the Tibetan appeal to the Security Council.[65] (Ironically, the Tibetan appeal to the United Nations had been written by the Indian representative to Tibet, based in Lhasa). Nehru's position would be summed up in a note written on November 18, 1950, a few weeks after the Chinese People's Liberation Army (PLA) entered Tibet: "We cannot save Tibet, as we should have liked to do, and our very attempts to save it might well bring greater trouble to it."[66] In just a month, one of the key fronts of the geopolitical system of Scientific Frontiers set in place by the British had broken down, and independent India was doing little to restore it.

Deputy Prime Minister Vallabhai Patel was the Indian National Congress Party's point man on domestic affairs.[67] Unlike Nehru, he did not write extensively on Indian defense and security; what little we know about his views comes from a few letters and memoranda he wrote to Nehru in response to the Chinese takeover of Tibet.[68] He died in 1951, and it is worth noting that much of what he did write on defense and foreign policy was written in the last two years of his life. Initially as minister of states and later as home minister, Patel was intimately involved in the transfer of sovereignty from the princely states to independent India.[69] Where peaceful methods worked, he was accommodating; when he faced resistance, he did not hesitate to use force, as demonstrated by the military annexation of Hyderabad and Junagadh. He was also closely involved in the power struggle in Nepal to remove the Rana shoguns and restore to effective power a monarchy loyal to India. With such a "realistic" approach to foreign policy, it is not surprising to find Patel thinking in the following terms.

In words that could have been taken directly from Viceroy Curzon or the influential colonial officer and geopolitical strategist Olaf Caroe,[70] Patel would respond to Bajpai's memorandum the very next day: "The Chinese advance into Tibet upsets all our security calculations. Hitherto, the danger to India on its land frontiers has always come from the Northwest. Throughout history we have concentrated our armed might in that region. For the first time, a serious danger is now developing on the North and Northeast side."[71] He would go on to identify the "weak spots" across India's northern and northeastern fronts: "Nepal, Bhutan, Sikkim, and the tribal areas of Assam . . . even Darjeeling and Kalimpong [in West Bengal]." Patel was too astute to see the dangers of the Chinese advance merely in terms of the perfidious tendencies of a Communist state. Although he had no doubt the Chinese were "irredentist . . . thoroughly unscrupulous, unreliable and determined . . . calculating, ruthless, unprincipled and prejudiced," undoubtedly harboring a "hideous design of ideological and even political conquest," these national and political character flaws alone were not the main problem. The real issue was the new frontier between India and China that had opened up with the annexation of Tibet. This was a frontier seething with "discontent" and lacking "close contact with Indians." Under these circumstances, the seductions of Communist ideology would make "the difficulty of the position . . . manifold."[72] Bajpai would write back at once in complete agreement. He would add his own concerns, couched in the racial terminology typical of contemporary Indian elites. Due to the poor administration of frontier areas, he noted, there was a great deal of disaffection among the "Mongoloid" tribes of Assam, Bhutan, and Sikkim, who were ethnically "of the same stock as the Tibetans." This meant there was "enough scope for political mischief by infiltrating Communists."[73]

This correspondence of views would be followed by a long and strongly worded letter from Patel to Nehru, asking him to reconsider what Patel saw as a dangerously accommodating approach to Chinese actions.[74] His letter begins by noting all the ways in which India had acted to engender recognition of the Chinese as a great power in the international system with little by way of return. India had served as a de facto spokesman for the Chinese; India had unilaterally pushed for China's entry into the United Nations; India had supported Chinese positions in secret discussions with the United States and Great Britain; and India had appointed a deeply sympathetic ambassador to represent her in Beijing. The ambassador was so accommodating, Patel pointed out, that the "External Affairs Ministry remarked in one of their telegrams, there was a lack of firmness and unnecessary apology in one or two of the representations that he made to the Chinese Government on our behalf." This ambassador was none other than the geopolitical savant K. M. Panikkar.

Once these preliminaries were out of the way, Patel went to the heart of the matter. "We have to consider what new situation now faces us as a result of the disappearance of Tibet, as we knew it, and the expansion of China almost up to our gates."[75] He would repeat what he had written to Bajpai, regarding the serious threat to India's geopolitical stability from an entirely different direction, the "domestic" Northeast: "Throughout history, we have seldom been worried about our northeast frontier. The Himalayas have been regarded as an impenetrable barrier against any threat."[76] But this was not the situation any more. The half-century-old agreement that made Tibet a buffer between India and China was now worthless. Patel would repeat what Bajpai had warned him: "We can therefore safely assume that very soon [the Chinese] will disown all stipulations which Tibet has entered into with us in the past."[77]

The threat to India from China was presented as a novel situation for Indian military planners. "Chinese irredentism and Communist imperialism are different from the expansionism or imperialism of the Western powers," Patel would write. This difference was "ten times more dangerous" than conventional forms of subversion.[78] Rather than seeking acceptance among the restive frontier people by promoting national or racial homologies, which were all too visible, the Chinese would begin by promoting Communist ideas, an even easier point of entry. Patel believed that Communist views would be an easy sell in the "weak spots" of "Nepal, Bhutan, Sikkim, Darjeeling, [and] tribal Assam" because of preexisting and serious class and national resentments. Communism would here cloak the real danger, namely Chinese expansionism, for under "the guise of ideological expansion lie concerned racial, national, and historical claims."[79] Communist infiltration into the Northeast would be the first wedge into the Indian national body, Patel felt, and there was a grave danger that a local movement might eventually link up with other Communist pockets in the heartland, such as Telengana in the Andhra region. But what was really at stake was an irredentism that would seek to absorb India's Northeast region into China. The real danger to India was Chinese imperial expansion under the red flag of international Communism.

Nehru's equally lengthy response to Patel would arrive a week later in the form of a Note to Cabinet.[80] After arguing that India could do little for Tibet without making the situation worse for itself, Nehru would make the following case why good relations with China were necessary for India at the present time. He first discounted the military threat from China. With Chinese involvement in the ongoing Korean War on his mind, Nehru was confident that any Chinese aggression toward India would lead to a world war. If war broke out, China would find itself exposed on too many fronts. It would have to concentrate its main forces in the south and east and hence was extremely unlikely to begin a "wild adventure across the Himalayas." Based on this reasoning, Nehru would conclude that "I think it is exceedingly unlikely that we may have to face any real military invasion from the Chinese side, whether in peace or in war, in the foreseeable future."[81]

Nehru rejected the idea that the inherent tendencies of Communism inevitably meant expansion and war, calling it "naïve." (He would later develop a strongly held, and prescient, position that the People's Republic of China was better understood as a nationalist force than a Communist one.)[82] Nehru also considered the costs to India of defending itself from a potential Chinese military attack as much too high. India simply could not afford to do so in a credible way if it was to continue to spend money on development and to defend itself from its "major possible" enemy, Pakistan. Maintaining good relations with China made good geopolitical sense because it would also prevent Pakistan from taking "advantage of this, political[ly] or otherwise," potentially trapping India in a "pincer movement." Peace with China would moreover "make a vast difference . . . to [the] balance [of power] of the world," which was probably why the United Kingdom, United States, and Soviet Union were not in favor of it.[83] Nehru accepted that "there are certainly chances of gradual infiltration [of men and ideas] across our border and possibly of entering and taking possession of disputed territory . . . we must therefore take all necessary precautions to prevent this." However, Communist infiltration needed to be countered in kind, especially by "other ideas."[84]

Faced with this newly emergent threat from China, the Indian government would move swiftly to restore its imperial relationship with the Himalayan buffer states of Nepal, Bhutan, and Sikkim. The External Affairs Ministry imposed bilateral treaties on these states that gave India an effective veto on the foreign and defense relations of these nominally independent countries. The treaties explicitly identified India as the guarantor of these states' security and sharply circumscribed their freedom of maneuver and sovereignty. The treaty with Sikkim (1950) defined the country as a protectorate of India and gave India the responsibility for its "defense and territorial integrity." It allowed Indian troops to be stationed anywhere in the country and denied Sikkim the right to have independent ties with any other state. India would bear the costs and responsibility of maintaining Sikkim's foreign relations, while the chief justice of India would adjudicate any disagreements over treaty provisions. Likewise, the 1949 treaty with Bhutan established Indian dominance emphatically. Article Two of that treaty established that Bhutan would be "guided by the advice" of India on its external relations, language that was taken directly from the Treaty of Punakha, signed between the British and Bhutan in 1910.

The treaty of "Peace and Friendship" with the Hindu kingdom of Nepal (1950) was driven by similar concerns. Discussing the treaty, Nehru would state in the *Lok Sabha* (People's House), "Much as we appreciate the independence of Nepal, we cannot allow anything to go wrong in Nepal or permit [the Himalayas] to be crossed or weakened because that would also be a risk to our security."[85] Nepal would be allowed to control its own external relations but not to establish an independent defense policy. The seemingly innocuous text of Article Five permitted Nepal "to import, from or through the territory of India, arms, ammunition or warlike material and equipment necessary for the security of Nepal," but what it did not say was that in practice Nepal had no choice but to depend solely on India for the supply of its arms and other "warlike material." India, in other words, would determine the security needs of the Nepali state. In return, India granted the residents of all three states the right to move freely within India and to be treated as equivalent to Indian citizens.

Given the substantial policy differences expressed in their correspondence and official notes, Nehru and Patel might have been surprised to realize how similar were their basic presumptions regarding military threats to the country. Both Nehru and Patel entirely subscribed to the geopolitical template set by prevailing strategic thought. Like their British predecessors, Nehru and Patel concentrated on the state of India's Himalayan buffers—Nepal, Sikkim, Bhutan, and the Northeastern region—and ignored the sea. Neither was particularly concerned about the sovereignty or autonomy of these small Himalayan kingdoms. They saw them much as the British did, namely as more important for their geopolitical location than anything else. Liberal concerns about the anachronism of monarchies in an era when republicanism and popular sovereignty were the prevailing political watchwords had no place in the Scientific Frontier scheme. The Himalayan kingdoms were the first line of defense against China, and that was why they mattered. Patel and Nehru also agreed entirely over the "essential characteristics" of the Chinese people and the "Mongoloid" people of the Northeast. Where they differed substantially was on the most effective policies to respond to the Chinese annexation of Tibet.

Patel's views on China were framed by his instinctive anti-Communism and traditional conservatism. He seems to have known little about China and its history and would conclude, with Bajpai, that China needed to be resisted militarily and at once. Nehru's views on China are often misrepresented, due to his penchant for framing issues in terms of the expansive epochal view of historical change that he drew from his prison reading of Arnold Toynbee. He would often draw parallels between the simultaneous, and historic, emergence of China and India from years of imperial subjugation. Even if it was currently obscured by years of colonial division, Nehru appeared confident that Asian civilizational solidarity existed, as he would propose during the Asian Relations Conference in 1947 and repeat at Bandung, eight years later. But when it came to policy making, he would think like a realist statesman. His views were shaped by a nuanced appreciation for the multiple challenges facing China, China's and India's places in the world, and the nationalist roots of the Communist revolution. This allowed him to set aside the significance of Communist ideology in understanding and shaping Chinese behavior. He would argue tactically that the need of the hour was for China and India to have good relations because peace between them "would make a vast difference to the whole setup and balance of the world." Good relations in the present were unlikely, however, in his view, to lead to a stable peace in the long run. The reasons why harked back to Curzon's view of the expansion of empires. Nehru would see a clash between India and China as inevitable as "India and China are two of the biggest countries of Asia bordering on each other and both with certain expansive tendencies, because of their vitality."[86] Even as they differed on the specifics of how to deal with China, neither statesman would question the deep logic of geopolitics or the importance of holding onto the strategic legacy of a colonial empire. The defense of postcolonial India, as with British India, would begin with the Himalayas.

Patel saw the threat from Chinese imperialism as beginning from the weakness of the Indian state's hold over the people of the Northeast. Nehru, too, acknowledged the lack of state legitimacy in this region but believed that India could win the battle of minds with the Northeastern tribespeople.

Patel saw the Northeast as a strategic frontier, only tenuously under India's control, while Nehru saw the same region as a tribal borderland, akin to the Federally Administered Tribal Area (FATA) region of what was now Pakistan. Guided by the English missionary-turned-anthropologist Verrier Elwin, Nehru would hope that enlightened behavior would create genuine goodwill among the tribal populations.[87] Where Nehru saw Indian territory inhabited by people who could be swayed in India's direction with the right ideas and actions, Patel saw a frontier inhabited by potentially disloyal people, facing an irredentist and expansionist Chinese state. Patel knew that the Northeast frontier needed to be territorially incorporated into India for his vision of security to prevail: what was once a strategic frontier needed to become an international border. In the end, both won this "debate." Nehru's temporizing view of China would prevail diplomatically. Patel's view of the Northeast would become Indian domestic policy.

The Northeast as a "Space of Exception"

Sanjay Chaturvedi's survey of geopolitical thought in modern India highlights the Indian Northeast as a region deeply resistant to the "singular and monolithic" project of national unity inaugurated by the postcolonial Indian state.[88] A long and continuing history of military violence and armed resistance is the most obvious indicator of this region's deeply troubled relationship to the Indian state. This concluding section locates the origins of militarization and resistance in the Northeast to the geopolitical practices of the colonial period and their seamless and expansive extension into the postcolonial.[89] The lack of meaningful political autonomy offered the inhabitants of the Northeast began with the actions of the Ministry of States during the transition to India's independence and continues with the imposition of illiberal legislation extraordinary in a democratic state. This final section goes beyond Chaturvedi's formulation and argues that geopolitics as a state territorializing practice has led to India's Northeast region becoming what might be called a "space of exception." This term applies to a political region—not a camp, in the sense used by Agamben[90]—where the "state of exception" has become normalized and ubiquitous across a territorialized political space.[91] "Space of exception" applies to a region where there are no legal restraints on the use of sovereign power, and yet this condition of legally sanctioned violence does not permanently undermine the liberal democratic credentials of the state or spill over regional boundaries to infect the entire body politic.

British expansion into what is now India's Northeast began in the first third of the nineteenth century, a decade before military victories in the Sindh, and later Punjab, would extend imperial hegemony past Peshawar in the west. The fall of the Ahom kingdom and the defeat of the expansionist Burmese kingdom in the east were closely tied to the economic extension of plantation lands and colonial governance into what had once been an "out of the way tract."[92] The conversion of the former Ahom kingdom of present-day Assam into a "planter raj," in Amalendu Guha's classic formulation, brought with it multiple changes: economic, ecological, demographic, and political.[93] Beginning around the same time, American, particularly Baptist, missionaries would enter the region bringing them epochal changes in the form of Christianity and standardized lexicons and linguistic grammars.[94] The expansion of British power to the Northeast combined efforts to settle a turbulent frontier via the geopolitical imperatives later theorized by Curzon, as well as a domestic version of what was taking place across the seas with the movement of indentured labor to the tea plantations and other Northeastern outposts of the colonial economy.[95] The need for plantation labor in Assam brought in migrants from eastern and central India, often indigenous themselves, and always poor. Their influx from the middle of the nineteenth century began to alter the population balance in a region that was always closer to Southeast Asia in many respects, but particularly one: people, not land, were the scarce resource from the point of view of a potential ruler.[96]

It took until the third quarter of the nineteenth century before the Northeast freed itself administratively from the Bengal presidency. Both economic and political reasons lay behind this move. Apart from planter interests who were keen to be free of the control of the Calcutta's colonial bureaucracy, between 1835 and 1871 there were no less than ten military expeditions to pacify the belligerent Naga tribes of the upper hill region.[97] Following the creation of Assam as a separate province in 1874, a major attack by the Angami Nagas on Kohima led to a devastating response and "the last major military encounter" for some time. British colonial governance would combine pacification with paternalism for the indigenous tribes of the region: colonial officials would call for "experienced and sympathetic handling [of the Nagas] and protection from economic subjugation by their neighbors."[98] Historian Peter Robb argues that, by the early 1880s, efforts to extend colonial governance into the hills of Nagaland by Chief Commissioner C. S. Elliott would become an early example of the colonial state's biopolitical power. Elliott's own view, however, saw his efforts at producing the extension of an "undivided" sovereignty, namely the conversion of an unruly frontier into a demarcated border.[99]

Seeking to order their new frontier, the colonial state drew an Inner Line along the foothills, separating the plains from the hills in the interests of communal "segregation," thereby creating an "Excluded Area" where the people of the upper hills could rule themselves according to their traditional customs.[100] Provincial governors were legally permitted to act "on their own discretion" in the Excluded Areas, a physical area which had now become a legal category. This new inscription on the land separated the indigenous people of the region, hill from plain, local from migrant, which would lead over the years to narratives that treated this geopolitical separation as proof of permanent distinction. The Excluded Areas marked by the Inner Line were more than just a strategic barrier to keep the tea plantations and plains-people safe. It had become a civilizational barrier, on one side of which lay the settled and civilized space of British India, tied together by capitalist relations and governed by law; beyond that lay a "primitive, innocent, and warlike" people who had to be kept away from modern civilization for their own survival and protection. The Inner Line and Excluded Areas would become spatial markers of cultural and other difference for those both outside and inside these incisions. Over time, Sanjib Baruah argues, the itinerant hill Nagas in particular came to see themselves in terms of colonial territoriality, as a separate people with their own homeland, erasing a long history of mobility and engagement with the plains. Bertil Lintner reports conversations with Nagas and Mizos who had mistakenly taken the term *Excluded Area* to mean that their homelands lay outside British India, a further justification to resist the imposition of an illegitimate Indian rule.[101] Reflecting this civilizational divide, an entirely different legal code governed this area.[102]

A series of governmental decrees would reinforce this separation over the next few decades. The Government of India Act in 1935, followed by independent India's liberal and republican constitution, would create a separate legal code to govern the Northeast, the Sixth Schedule.[103] Although, on the face of it, the Sixth Schedule is a document that respects the cultural autonomy of the indigenous people of the Northeast and allows for a measure of self-governance, it is also a document that reinforces the region's difference for reasons of geopolitical security. The Northeast's location as a border region that joined India, Burma, and China was never far from the minds of colonial as well as postcolonial administrators.[104]

When Partition provisions drew East Pakistan's borders in such a way that the physical connection between peninsular India and the Northeast was reduced to a narrow and militarily vulnerable corridor, official insecurities over the Northeast were greatly increased. The combined effect of these two forces, a history of social separation that had been formalized through the Sixth Schedule on the basis of civilizational difference and the particular demands of geopolitical security of a frontier region that bordered other, assumed unfriendly, states, reinforced the separation of the Northeast from the rest of the country. Recent critical scholarship has further nuanced this account by locating the exceptionalism of the Northeast as also discursively produced through dominant understandings of the region as economically underdeveloped and in need of external and rational intervention. In a territorial imaginary still dominated by colonial categories, the tribal people of this region are represented as simple and feminized, on the one hand, and irrationally prone to violence, on the other.[105] The geopolitics of location, the power of dominant representations, the political economy of development, and the cultural and religious (the Northeast is predominantly Christian) distance of this region from the Indian heartland work in conjunction to produce the Northeast as a zone apart where the normal codes of governance and citizenship do not apply.

Sardar Vallabhai Patel's vision of the Northeast as an always recalcitrant and disloyal space would set the terms for postcolonial India's relation with this region. Independence for India would mean little in the Northeast: legal and social continuity with the parameters of governance established during colonial rule would mean that little changed in terms of political autonomy. If anything, political freedoms would become even more restricted, as the spatial definition of the Northeast shifted from turbulent frontier to vulnerable border region. As in the rest of India, the spatial unevenness of British India would be smoothed out into a single principle of sovereignty, sweeping the principalities and kingdoms of this region into a uniform political space. Consider, for example, the Khasi states of the Garo and Jaintia Hills, small semisovereign political entities that had signed treaties of subordination to the colonial state. Although they may have hoped, as did many such semisovereign entities, that the departure of the British would lead to greater freedom for them, the Indian Ministry of States had no compunctions about quickly disabusing them of that possibility. The Khasis were informed on December 2, 1947, that they would be signing legal instruments of accession to the Indian Union two weeks later.

Two *syiems* (chieftains) who refused to do so on the basis of their inability to consult with their people found "a government mission, with military escort" at their gates. The two holdouts followed suit in March 1948.[106]

The Manipur kingdom also received the Khasi treatment. Subordinated to British India after the war of 1891, Manipur's long history of political autonomy soon converted into a modern "cultural and national reawakening" that continued resistance against the authority of British rule.[107] After the British left, the maharaja of Manipur hoped to become a constitutional monarchy and passed an act creating an appointed constituent assembly on August 15, 1947. A year later, in October, the first elected representatives of Manipur took their places in the new State Assembly. In his inaugural speech to the assembly, the maharaja made it clear that Manipur was not an independent and sovereign state. The speech made repeated references to the "Central Government" and to the loyal role that Manipur would play in the defense of the frontiers of India.[108] In September 1949, the maharaja, constitutional head of the new entity, was invited to the regional capital, Shillong, for discussions with the governor of Assam. On arriving there, he was detained, held incommunicado, and not permitted to leave before signing an Instrument of Accession to India. With that signature, Manipur's modest bid for political autonomy within the Indian state structure ended. In the first few years of independence, it became clear that, whatever autonomy was to be granted to the Northeast, it would be on terms decided by Delhi, not the people of the region. The meaning of autonomy, in any case, would fall far short of territorial sovereignty.

The most celebrated case of resistance to incorporation into the strategic-territorial scheme of British India belongs to a group of hill tribes who came to be collectively known as the Nagas.[109] As noted earlier, it was only after the Nagas were "pacified" that the British would draw an Inner Line to segregate the hills from the plains of the Northeast. Naga tribes had a long history of self-organization, starting with political clubs and other social organizations creating forums for political engagement, education, discussion, and mobilization from the early twentieth century. The Naga National Council (NNC), an umbrella group of Naga tribes, met with the governor of Assam, Sir Akbar Hydari, in June 1947, as well as with Gandhi, to hammer out the details of their fate as the departure of the British became imminent.[110] Receiving strong assurances from both of the bona fides of the Indian state, the NNC agreed to sign a nine-point agreement spelling out the terms of the political relationship between itself and the Indian government. The final point specified that the bilateral agreement would be in place for the next ten years, following which the Nagas would decide whether to extend it or make other arrangements for the future of the Naga people.

In 1950, the Naga leader Phizo would meet Nehru, who would call independence for the Nagas an "absurd demand." Although turning his back on past promises, Nehru was at least being consistent. At the same moment as the struggle with the Nagas was increasingly becoming militarized, India was also providing arms to the new Burmese government to put down armed rebellion by their own tribal minorities living on the other side of the international border.[111] By the early 1950s, goodwill on both sides had broken down, and it became clear to the Naga political leadership that India was not going to honor its promise of allowing for the possibility of an independent Naga state after the ten-year waiting period was over. Political violence broke out, and the original agreement signed between the NNC and India became moot. In 1956, the NNC would declare Nagaland's independence, just two months after the Indian government reclassified the Naga Hills as a "disturbed area."

The Naga insurrection, building in strength and violence, led to the induction of large numbers of Indian army units into the Northeast from the early 1950s onwards. In May 1958, the president of India issued an ordinance that was passed into law by Parliament as the Armed Forces Special Powers Act (AFSPA). The bill was a postcolonial updating of an ordinance first issued by the British Indian government in 1942, when Japanese armies were knocking at the gates of Kohima. This extraordinary piece of legislation would apply only to India's Northeast region and is draconian by any standards.[112] Following an executive decision to declare any part of this region a "disturbed area," state authorities were empowered to introduce the provisions of the act. AFSPA permits any member of the armed forces at the rank of a noncommissioned officer or above to enter any premises in search of people or weapons; it permits arrest of any person involved or suspected of being involved in insurgent activities; it also permits the destruction of any structure that may potentially be used for belligerent purposes. Most important, these activities may be carried out without judicial warrant or oversight, using whatever force is deemed necessary, including deadly violence. Perpetrators of official violence have complete immunity for their actions and are entirely unaccountable. Under the provisions of the law, no "prosecution, suit, or other legal proceeding" may be brought against them in a civilian court. This extraordinary legislation does not apply to any other part of the country except another "disturbed area," namely the state of Jammu and Kashmir, since 1990.[113]

Abuses against individuals under this legal umbrella of complete immunity under the provisions of this act are legion, but far more than isolated individuals were the victims of geopolitical militarization in the Northeast.[114] When the Mizos erupted in violence in March 1966, the region was at once declared a disturbed area.[115] The AFSPA came into effect. For the first time in independent India, air power was used against civilians and its own citizens. Sajal Nag has used multiple sources, including evidence drawn from military commanders involved, to show that, on March 5, 1966, the Indian Air Force was used to attack guerilla positions in Aizawl town to protect the army garrison from Mizo insurgents.[116] Bombing and strafing of the town over a week led to loss of life and a huge outflow of civilians. This would be followed by the relocation of Mizo communities, following the example set by the British in colonial Malaya, to areas where they could be more easily observed and monitored by the armed forces. A near-contemporary account notes that 50,000 villagers from 106 villages were relocated to eighteen fortified villages in just six weeks.[117] Relocation had been first tried in the Naga region in the late 1950s, and although it was not successful from a military standpoint, the tactic had become a part of the military's political arsenal. It was hoped that relocation would make it more difficult for insurgents to get help and support from Mizo village communities and make it easier for the army to spot infiltrators when they tried to cross the international border with East Pakistan. Eventually, 82 percent of the state's population, or over 200,000 people, were resettled in this manner.[118]

Nag quotes at length one Army officer's description of the process: "[After much persuasion], all the villagers were assembled outside their houses with whatever possessions they could carry." Then they were told to set fire to their houses. They couldn't bring themselves to do it, so

> ... ultimately I lit a torch myself and set fire to one of the houses ... soon the place was ablaze ... but there was one more thing to be done. I called the [village headman and elders] and ordered them to sign a document saying that they had voluntarily asked to be resettled in Hnahthial [the relocation village] ... as they were being harassed by the insurgents ... Another document stated that they had burnt down their own village and that there was no coercion used by the security forces. They refused to sign. So I sent them out again and after an hour called them in again, this time one man at a time. On my table was a loaded revolver and in the corner stood two NCOs with loaded sten guns ... One by one they signed both documents.[119]

Mizoram's insurgency was eventually stamped out, reducing the incidence of armed violence taking place between the Army and local inhabitants. The AFSPA remains in force at the time of this writing, notwithstanding legal challenges and other protests that continue into the present, led by national and international human rights and civil society groups (including some based in the Indian heartland). In 1997, the Indian Supreme Court upheld the constitutionality of this legislation. Other comparable legislation, including the notorious Maintenance of Internal Security Act (MISA) and Prevention of Terrorism Act (POTA), has been repealed by Parliament or declared unconstitutional by the courts, but the Armed Forces Special Powers Act remains in force.[120]

Exception and the Permanent Emergency

The Armed Forces Special Powers Act (AFSPA), which allows sovereign power full rein without judicial accountability in the seven states of the Northeast, falls under the legal jurisprudence of the "Emergency." Emergency legislation may be introduced in democracies as a result of extraordinary circumstances, including civil wars, economic collapse, riots, mutinies, and the threat or fact of external conflict. The jurisprudential emergency in a liberal state, Nasser Hussain points out, is rationalized on the basis of extraordinary circumstances, and, by the same token, can be in place for only a limited period of time. Once a state of order—normalcy—is restored, the emergency comes to an end, and with it, the application of these special laws. Two normative conditions, in other words, structure the jurisprudential emergency. The first is a recognizable state of normalcy as an implicit counterpoint for the exceptional conditions of the emergency. The second is the *temporary* nature of the emergency, making the emergency a period preceded and followed by the "normal."

Colonialism, Hussain argues, violates both these norms: The colony becomes a space where the emergency is a permanent state of being. In seeking to understand how a liberal metropolitan state sustains the illegitimacy of colonial rule, Hussain proposes that the racialized world of colonial discourse produces the colony as a space where extraordinary circumstances always apply. The application of emergency provisions in a colonial setting is not justified in terms of the *restoration* of law and order, as it would be in a liberal democracy, as the colony is represented as a space that has never had or known normalcy. Thus, the emergency is legitimized as a claim to produce law and order in the colony *for the first time*. Under these conditions, the application of sovereign power in the name of the emergency becomes a prepolitical act that seeks to constitute the foundations on which law, order, and a normal society can be built. Extraordinary state violence is justified, Hussain proposes, in relation to "the more general purpose of establishing the [initial] authority and force of the state at large."[121] The permanent emergency in the colony is ultimately justified as a means to engendering civilization and, thus, bringing into being something recognizable as a condition of normalcy. Hussain's argument links the colony and the emergency through a spatial boundary: it depends crucially on the imposition of a cordon sanitaire between the "normal" metropole and the "extraordinary" colony for these master terms, *normal* and *extraordinary*, to make sense. Applying these insights to the Northeast, it becomes possible to see that the continued use of the extreme and illiberal measures of the AFSPA likewise depend on and are conditioned by the difference of the Northeast from the rest of India. AFSPA is ostensibly applied to deal with the "emergency" in this region. In fact, the geopolitics of state violence both produce and reproduce the extraordinary conditions that makes the Northeast a permanent "space of exception."

To summarize: Geopolitical territorial practices began with the imperial logic of the "unruly" frontier that supplemented the buffer state. From the state's standpoint, this frontier was a zone that could remain underdeveloped precisely to protect the more valuable (in both economic and moral terms) settled and civilized areas from foreign attack. Although this frontier area might initially have been, from this set of eyes, unruly, it was also understood to have great economic potential due to its untapped physical and natural resources. The ensuing drive to settle this region for economic exploitation would lead to the importation of workers from peninsula India to clear the land, extract the timber, and work the plantations, mines, and oil refineries, creating a capitalist enclave that had little to do with its hinterland. The indigenous people of this region were considered warlike nomadic people organized in tribes who lived by swidden cultivation, without the recognizable institutional structures and legal order of a settled civilization. Due to their primitive material conditions, the indigenous inhabitants could be defined in terms that placed them on a civilizational scale lower than the people of the Indian heartland. The attitudes and behavior of colonial administrators and Christian missionaries to the Northeast may have differed in style but not in terms of their starting assumptions. Official reactions to the people of the Northeast would range from, at best, a benevolence that came from a misguided "*mission civilisa-*

trice," to, at worst, an indifference that permitted all kinds of abuses justified by their alleged lack of civilization.

Visible ethno-racial contrast would join the rise of Christianity among tribal populations to create a particularly sharp distinction with the Indian national heartland. Social, cultural, economic, and political difference would be materialized and segregated through a territorial boundary known as the Inner Line. This line not only demarcated different kinds of land and social habitus; it also marked a civilizational and political difference that could be bridged only by assimilation to the culture of the dominant power. After the redrawing of maps to define the new states of Pakistan and India in 1947, the Northeastern region would be joined to the rest of India only by a narrow and vulnerable land corridor. At this point, physical distance and remoteness would join cultural alienation to make the "Northeast" a metaphor for absolute difference. This was a part of India that looked, sounded, and behaved differently from the rest of the country yet shared the same state territory: Geopolitics had produced "outsiders within."

The seemingly endless violence that made the Northeast a de facto war zone from India's independence onwards was not seen as the outcome of histories of imperial expansion that had joined very different geocultural zones into a national heartland and a marginal area that was also a strategic frontier. The worldview of Indian elites is exemplified by Sardar Patel's geopolitical view of the Northeast as first and foremost a sensitive border region with China, inhabited by culturally distinct "Mongoloid" people whose loyalty to India was highly tenuous. Long-established forms of difference would be multiplied by the military exigencies of defending this region from restive "tribal" insurgents and revolutionaries seeking meaningful forms of political autonomy and from a threatening Communist neighboring state that was unwilling to accept an international border imposed on it during a period of political and military weakness. The fear of territorial loss, combined with distance and difference, would come together to create a space that stood apart in every possible way. As a constituent territory of the Indian state, defined by the Sixth Schedule, the Northeast had to be defended. Although the people of the Northeast may have been Indian citizens, that formal condition did not mean they belonged to the Indian nation. The Northeast became, following Agamben, that "extreme form of relation by which something is included solely through its exclusion."[122] The Northeast is a "space of exception": in India but not of it.

Extending Hussain's argument of the colony as a permanent state of emergency to the Northeast allows us to see this region as a permanent *space* of exception. But there is a corollary to his argument. The exceptional condition of the colony also allows the metropole to be constituted as its legal and constitutional other, a space of normalcy and civilization where the emergency is only a temporary condition imposed under extraordinary circumstances. The exclusion of the Northeast and its legal definition as a permanent space of exception through the Sixth Schedule and laws such as the Armed Forces Special Powers Act plays an analogous role for mainland India. Thanks to the Northeast, the rest of India can now be constituted as a "normal" space. When emergency legislation is introduced in other parts of India due to extreme political circumstances, "extreme" comes to be defined through the tacit counterpoint of the Northeast. The presence of the Northeast as a permanent space of exception makes possible two necessary legal presumptions for the application of emergency legislation for the rest of India, namely that this emergency legislation is only "temporary" and, second, that there is a normatively known "normal" condition that will return when the emergency is over.

In other words, India needs the Northeast to assure itself that emergency legislation in the national heartland has a temporal limit and that political space outside this permanently disturbed region is defined in normative terms. No matter how extreme the conditions faced in the heartland, the Northeast is always worse. The containment of the Northeast through special laws and civilizational boundaries reassures the rest of the country that it is in fine working order. The space where the sovereign need respect no limit to the exercise of its power becomes the standard against which the everyday operation of the law and the meaning of normal are measured. Geopolitics as foreign policy produces much more than a space of exception. The permanent spatial emergency that is the outcome of geopolitics, the Northeast, is foundational to the representation of the rest of the postcolonial state as a normal, legally constituted, and ordered political space.

Conclusion

Indian Territorial Disputes

Few commentators appeared to realize the larger significance of the historic September 7, 2011, agreement between India and Bangladesh.[1] This agreement included a protocol seeking to resolve long-standing issues of territorial sovereignty that had long troubled good relations between the two countries, regardless of the respective political parties in power. The protocol addressed an unmarked section of the international boundary line, the question of "adverse possession" of each other's land, and the long-standing problem of the sovereignty of "enclaves" lying in each other's countries.[2] Jyoti Malhotra was one of the very few journalists to realize that: "The reason the Manmohan-Hasina agreement is so important is because for the first time since 1947—not counting the ceding of the uninhabited island of Kachhateevu to Sri Lanka in 1974, amounting to only 285 acres, or the so-called 'return' of the Haji Pir pass to Pakistan after the 1965 war—India has agreed to give up some of its territory to another country."[3]

The uncontroversial premise that India's unresolved territorial disputes—most notably with Pakistan and China—are among the country's most urgent problems of foreign and security policy is the starting point for this conclusion. These disputes are long-standing and seemingly intractable and have been the proximate cause for repeated militarized interstate conflicts. The dispute over Kashmir has been the flash point for at least three wars between India and Pakistan, the last as recently as 1999. Half a century on, bitter memories of the war with China in 1962 continue to rankle in the minds of Indian policy makers and foreign policy elites. The humiliating outcome of 1962 has left a lingering fear of China that can be drawn on at will to create a stifling climate of anxiety, even in the absence of manifest threats to India's military security. All these themes are clearly expressed in Prime Minister Vajpayee's leaked letter to President Clinton in the wake of India's nuclear tests in 1998, identifying territory as the root problem, with China as the primary and Pakistan as the secondary reason for India needing to develop a nuclear deterrent:

We have an overt nuclear weapon state on our borders, a state which committed armed aggression against India in 1962. Although our relations with that country have improved in the last decade or so, an atmosphere of distrust persists *mainly due to the unresolved border problem.* To add to the distrust that country has materially helped another neighbour of ours to become a covert nuclear weapons state. At the hands of this bitter neighbor we have suffered three aggressions in the last 50 years. And for the last ten years we have been the victim of unremitting terrorism and militancy sponsored by it in several parts of our country, specially Punjab and Jammu & Kashmir.[4]

India–Pakistan border disputes find their most extreme expression in the so-called Siachen Glacier conflict. When the international boundary between the two countries was mapped following the 1948 war, it was mutually agreed that there was little need to go beyond map coordinate NJ9842 on the original cease-fire line, given the absence of troops and fighting in this area and due to the extremely forbidding physical terrain and weather conditions. Both sides assumed at the time that this was a region of no strategic value and that it was impossible to imagine actually occupying this harsh environment. Indian and Pakistani military negotiators agreed that the international boundary would proceed "north to the Glaciers" in the now well-known, if highly contested, phrase. Pakistan took "north to the Glaciers" to mean that they could draw a straight line from NJ9842 to the Karakoram Pass, which they controlled; the Indian side took the same injunction to mean that they would follow the watershed line of the Saltoro Range up to the Chinese border. This ambiguity remained in place during the post-1971 war Simla Agreement that led to the establishment of today's line of control, the de facto international boundary between the two states.[5] In 1984, as V. K. Raghavan points out in his detailed study of the conflict, all this changed, when India decided to control the high point of the then-uninhabited Saltoro range for newly discovered "strategic" reasons.[6] What had been left unclarified because it was of no apparent value to either side was transformed, overnight, into the zero-sum logic of strategic advantage. The key decision maker on the Indian side appears to have been the director general of military operations, not the top military or political leadership. But once the heights were controlled by Indian forces, they could not be given up without being seen as a loss of "Indian" territory. Pakistan had no choice, by the same logic, but to seek to reclaim "its" land, and what followed can be described only in terms of ridiculous extremes.

At nearly 6,000 m above sea level, the Siachen Glacier easily lays claim to being the world's most extreme war zone. It is the highest battlefield in the world, the coldest, and the most expensive to operate in. The greatest danger to combatants comes from the environment, not the opposing military force. Journalists have estimated that between 1984 and 1992, India and Pakistan spent nearly US$6 billion on the conflict.[7] A decade later, in the absence of direct contact with the enemy but with access to better equipment and improved logistics, India managed to bring casualties down to thirty soldiers a year and, since 2003, about ten annually.[8] Neither side can step away from this conflict if it appears to give up territory in the process of seeking a reasonable end to the conflict: high-level talks between the two governments on Siachen have repeatedly stalled. In the wake of the 1999 Kargil War, political scientist Sumit Ganguly is of the opinion that "the prospects of conflict resolution [have] probably further diminished."[9] No better example need be cited how territory, or more precisely territorial loss, has become so intimately associated with (the loss of) state power. The logic of the inherent value of territorial control is so internalized that it no longer needs to be explained why a forbidding and worthless piece of land is worth the cost of three decades' loss of blood and treasure.

Over the last six decades, all sorts of efforts have been made to resolve India's territorial disputes. These include multiple rounds of direct talks between the states in question, discussions at the Track Two level, and interventions involving the international community.[10] Some progress has been made, including, for example, the opening of the Nathu-La Pass between Tibet (China) and Sikkim (India) in 2006 and the relaxation of border controls for divided families in Kashmir; nevertheless, the core concerns underlying these disputes remain unresolved and continue to act as potential triggers for interstate conflict.[11] Even as Indian foreign policy is increasingly challenged by demands emergent from the need to take on greater responsibilities in a rapidly evolving international order, from global economic governance to trade pacts to new international groupings, long-standing territorial disputes continue to stand in the way of allowing India to fully embody this new and preferred global identity.[12] Under these circumstances, it becomes a question of the highest importance to understand why territorial conflicts are so protracted and appear to be so difficult to resolve.

India is hardly alone in facing the problem of long-standing territorial disputes. Throughout Asia, from Japan to Afghanistan, various bits of land and sea are the objects of interstate contestation.[13] Few observers are unaware of the ongoing conflict over the 650-odd island archipelago spread over 400,000 square kilometers in the South China Sea collectively called the Spratly Islands. These islands are variously claimed by Vietnam, the Philippines, Malaysia, Brunei, China, and Taiwan; increasingly belligerent

Chinese efforts to claim these islands exclusively have led to concerns that interstate conflict over this issue cannot be ruled out in the near future.[14] The Philippines has now turned to the International Court of Justice (ICJ) for a ruling on the matter.[15] But this is hardly the only territorial dispute in Asia. Afghanistan and Pakistan have long disagreed over the status of the Durand Line that ostensibly divides their two countries.[16] The Japanese and the Korean people are both outraged when each is reminded that the other claims the tiny rocky islands that lie in the sea between them. Indeed, they even refer to them differently: the Japanese call the islands Takeshima, and the Koreans call them Dokdo.[17] With the potential of exclusive economic rights accruing to the legitimate "owner" of these islands, the battle over these tiny islands has now even more at stake for the three countries involved, namely, South Korea, North Korea (DPRK), and Japan. The Japanese are also involved in a dispute with the Russians over the Kurile Islands in the north, dating back to World War II, and with China over the Senkaku/Diaoyu Islands, which are increasingly considered a major regional flashpoint.[18] Indonesian claims to former British Malayan territories on the island of Borneo led to the *Konfrontasi* conflict in the 1960s.[19] Thailand and Cambodia have long had a diplomatic standoff over the status of the ancient Preah Vihear temple, which lies on a disputed strip of land between the two countries.[20] The ICJ has now ruled that the temple lies on Cambodian land but has declined to resolve the underlying border issue. As recently as February 2013, an armed militia based in the Philippines claiming to represent the descendants of the former sultanate of Sulu "invaded" the Malaysian province of Sabah in an effort to reclaim it, leading to an intense military encounter with the Malaysian armed forces. Perhaps most existential of all the disputes is the conflict between China and Taiwan, which can only truly end with the dissolution of one of the parties to the conflict.[21]

This far from complete list makes it clear that India is hardly alone in Asia when it comes to disputed territories. The majority of these disputes owe their origins to the period when Asia was dominated by imperial formations, from the British in the West to the Japanese in the East, a period from the mid-nineteenth century until after World War II. Some of today's disputes originate from inter-imperial cartographic carelessness, problems with translation, and callous indifference; others from the unequal encounter between an empire and a nominally independent state. What is not under dispute is that the majority of Asian territorial disputes originated during the period of decolonization, when empires collapsed into nation-states transmuting existing cartographic ambiguities into interstate disputes. Notwithstanding their origins, what this accounting reinforces are the simple conclusions that territorial disputes are, first, widespread and, second, difficult to resolve. Given the number and intensity of these ongoing tensions, it now becomes easier to appreciate the rarity and significance of the India–Bangladesh agreement of 2011.

Forms of territorial disputation are not restricted to diplomatic démarches and Notes circulating in the corridors of power. The domestic public's reaction to perceived territorial losses is usually loud and angry, expressed through a variety of mediums, even in countries where freedom of speech is restricted, for example, China. Governments often find themselves on the defensive vis-à-vis their domestic populations when it appears that suitably vigorous and muscular responses to alleged territorial encroachments are slow in coming. Restricting our analysis to understanding the *origins* of territorial disputes still leaves us very far from understanding the more practical (and policy-relevant) questions of why they matter so much in contemporary international relations. Two questions in particular stand out: First, why do territorial disputes raise such intense passions among elites and domestic publics, even if the land involved is economically and politically worthless; and, second, why is the exchange of territory between states almost always portrayed as a net loss to state power even when the objective benefits of resolving territorial disputes include a mutual improvement in bilateral relations and greater regional peace and stability? Complicating matters, these passions have also to be squared against those rare moments when countries have given up land or other territorial claims with little or no hostile reaction from their people.

Seeking to understand the persistence of territorial conflicts in Asia begins from the political history of the modern nation-state. This history does not begin from putative origins in a mythical European past but rather starts from the articulation of the nation-state model as a universal standard for political self-determination and sovereignty, following the end of World War I. Once Wilson put forward the Fourteen Points, anticolonial movements around the world took his statement as an affirmation of the legitimacy of their demand for political sovereignty, despite Wilson's inability to define the nation-state unambiguously and, more important, despite the rank unsuitability of this model for the multicultural, polyglot, mobile world of Asia. Unable to conform to the normative standards of the modern nation-state, summarized as one people–one land–one state, anticolonial nationalists fell on territorial sovereignty as the measure of their right to political freedom, thereby reifying territory as the prime means by which their claims to independence as political entities could and should be assessed.

Territorial control thus became the most important channel through which modern political identity could be established. Territory would become the embodiment of the national homeland through spatializing techniques, including measurement, narration, mapping, and visualization. Once territorial boundaries and limits were established, national myths and stories were produced to conform to these boundaries, engendering an uneven national space overwritten by topographies of legend and history. Through this process, multiple histories of place were condensed into the singular history of a bounded nation-space authorized in the name of a single and immobile autochthonous and/or majority population who had "always" lived there. Other visible populations were identified under the sign of the Minority, a category that could include ethnic, cultural, religious, civilizational, and/or linguistic difference. The object of this exercise was to make territory so obviously the ground of political identity that it became invisible: as Paul Allies notes, territory gives the state "a physical basis which seems to render it inevitable and eternal."[22] Given these powerful inscriptions, it is often difficult to remember that territory preceded nation. Postcolonial nation-states were produced by the retrospective nationalization of the territories under the state's control.

The extent of state territorial claims was typically determined by the boundaries of the predecessor state. Postcolonial nation-states did not identify with their British, French, and Dutch predecessors but had little choice but to claim their territorial boundaries for the advantages of legacy and international legitimacy they conferred. Modern nationalism is typically narrated in terms of the historic culmination of the nation "coming into its own" by finally acquiring its own state. In fact, the reverse is true. Territorial possession is the historical starting point for the authenticity of the claim to be a legitimate nation-state. Yet, the narration of the national homeland necessarily reverses that history, giving the appearance that the existence of the nation and its self-evident homeland *preceded* territorial control, in order to conform to the normative dictates of "national self-determination." The process of postcolonial nation building is the suturing of territory to nation and state through processes that begins from the disavowal of recent political history. For most postcolonial states, territorial "loss" threatens not only to undermine their standing as legitimate states, and also to expose the fault lines of history, migration, and ethnicity, in the process revealing a past still too recent and politically charged to be consigned to the margins of official memory.

Hence, what is really at stake in the loss of territory, whether real or imagined, is the return to collective consciousness of the historical process whereby a national past is inscribed onto state land, exposing the nation's contingent and post hoc emergence. Territorial disputes are a public disavowal of both the nation's narrative of always having been there and the state's resolute claim to represent this nationality.[23] When nation formation follows territorial control, the loss of territory opens up to outside scrutiny the historical artifices of the material scaffolding over which the national imaginary has been produced. This exposure threatens the coherence of the existing national idea by interrupting a carefully scripted collective amnesia and reminds the nation of other historical possibilities that existed and that might have been equally plausible as political outcomes. This is what is at stake in Asia's territorial conflicts. This explains why the loss of territory is represented as a foundational crisis. This is why today's territorial conflicts are so protracted and difficult to resolve.[24]

Chinese Territorial Exceptionalism?

Under these circumstances, how is it possible for any Asian interstate territorial conflicts ever to be resolved? The Chinese case is the most prominent example of an unlikely state that has been able to settle a number of border disputes with its neighbors.[25] M. Taylor Fravel has forwarded a series of carefully reasoned and well-documented arguments regarding China's approach to territorial disputes.[26] He begins from the observation that China has behaved in an unexpected way in most territorial disputes with its neighbors:[27] "China has not used its power advantages to bargain hard over contested land . . . nor has it become less willing to offer concessions . . . as its power has increased." Fravel's "diversionary peace" argument suggests that China's real concern is domestic insecurity. He finds that where China faces threats to its territorial integrity from movements of ethnic minorities who live on or near international borders, it has tended to make concessions on boundary disputes with neighboring states. The logic of this pragmatic approach is as follows. China seeks to reduce the likelihood that ethnic minorities will find refuge across international borders as well as the possibility that neighboring states will use ethnic unrest to destabilize China's borders. The argument is well supported by his data and makes a considerable advance in our understanding of China's ostensible motives in resolving seventeen of its twenty-three territorial disputes since 1949.

Fravel divides China's territorial disputes into three kinds: *frontier* (for example, the borders with Mongolia or Myanmar), *offshore* (the Spratlys), and *homeland* (Taiwan, Macau, and Hong Kong). China is most willing, he argues, to make concessions on frontier disputes for the pragmatic security-related reasons outlined earlier. Offshore disputes offer a mixed picture, with China holding on to its claims for potential economic benefits (although today these have become sites of greater tension). On homeland disputes, however, Fravel argues that China will not compromise under any circumstances.[28] As he says: "The overriding importance of completing national unification suggests that these conflicts are basically non-negotiable."[29] In the discussion leading up to this unambiguous conclusion, Fravel variously identifies these "homeland" disputed territories as "areas linked to the Han Chinese core" and "China proper."[30] China, by this reading, is in the eyes of its ruling elites first and foremost a territorially incomplete nation, hence the "non-negotiable" and overwhelming importance of restoring its dismembered territories to the homeland. Territorial loss, we are told, is a reminder of the historical humiliations of the Chinese nation. In other words, Fravel argues that one set of territories may be bargained away because their "loss" makes the Chinese state more secure even as another set of territories are "non-negotiable" because they represent core areas of the Chinese national homeland. Note that one reason is offered for giving up land (state insecurities) and quite another for demanding its restoration (nationalist passion). This leads to an intriguing puzzle. The long-standing Chinese territorial dispute with India is, in the last instance, a dispute over the borders of Tibet. There is little question that resolving this dispute would allow Chinese military planners considerable relief on their southwestern front, and Tibet is unquestionably a frontier. By the logic of Fravel's argument, China should be willing to make concessions to India to resolve the dispute as it has done with many of its other neighbors. But it has not. What then explains China's unwillingness to offer territorial concessions in its dispute with India? Why is Tibet, anything but a core area of the Chinese homeland, not a site of territorial compromise? After all, territorial compromise over the disputed Tibet–India border would allow the Chinese state to reduce its insecurities on its southern frontiers, as it has done successively with Vietnam, Burma, Laos, and Cambodia. What is missing in this account is any consideration of the national question. As we have seen in the case of India, territorial issues are also always issues involving the nation.

Fravel offers a picture of Chinese territory as a hierarchical and heterogeneous distribution of space built around two orders of distinction. He implies that, depending on where one stands, "Chinese territory" can mean entirely different things and, hence, can lead to very different state behaviors. The first mark of spatial distinction is ethnic, that is, based on the occupants of the land (Han versus non-Han), while the second is locational, depending on the meaning attributed to place (homeland versus frontier). The first distinction speaks to a national formation; the second, to a category that belongs to the territorial state. The overlap between the two—Han/homeland—defines the Chinese heartland. As a result, the values that accrue to each spatial category are quite different. Tibet is different from, say, Hong Kong, not only on the basis of the ethnicity of its majority population but also because the "restoration" of Hong Kong was deemed necessary for the project of "completing national unification." Clearly, the lack of territorial compromise with India over the Tibetan border cannot be explained by the story of national restoration. But the absence of compromise cannot be reduced to strategic reasons either, or China should have been willing to take the step of unilaterally making concessions as it has done in other cases. Indeed, China did make an offer of a territorial swap in the early 1950s, long before it settled territorial disputes with other countries, only to be rejected by India.[31] Since 1959, however, the Chinese have taken a harder line on settling this border dispute. This suggests that India is the problem. Although this conclusion is not entirely incorrect, it is not sufficient. I argue that a fuller understanding of China's concern over its Tibetan border with India must also come from another source, namely the question of the Chinese nation. This involves unpacking the contradictions of territorial claims emanating from China's need to be accepted as the official legatee of the Qing Empire as well as the sole legitimate representative of the Chinese nation. The Chinese territorial story is not an exception as it first appears—namely, its willingness to resolve territorial disputes in spite of being the more powerful of the two parties—but rather exemplifies the double bind of a postcolonial nation-state seeking international recognition and legitimacy while making a singular claim to territorial control.

Unlike the case of most postcolonial Asian states that are the inheritors of a Western colonial state or imperial territory, China's Communist leadership adopted the imperial boundaries of a Chinese/Manchu lineage, the Qing, as the borders of their new nation-state. To claim to inherit the Qing legacy was not an obvious or necessary choice for a revolutionary state.

Taking on the troubled inheritance of a political entity that was an avowedly imperial and feudal state was at one level finessed for the People's Republic by the historicist logic of Communism. Communism is, in its own terms, a historical advance over feudalism. Hence, there need be no fear from an ideological point of view of the contamination of the modern Chinese state by its feudal past, as the revolution itself was "scientific" confirmation that an irreversible and progressive historical change had taken place.

Understanding China's problems in becoming a territorial nation-state begins by acknowledging the intricate combination of imperial and national formations that constitute the modern Chinese state. The Qing Empire had, from the Opium Wars onward, been steadily weakened by external military and commercial pressures and forced to cede sovereignty over territories, control over trade, and judicial jurisdiction over Western citizens.[32] At the beginning of the twentieth century, Japanese annexations of Taiwan and later Manchuria left territories once deemed to be subordinate to the Qing alienated from the imperial state.[33] Although, historically, the meaning and practices of Chinese imperial hegemony did not correspond to the Western definition of sovereign territorial control, once China was redefined as a nation-state, the need for singular territorial control followed.

Imported conceptions of territorial sovereignty had to contend with the problem that Chinese imperial territory was not a stable or fixed entity. The territorial imagination of China, William Callahan argues, is a palimpsest of "imperial domain and sovereign territory,"[34] an asymmetric overlay of "the ambiguous frontiers of the imperial domain and the clear national boundaries of the international system."[35] He shows that edges of the Chinese geobody are "fluid and contingent boundaries produced by historical events framed by multiple cartographic conventions."[36] Cartographic conventions include "premodern unbounded understandings of space and territory" that foreground civilizational distinctions as well as more familiar bounded and modern maps of sovereign territory.

The transition from the Qing Empire to the modern Chinese nation-state required dealing with a far-reaching legacy, the simultaneous ethnicization of Chinese identity and identification of the Mandarin-speaking Han people as the majority national population. A critical point of mobilization for modern Chinese nationalists in the early twentieth century was the rejection of the Manchu Qings as non-Han outsiders.[37] This bitter dispute over the very "Chinese-ness" of the Qing Empire had led to the rewriting of Chinese identity in ethnic terms, building on Sun Yat-Sen's nationalist reformulation of the "Five Peoples of China": Han, Manchu, Mongolian,

Tibetan, and Hui (Muslim). Following Communist theoreticians from Stalin onward who took an early stand on the question of national self-determination in multiethnic states, the PRC could have decided that the many ethnic minorities subsumed under the Qing were legitimate entities for self-determination, but they did not.[38] Dru Gladney argues that objectified and eroticized representations of ethnic minority identities played a critical role in permitting the Han majority to become the "unmarked" center of the nation, connoting civility and modernity. Marginalizing China's "ethnic" populations made possible the "homogenization of the majority at the expense of the exoticized minority."[39]

Further complicating the question of historical legacy and the modern Chinese state's claim to be the sole representative of the Chinese people was a globally dispersed diaspora (*huaqiao*). Following centuries of travel and "sojourning" from Nanyang, the Chinese name for the Southern Seas, to such far-flung locations as Cuba and Australia, the Chinese nation was, by 1949, a globally dispersed deterritorialized entity.[40] Although the official relation to the diaspora was not consistent, ranging from outright rejection to welcoming, the Chinese state always considered Chinese national identity to be a nonideological condition.[41] Even if Chinese nationals had lived outside the official borders of the Chinese homeland for generations, they were considered to remain Chinese in essential respects, a view that was reinforced by colonial governmental practices of enumeration and ethnicization.[42] For the Chinese state, Chinese-ness would not fade with time or distance as Indian leaders would claim for their own overseas populations in 1947. The deterritorialized boundaries of the Chinese nation remained constant through hereditary and cultural transmission even as centuries of political turmoil and "humiliation" moved and removed Chinese territorial borders.

Modern China's territorial borders would follow the boundaries of the Qing Empire to establish that first the Nationalist and then the Communist states were the Qing's legitimate historical successors. For the Communist state, this claim came immediately into question during the Cold War. Due to U.S. hostility and support for the Republic of China, or Taiwan, the People's Republic of China (PRC) would remain unrecognized by much of the world and unable to join the United Nations until 1971.[43] This lengthy period without external recognition only intensified the need to resolve the territorial and national contradictions of the PRC, problems that can be summed up under the mark of continuity. Establishing unbroken territorial and national continuity was a requirement for the PRC to successfully claim the legacy of the Qing Empire. The PRC's claim to be the inheritor of the Qing required that the borders of Communist China coincided with the borders of the erstwhile empire. Moreover, the PRC's simultaneous claim to be the sole representative of the Chinese nation required that overseas Chinese loyalties be directed solely at it and especially not at the pretender claimant, Taiwan. The urgency of establishing continuity would lead to serious politico-ideological complications for the PRC that become visible through the lens of territorial "loss," disputes, and their resolutions.

The borders claimed by the PRC correspond to the Qing Empire at its most expansive, an expanse far greater than the territory actually inherited by the Nationalist regime at the fall of the empire. In other words, seeking to restore Qing boundaries as China's new borders created territorial loss as a foundational condition of modern statehood. Alienated Qing lands at once became "lost" territories that had to be regained for the Chinese state to be considered the legitimate successor to the Qing. Due to the decision to take Qing boundaries as their own, the Chinese state had also now to come to terms with ethnic—non-Han, non–Mandarin-speaking—nationalities with their own histories and cultures living within newly claimed Chinese state borders. Although Communist ideology initially made space for a working multinational political formation, this would only be a temporary solution, as ongoing insurgencies in China's western provinces make most clear.

At the same time, the Chinese state sought to be acknowledged as the sole representative of a globally dispersed Chinese nation. What remains unstated in the official account of Chinese national identity is that the core nation identified through geography and history is the Mandarin-speaking Han people. A substantial proportion of overseas Chinese, some of whom had left the country in resistance to Qing dominance, were non–Mandarin-speaking people, albeit identified as ethnically Han. Predominantly drawn from southern and eastern China, overseas Chinese allegiances were more likely to have been to ancestral villages and provinces than the faraway imperial capital. A case in point is the overseas Chinese millionaire, Tan Kah Kee, who founded Amoy (now Xiamen) University in his native Fujian province in 1921. Beijing could hardly count on diasporic Chinese with similar histories to identify with the new, Communist, aspirant nation-state. In other words, the political transition from the Qing to the PRC brought with it the following contradictions. The new state's claimed territorial borders incorporated people who tacitly brought into question the articulation of the Chinese nation as an ethnically Han, Mandarin-speaking population and, at the same time, tested the new state's claim to be the sole representative of the Chinese nation, a social body that far exceeded the state's territorial borders. As in India, efforts to resolve these contradictions would begin with territoriality.

The standard account of the demand for the restoration of alienated territories to the Chinese state is that they are non-negotiable because their "loss" is a constant reminder of the period of foreign domination. No small part of official Chinese state nationalism is built around overcoming "humiliations" of the past at the hand of foreigners; in that context, these "lost" homeland territories are a synecdoche for national dismemberment.[44] In other words, Hong Kong, Macau, and Taiwan do not just represent territorial disputes with other countries but are also conflicts in which historical memory is a central disputant. Although this is surely no small concern, demanding the return of lost territories is also a necessary condition for the Chinese state also to claim to be the legitimate representative of the entire Chinese *nation*. Reclaiming "lost" territories addresses two important and unresolved contradictions of Chinese nationalism. The first is the representation issue, "insiders without"; the second is the ethnic minority question, or "outsiders within."

In the standard account, the restoration of Hong Kong and Macau, and eventually Taiwan, compensates for historical humiliations and also removes any lingering doubts that the PRC state is the legitimate territorial successor to the Qing Empire. The emphasis on restoring the original geobody of the Chinese state finesses a major contradiction within official Chinese nationalism, namely, the PRC as the legitimate representative of the Chinese nation understood as a global social body. However, state nationalism and national patriotism are not identical. The overseas Chinese community holds complex relations of both attachment and distance with respect to their natal villages, regions, and languages and to China as a whole. Beijing cannot assume that it will naturally represent them. By restoring Qing territories to the Chinese state, by regaining Taiwan and other "homeland" territories, the essential continuity of a deterritorialized Chinese nation is affirmed, reinforcing the claim of the Chinese state as this nation's legitimate political representative. Territorial restoration, in other words, allows the modern Chinese state to claim the Qing Empire's standing and authority as the highest political embodiment of the Chinese *nation*, without however actually testing that claim. What is at stake in the unwillingness to "lose" Taiwan is the Chinese Communist state's claim to be the sole legitimate representative of the Chinese people, not only in China but across the world.

Locating the restoration of national territories as a major imperative of state policy also finesses the problems of "outsiders within." Making it appear that the problem of "lost" homeland territories is the major issue facing Chinese nationalism successfully glosses Han identity as the unspoken center of the Chinese nation. To the extent this national erasure can be sustained, it affords an alibi to the Han majority from needing to acknowledge themselves as the dominant majority in a multiethnic state. It also allows the state to deny the political resistance of minority ethnic groups as a legitimate political aspiration. Yet, ongoing insurgent movements show most clearly that the national question in China is far from fully resolved. From the point of view of the western margins, historical tributary relations of these vast regions to the Qing does not entitle the modern Chinese state to claim territorial sovereignty over them.[45] Moreover, ethnic nationalists argue, they can never be more than minorities in a majority Han Chinese state. Seen from its territorial edges, China is an unequal and hierarchical state dominated by the Han. Such a reading is buttressed by China's resolution of some territorial disputes. From Beijing's point of view, the territories inhabited by the ethnic minorities of China are qualitatively inferior lands. They can be given up in the interests of interstate harmony because they do not impinge on national space. China, in other words, is able to resolve the majority of its territorial problems precisely because the inhabitants of those border regions are not considered truly Chinese: giving up these lands thus comes at no cost to the Chinese nation. In other words, Fravel is partly correct. He is correct to note that "homeland" territories cannot be given up because they are central to national identity; what he fails to see is that this maneuver is also a claim to represent the global Chinese nation, as explained earlier. Fravel is also correct to see a pragmatic strategic interest in China's willingness to cede frontier lands. But what he does not appreciate are the implications of the finding that frontier lands can be given up at little cost because they are not central to Chinese national identity. The reason why some lands matter more to the Chinese state is exactly the same reason that other lands matter less. The variation among them comes from the degree to which these lands are deemed national spaces. Nation is the critical missing element from conventional accounts of disputed and lost Chinese territories.

Seen in this light, what about Tibet? As already mentioned, China did show some willingness to trade disputed territories with India in the 1950s, in effect giving up the Tibetan claim of (nonterritorial) sovereignty and tributary relations over parts of northeastern India in exchange for sovereign control over Aksai Chin. India refused this offer, for a number of reasons. Today, the possibility of territorial concessions from the Chinese side, as offered to other countries in the region, is unlikely, although it would help reduce state insecurities. The reason is due to the formation and consolidation of an overseas Tibetan community. The escape of the Dalai Lama to India in 1959 and the creation of a Tibetan diasporic enclave in India have created an untenable situation for the Chinese nation-state, making it impossible anymore to consider territorial concessions or a land swap.

It is easy to understand the logic of China's territorial claim over Tibet. Claiming Tibet for China follows from the need to claim all territories subservient to the Qing: territorial continuity. With this claim, however, also comes a tacit demand for the allegiance of the people resident within that territory. Within the territorial bounds of the Chinese state, that is, the Tibetan Autonomous Region, this demand has been met to a considerable extent through cooptation, tacit hegemony, and physical coercion, broken only by the constant and tragic flow of Tibetans resisting through self-immolation. The overseas Tibetan community is another story. The Tibetan diaspora will never agree to be identified primarily as Chinese, even as younger Tibetans increasingly may trade on connections in China to take advantage of business opportunities.[46] There is plenty of variation among the political views of the Tibetan overseas community, but one constant is their unwillingness to see themselves as representatives of the overseas Chinese nation. To a lesser or greater extent, they are (Overseas) Tibetans. The overseas Tibetans thus represent a "Chinese" nation that refuses to be acknowledged as Chinese. The Chinese state cannot expect their loyalty or recognition as the legitimate representative of the Chinese people. With the formation of an overseas diaspora, Tibet cannot anymore be considered a strategic frontier or a potential territorial asset to be traded away as state dictates demand. With every self-immolation, the legitimacy of the Chinese claim to Tibetan territory is questioned. Further afield, the presence of a Tibetan diaspora that will not be identified as Chinese stands as a permanent reminder that the Chinese state will never fully command the allegiances of all peoples whose origins now lie in the PRC. National continuity is broken twice, over territory as well as people. This is why China has a protracted territorial dispute with India.

Pakistan

Chapters 3 and 4 have presented a critical discussion of two core practices that established territorial boundaries between India and the world, before and after it became a sovereign state. The first boundary addressed the territorialization of India from the point of view of its global nation or diaspora, showing how divisions were variously inscribed within the national body, selectively separating and joining the residents of the Indian homeland from/with a globally dispersed nation. As a direct result of this process, political exclusions around the categories of caste and class were written into the nation, reinforcing a hierarchical social order that privileged the middle-class and upper-caste political subject. The second boundary sought to territorialize a strategic frontier between the cartographed body of the Indian state and perceived external sources of political and military insecurity. Drawing on the postcolonial legacy of British imperial geopolitics, independent India's efforts to reterritorialize itself after becoming independent have led to the creation of a space of exclusion in its northeastern region. In the process, the Northeast has become a spatial exception to the rest of the country, defined around a permanent state of emergency. Spatially containing the Northeast permits the rest of India to be identified as its normative counterpoint; the sphere of the normal, ordered, and civilized is produced by its putative difference from the always-othered Northeast. These chapters demonstrate that diaspora and geopolitics, two key territorializing practices of foreign policy, have had far-reaching domestic political effects. The uneven quality of postcolonial Indian citizenship, I argue, is the direct result of defining the nation-state in territorial terms.

The conjoined effect of these two foreign policy practices also offers a novel perspective on India's inability to stabilize good relations with its neighbor, Pakistan. As is all too well known, India and Pakistan have been in a constant state of militarized tension since 1947, a condition that has erupted into war on at least four different occasions. Conventional explanations for this perpetual state of conflict always return to the centrifugal dynamics of joint histories and oppositional religio-national ideologies, grounded in the unresolved legacy of territorial disputes—including but not restricted to Kashmir—that inaugurated bilateral relations between the two successor states of British India.[47]

Based on the findings of this study, I propose that, even if independent India had had no territorial disputes with Pakistan, it would not be able to have good relations with its neighbor. This condition holds true as long as Indian foreign policy is territorialized through diaspora and geopolitics. The reason is that the very existence of Pakistan, as the following discussion explains, stands as a permanent repudiation of these core Indian foreign policy practices.

Since Curzon, India's strategic vision has taken the Himalayan mountain ranges as the country's first line of defense. Eschewing potential threats facing India from the sea in spite of the historical experience of the last three centuries, defense planners have always looked to the north as the most likely source of military danger. Afghanistan and Tibet, so-called buffer states to the northwest and northeast, were propped up to keep the great land empires of Russia and China a safe distance away. To sustain further this strategic vision, the Himalayan kingdoms of Nepal, Sikkim, and Bhutan were written into India's defensive horizon and prevented from having independent defense or foreign policies. Whenever Nepal or Sikkim began to show signs of behaving in an autonomous fashion, they could count on the wrath of Delhi's proconsuls. Both economic blockades and outright annexation were used by postcolonial India to keep these vassal states in line and properly subordinate to India's wishes. And it had worked. Only the Japanese, during World War II, had come close to threatening India's military security, and they had been beaten back in a series of battles in the frontier zone of northeast India.

The creation of Pakistan in 1947 changed this strategic map fundamentally. Seen from New Delhi, the creation of Pakistan was a severe setback to the existing defense policy of territorial India. The creation of Pakistan as a spatially bifurcated country flanking the Gangetic floodplain, northern India's heartland, restructured the geopolitical map of British India fundamentally. Military planners were forced to refashion entirely their plans to deal with these new scales of military vulnerability. The borders of East Pakistan, now Bangladesh, left the already-suspect Indian Northeast physically connected to the mainland only through a narrow land corridor, creating an extremely vulnerable strategic chokepoint. The former imperial capital of Calcutta became in effect a border town. With Lahore now the capital of the Pakistani province of Punjab, the traditional land route to Kashmir was no longer in Indian hands. The new international borders of West Pakistan were dangerously close to New Delhi and Bombay, making cities once considered relatively deep in the Indian hinterland now proximate to a belligerent international foe. What was once imagined as a "scientific frontier," a means of forcing potential invaders to pass through the hostile buffer state of Afghanistan limned by the tribal frontier regions of the Northwest Frontier Province before reaching the most valuable civilized and settled regions of British India, had disappeared overnight. The creation of Pakistan led to the layers of geopolitical protection once offered by the frontier policy and the Himalayas being stripped away, leaving India exposed to conventional military threat as never before.

The easiest way for India to accommodate this enormous geopolitical transformation would have been if Pakistan, like the Himalayan kingdoms, had been forced to subordinate its security policies to Indian needs. In other words, Pakistan would have had to relinquish its newly gained sovereignty to allow the region to return to the pre-1947 geopolitical map. That this likelihood was highly improbable was empirically confirmed when the first India–Pakistan war broke out over Kashmir in 1947–1948. Pakistan, even more than India, saw itself as under a constant existential threat of dissolution. Few Pakistani leaders were confident that the new country would survive long enough to become truly sovereign.[48] The pressures it faced in the early years of independence, from the political to the humanitarian, were extraordinary. Overriding everything else was the fear that India would not permit Pakistan's continued existence and would act militarily to restore British India to its original territorial extent. India's refusal to relinquish the Muslim majority state of Kashmir, in spite of the partition provisions, only confirmed this fear. To balance India's far greater military power and economic resources, Pakistan's political leadership eagerly sought external allies for protection and aid.[49] When a weakened postwar British government proved unable to offer significant resources and support to Pakistan, it turned to the United States.[50] By the time of the Bandung conference in 1955, Pakistan had become the geopolitical hinge between two U.S.-sponsored Cold War treaty organizations stretching from Turkey to the Philippines seeking to "contain" the spread of international Communism. With this international support behind them, Pakistan ensured that there was no possibility of returning to British imperial geopolitics.

If the creation of Pakistan was a geopolitical disaster for the Indian state, the national problem epitomized by the new Muslim-majority state on India's borders engendered its own crisis. Willy-nilly, the independent state of Pakistan had overnight become India's largest and most proximate diaspora. Until August 15, 1947, the date of Indian independence, every resident of the territories that had become Pakistan the day before had been an Indian national. With dual citizenship out of the question, drawing a line between Indians and this "near-abroad" diaspora could hardly follow the traditional criteria for establishing national identity. Whether the standard applied was citizenship by blood/descent (*jus sanguinis*) or citizenship by place of birth (*jus soli*), the same outcome applied. All Pakistan's residents, other than those born after August 14, 1947, were potentially Indian citizens. The new state of Pakistan was comprised of a large Muslim majority as well as significant Hindu and Sikh minorities. What needed to be found was a formula that admitted Pakistan's minority communities to Indian citizenship, but not its Muslim majority, though this could never be stated officially.

Faced with this problem, India developed a hybrid model to deal with the particular founding conditions of a formally secular state. Indian legislators particularly struggled with deciding how to prevent Muslim residents of the new state of Pakistan from also being eligible for Indian citizenship, without saying so explicitly. Eventually, a complex spatio-temporal threshold was established for establishing eligibility for Indian citizenship. The first mark of distinction was a person's current location on March 1, 1947. Anyone currently living within what would become India's new territorial borders on that date was eligible for Indian citizenship. Anyone resident in what had now become the new state of Pakistan on that date would not be permitted to take Indian citizenship. However, a person who had been born in what was now Pakistan but had moved to India as a refugee could also become an Indian. No explicit reference was made to the religious identity of a potential citizen, but, in practice, Hindus and Sikhs who had been born in what was now Pakistan would not be denied citizenship on arrival in India, regardless of when they moved.[51] However, all those who may have been born in British India but had left the country for what was now Pakistan after March 1, 1947, were denied Indian citizenship. Moving from India to what was now Pakistan after March 1947 was taken to mean the intention of a migrant to renounce Indian nationality. It was further assumed that all those who had moved after this date were Muslims. The act of movement after this arbitrary date, in other words, would become a legal proxy for deciding the true intentions of individuals and, hence, could be used as a means for establishing their bona fides as legitimate national citizens. The newly independent state of India did not define itself in religious terms, but it was universally assumed that Muslims "belonged" to Pakistan and other religious affiliations, especially Hindus and Sikhs, to India. Muslims had a lesser claim to Indian citizenship, especially if they were in motion.

Between 1950, when the Indian constitution came into effect, and 1955, when the Citizenship Act was passed, Anupama Roy argues, the rules defining Indian citizenship were in a state of "liminality."[52] Although the constitution had laid down broad principles for the awarding of citizenship, it was only in 1955 that the citizenship act was officially passed, establishing the legal terms by which Indian nationality could be established. The interim period is notable for a host of judicial efforts to deal with a series of anomalous cases, especially involving Muslim women and children moving between India and Pakistan. As her study shows, divided families, abducted women and children and new spouses, as well as those ignorant or doubtful of the permanence of these new national arrangements all fell between the gaps in the law and had to be dealt with on a case-by-case basis. Roy explains that Indian citizenship laws have always struggled with the problem of migration. People born in one country seeking to move to the neighboring country, whether for personal and professional reasons, became the multiple exceptions on which the apparent clarity of the law broke down. In later amendments to Indian citizenship laws, seeking to deal with the political and demographic transformations of the northeastern state of Assam, the year 1966 would acquire similar foundational status as the temporal divide separating the legitimate citizen from the illicit or illegal resident.

To repeat, what was at stake in these arbitrary dates but could not be stated explicitly in the official files was the religious identity of the migrant or claimant. Hindus and Sikhs, denoted as Pakistan's "minority community" in Indian citizenship files, were easily accommodated in India. Muslims were less easy to "fix," as their claim on Indian citizenship was compromised, in legal terms, by their movement between the neighboring Muslim majority state (east or west Pakistan) and nominally secular India. The act of mobility became, for the courts, an assessment of the measure of commitment to India or, put another way, a measure of the divided loyalties between a confessional and national-territorial identity. "Moving while Muslim," to modify a notorious epigram, immediately weakened the strength of plaintiff's claim to Indian citizenship. Pakistan represents the Indian diaspora that can never be acknowledged or claim a right of return due to the religious identity of the majority population.

To sum up, from India's point of view the formation of Pakistan both was a geopolitical disaster and produced a crisis of nationality. The creation of a new northern neighbor that was not subordinate to Indian strategic interests meant the end of the carefully crafted geopolitical defense of the subcontinent and the creation of new military vulnerabilities dangerously close to the Indian heartland. As long as imperial geopolitics shapes India's defense thinking, Pakistan can be seen only as a permanent military threat, regardless of the other issues that may bedevil bilateral relations. The other problem with Pakistan was what it meant for Indian national identity. India did not define itself officially as a Hindu-majority state but a long history of spatial politics had identified the Muslim as a permanent outsider and threat to Hindu identity. The difficulties of preventing a nation of Muslims from claiming Indian citizenship was compounded by the strategic anxieties attendant on having a religiously identified neighbor with the same confessional identity as India's largest minority. The creation of Pakistan as a rejection of the terms of Indian national identity, and the tense histories of intercommunal violence capped by the extraordinary violence of the partition, framed the Indian Muslim as a constant threat and potential fifth column. From both within and without, the formation of the state of Pakistan engendered a perceived existential threat to the new Indian state. Even in the absence of hatreds engendered by massive communal violence and personal animosities, independent India would have had to confront the foundational crisis produced by the creation of a Muslim-majority country on its eastern and western flanks. Pakistan represents a structural contradiction of India's core territorial practices, geopolitical as well as diasporic. This is why relations between the two countries began from a position of ambivalence and heightened tension that has only gotten worse with time. Even in the absence of territorial disputes, I argue, India's conflict with Pakistan was entirely overdetermined.

Given this, the only way for India's relations with Pakistan to improve is for India to see Pakistan and its people entirely differently, a process that involves fundamentally reconsidering its foreign policies of diaspora and geopolitics. To do so requires extending still further the underlying logic of its changing diaspora policies and turning away from a static geopolitical calculus as the prime measure of national security. As we have seen, India's new diaspora policies have already led to a delinking of formal citizenship from national identity and of national identity from territorial location. This process, which tacitly admits to the presence of multiple identities as a social commonplace, could be extended still further by officially acknowledging the prior territorial histories and collective memories of the people of Pakistan who once lived in an undivided British India. By treating these living pasts as tantamount to holding a legitimate claim to being identified as a "people of Indian origin," such a policy recognizes the multiple social identities inhabited by millions of Pakistani families, identities that include Indian places and people in some way or form. It also permits India to begin the process of fully coming to terms with its own alienated heritage, permitting some Indians to acknowledge that their pasts may have Pakistan-located identifications. Taking this step particularly offers *muhajirs* (migrants from India to Pakistan) and their Indian counterparts the ability to begin to resolve the broken pasts that they live with and pass on to future generations. The ability to recall and in some cases to reclaim lost memories, divided families, and alienated properties lying in another territorial space is the first step to dissolving the tensions that come from the current lack of psychic and material closure. This lack of closure is today sometimes expressed in the form of nostalgia and affection but more often emerges in the form of hostility. This is not a proposal that calls for millions of Pakistanis claiming a right of return to India; rather, it is a long-overdue recognition that the histories of modern India extend beyond its current borders and are also claimed by millions of people who no longer live within its territorial boundaries.

The most critical transformation requires a reformulation of what constitutes national security. As long as national security is defined in fixed territorial terms, postimperial geopolitical practices hold sway. By contrast, the more that national security is defined in terms of well-being, especially economic, the more likely it is that the loss or gain of land loses its power to disturb the political balance. The changing economic geography of India is an important facilitator of this outcome. The last three decades have seen a shift in the relative wealth of the country to the south and the west, away from the Himalayas, effectively reducing the perceived value of regions closer to disputed lands. Overcoming the geopolitical logic of zero-sum relations between India and Pakistan does not entail giving up claims to lands now occupied by the other. Rather it seeks a shift away from competition over whose territorial claim is more legitimate. The long-term objective is to transform the deadly affect produced by the impression of territorial loss or gain. Both India and Pakistan have in the past given up lands to other countries without the loss of state power. The question is how to convert disputed territories into spaces that do not produce the extreme nationalist reaction of state treason. Proposals that have long circulated in the public domain, including jointly administering or sharing disputed lands such as the Siachen Glacier and/or converting it into an international scientific station, are eminently practical steps in that direction. In addition, recent measures taken by the Indian government of easing restrictions on allowing Pakistanis to obtain business visas without onerous requirements are the kinds of action that need to be multiplied. Equally important is the admirable restraint shown by the Manmohan Singh government not to let the actions of terrorist groups and sectarian extremists dissolve the momentum toward better relations.

One of the most encouraging signs of positive change comes from a most unlikely place, driven by a charge that rarely appears in unqualified form in international relations, namely, a genuinely humanitarian impulse. As is well known, the Kashmir Valley has long been divided between India and Pakistan, or, to put it less geopolitically, Kashmiris are a people divided between two hostile states and an overseas diaspora. A militarized border has separated families, social networks, landed properties, and collective memories for more than half a century, during which time India and Pakistan have fought multiple battles across numerous arenas both local and global. Kashmir, during this period, has become a globally acknowledged metaphor for a zero-sum territorial dispute between states leading to multiple accounts of human tragedy. Yet, in 2005, a bus service connecting Srinagar, capital of the Indian state of Jammu and Kashmir, and Muzzafarabad, capital of Pakistani "Azad" Kashmir, came into being. A year later, another bus line joining Poonch in India and Rawalkot in Pakistan followed. Two years later, both bus services began weekly schedules of travel that continue into the present. Kashmiris living on either side of the border are now eligible to travel on the bus without visas after fulfilling a number of requirements imposed by both governments. It is still not easy to get permission to travel across the Line of Control, as the de facto border is called, but it is now possible. The change in the status quo such a development implies is considerable.

A weekly bus line may not appear to be an obvious harbinger of change, but what is most notable about this modest effort at improving the lives of people living in a war zone is that it is the product of official recognition of human suffering. Neither government benefited materially from the creation of the bus service; indeed, both took heat from political extremists for letting it go ahead. Both sides also made clear that permitting the movement of Kashmiris across the border did not in any way prejudice their respective and mutually exclusive claims to lands occupied by the other state. Each government was responding to public appeals for the chance to be temporarily reunited with people and places that had long been, to quote the Kashmiri poet Abdul Ghani Sheikh, "like a star in the sky that [one] can see but not touch."[53] Given the relative lack of political rights available to Kashmiris living on both sides of the border, it would have been all too easy to ignore these popular calls for spatial redress. Yet the highest levels of the state did respond and, after long negotiations, decided they could go ahead with this modest response to the human plight of a divided people. Indian and Pakistani officials took this unlikely step for humanitarian reasons, drawing on resources that lie beyond reasons of state. And that unlikely outcome is what gives particular hope that the confinements engendered by the territorial nation-state will eventually be bypassed by what Ranabir Samaddar calls the politics of dialogue.[54]

Last Words

This study has argued that the logic of the territorial nation-state, with its in-built hierarchies and exclusions, is hostile to the provision of equal citizenship. State policies that territorialize state and nation lead inevitably to the marginalization of some groups and the elevation of others. These unequal outcomes are not the actions of political extremists that can be reversed by legal proscription or political debate. The process described here is structural. Once territorial sovereignty became the ground on which the new nation-state finds itself and demands recognition, processes that lead to uneven and unequal outcomes are set into motion. The idea of the nation-state as a hierarchical political community that defines minorities as social collectives of lower standing remains unchanged. Political contingencies might govern which minorities or regions are excluded, but there is no doubt that there would be exclusions, majorities, and centers. The imagination of new states follows exactly the fault lines of past political grievances and conflicts, albeit with newly formed majorities producing newly subordinated minorities. Such outcomes are endemic to the working of territorializing practices and constitute the political bedrock of modern nation-states. The prevailing tendency of the international community has been to affirm how important it is for global order not to challenge or overturn existing territorial boundaries. The far greater and important challenge, in my view, is how to transcend territory as the basis for the formation of political community.

Notes

PREFACE

1. This study also does not address, unfortunately, important foreign policy themes that have long suffered from intellectual neglect, namely the political economy of foreign relations and India as an exporter of capital, except in passing.

2. A caution: By demonstrating institutional continuities in foreign policy behavior, I do not intend to imply that all or important postindependence policies such as nonalignment were products of colonial thought or practice. What I will claim is that concepts like nonalignment have histories independent of state sovereignty and that these histories are indispensable to understanding postcolonial Indian foreign policy.

INTRODUCTION

1. In International Relations (IR), this is referred to as a "second-image reversed" problem. Peter Gourevitch, "The Second Image Reversed: The International Sources of Domestic Politics," *International Organization* 32, no. 4 (October 1, 1978): 881–912. Chapter 2 in this volume addresses what Stephen Krasner has called the "structural power" of the international system in a recent review of Gourevich's original article. Stephen D. Krasner, "Revisiting 'The Second Image Reversed'" (paper presented at the Conference in Honor of Peter Gourevich, San Diego, CA, 2010); retrieved on June 19, 2013, from http://empac.ucsd.edu/assets/006/11458.pdf.

2. Vijay Prashad, *The Darker Nations: A People's History of the Third World* (New York: The New Press, 2007).

3. David Campbell, *Writing Security: United States Foreign Policy and the Politics of Identity* (Minneapolis: University of Minnesota Press, 1998). R. B. J. Walker, *Inside/Outside: International Relations As Political Theory* (Cambridge, UK: Cambridge University Press, 1993). Sankaran Krishna, *Postcolonial Insecurities: India, Sri Lanka, and the Question of Nationhood* (Minneapolis: University of Minnesota Press, 1999).

4. Timothy Mitchell, "Society, Economy, and the State Effect," in *The Anthropology of the State: A Reader*, ed. Aradhana Sharma and Akhil Gupta (Oxford, UK: Blackwell Publishers, 2006).

5. J. David Singer, "The Level-of-Analysis Problem in International Relations," *World Politics* 14, no. 1 (1961): 77–92.

6. Walker, *Inside/Outside*.

7. Neil Brenner, "Beyond State-Centrism: Space, Territoriality, and Geographic Scale in Globalization Studies," *Theory and Society* 28, no. 1 (February 1999): 39–78.

8. Erik Swyngedouw, "Excluding the Other: The Contested Production of a New 'Gestalt of Scale' and the Politics of Marginalisation." In *Society, Place, Economy: States of the Art in Economic Geography*, edited by R. Lee and J. Willis, J, 167–176 (London: Edward Arnold, 1997).

9. Willem van Schendel, "Geographies of Knowing, Geographies of Ignorance: Jumping Scale in Southeast Asia," *Environment and Planning D: Society and Space* 20, 6 (2002): 647–668.

10. Daniel Philpott, *Revolutions in Sovereignty: How Ideas Shaped Modern International Relations* (Princeton, NJ: Princeton University Press, 2001).

11. Kalevi Jaakko Holsti, *Taming the Sovereigns: Institutional Change in International Politics* (Cambridge, UK: Cambridge University Press, 2004).

12. Christopher A. Bayly, *The Birth of the Modern World: 1780–1914* (Oxford, UK: Blackwell Publishers, 2004). Charles Tilly, ed., *The Formation of National States in Western Europe* (Princeton, NJ: Princeton University Press, 1975). James Der Derian, *On Diplomacy: A Genealogy of Western Estrangement* (Oxford, UK: Basil Blackwell, 1987).

13. James N. Rosenau and Ernst-Otto Czempiel, eds., *Governance without Government: Order and Change in World Politics* (Cambridge, UK: Cambridge University Press, 1992).

14. Antony Anghie, *Imperialism, Sovereignty and the Making of International Law* (Cambridge, UK: Cambridge University Press, 2007).

15. Mark Mazower, *No Enchanted Palace: The End of Empire and the Ideological Origins of the United Nations* (Princeton, NJ: Princeton University Press, 2009). R. P. Anand, *New States and International Law*, 2nd edition (Gurgaon: Hope India Publications, 2008). Manu Bhagavan, *The Peacemakers: India and the Quest for One World* (Delhi: HarperCollins, 2012).

16. Rotem Kowner, ed., *The Impact of the Russo-Japanese War* (London: Routledge, 2007).

17. David Arnold and Erich DeWald, "Cycles of Empowerment? The Bicycle and Everyday Technology in Colonial India and Vietnam," *Comparative Studies in Society and History* 53, no. 4 (2011): 971–996. Rudolf Mrázek, *Engineers of Happy Land: Technology and Nationalism in a Colony* (Princeton, NJ: Princeton University Press, 2002).

18. Michael Adas, *Machines as the Measure of Men: Science, Technology, and Ideologies of Western Dominance* (Ithaca, NY: Cornell University Press, 1990).

19. Partha Chatterjee, *The Nation and Its Fragments: Colonial and Postcolonial Histories* (Princeton, NJ: Princeton University Press, 1993).

20. Pheng Cheah, *Spectral Nationality: Passages of Freedom from Kant to Postcolonial Literatures of Liberation* (New York: Columbia University Press, 2003), p. 394.

21. Benedict Richard O'Gorman Anderson, *Under Three Flags: Anarchism and the Anti-Colonial Imagination* (London: Verso, 2005).

22. Faisal Devji, *The Impossible Indian: Gandhi and the Temptation of Violence* (Cambridge, MA: Harvard University Press, 2012), 49.

23. A comprehensive account of international space (which is beyond the scope of this study) would also include such events as the 1893 World Congress of Religions and other events that tacitly invoked a transnational and relativized global space.

24. Robert J. C. Young, *Postcolonialism: An Historical Introduction* (Oxford, UK: Blackwell Publishers, 2001).

25. Sanjay Seth, *Marxist Theory and Nationalist Politics: The Case of Colonial India* (Delhi: Sage Publications, 1995), pp. 60–61.

26. T. A. Keenleyside, "Prelude to Power: The Meaning of Non-Alignment before Indian Independence," *Pacific Affairs* 53, no. 3 (1980): 461–483.

27. David Arnold, *Colonizing the Body: State Medicine and Epidemic Disease in Nineteenth-Century India* (Berkeley: University of California Press, 1993). Christopher Bayly, *Imperial Meridian: The British Empire and the World, 1780–1830* (London: Longman, 1989). Gauri Viswanathan, *Masks of Conquest: Literary Study and British Rule in India*, reprint (Delhi: Oxford University Press, 1998).

28. Hannah Arendt, *The Origins of Totalitarianism* (New York: Harcourt Brace Jovanovich, [1968] 1976), p. 154.

29. Walter Mignolo, *The Darker Side of the Renaissance: Literacy, Territoriality, & Colonization*, 2nd edition (Ann Arbor: University of Michigan Press, 2003).

30. B. R. Tomlinson, *The Economy of Modern India, 1860–1970* (Cambridge, UK: Cambridge University Press, 1993).

31. Nicola Cooper, *France in Indochina: Colonial Encounters* (Oxford, UK: Berg, 2001).

32. Tyler Edward Stovall and Georges Van den Abbeele, eds., *French Civilization and Its Discontents: Nationalism, Colonialism, Race* (Lanham, MD: Lexington Books, 2003).

33. Susan Pedersen, "Back to the League of Nations: Review Essay," *The American Historical Review* 112, no. 4 (2007): 1091–1116.

34. Sunil S. Amrith, *Decolonizing International Health: India and Southeast Asia, 1930–65* (London: Palgrave Macmillan, 2006).

35. J. Krishnamurthy, "Indian Officials in the ILO, 1919–c.1947," *Economic and Political Weekly* 46, no. 10 (2011).

36. Erez Manela, *The Wilsonian Moment: Self-Determination and the International Origins of Anticolonial Nationalism* (New York: Oxford University Press, 2007).

37. Mark Mazower, "Minorities and the League of Nations in Interwar Europe," *Daedalus* 126, no. 2 (Spring 1997): 47–63. Quotation from p. 50.

38. Arjun Appadurai, *Modernity at Large: Cultural Dimensions of Globalization* (Minneapolis: University of Minnesota Press, 1996).

39. Stuart Elden, "Land, Terrain, Territory," *Progress in Human Geography* 34, no. 6 (December, 2010): 799–817.

40. J. Penrose, "Nations, States and Homelands: Territory and Territoriality in Nationalist Thought," *Nations and Nationalism* 8, no. 3 (2002): 277–297.

41. Andrew Moseman, "Tiny Island, Fought over by India and Bangladesh, Vanishes into Sea," *Discover Magazine*, March 25, 2010. J. Penrose, "Nations, States and Homelands: Territory and Territoriality in Nationalist Thought," *Nations and Nationalism* 8, no. 3 (2002): 277–297. Sumathi Ramaswamy, *The Lost Land of Lemuria: Fabulous Geographies, Catastrophic Histories* (Berkeley: University of California Press, 2004).

Chapter 1

1. One scholar summarizes the importance of territorial disputes as follows: "[They have been] the major cause of enduring inter-state rivalries, the frequency of war, and the intensity of war." Mark W. Zacher, "The Territorial Integrity Norm: International Boundaries and the Use of Force," *International Organization* 55, no. 2 (2001): 215–250; quotation from pp. 215–216. See also D. B. Carter and H. E. Goemans, "The Making of the Territorial Order: New Borders and the Emergence of Interstate Conflict," *International Organization* 65, no. 2 (2011): 275–309. Paul Francis Diehl, ed., *A Road Map to War: Territorial Dimensions of International Conflict* (Nashville, TN: Vanderbilt University Press, 1999). Gary Goertz and Paul Diehl, *Territorial Changes and International Conflict* (London and New York: Routledge, 2002). Paul K. Huth, *Standing Your Ground: Territorial Disputes and International Conflict* (Ann Arbor: University of Michigan Press, 1998). For a functionalist account of the significance of boundaries and borders, see Friedrich Kratochwil, "Of Systems, Boundaries, and Territoriality: An Inquiry into the Formation of the State System," *World Politics* 39, no. 1 (1986): 27–52. For recent reviews of the extensive literature on territory and conflict in IR, see M. Taylor Fravel, *Strong Borders, Secure Nation: Cooperation and Conflict in China's Territorial Disputes* (Princeton, NJ: Princeton University Press, 2008), and George Gavrilis, *The Dynamics of Interstate Boundaries* (Cambridge, UK: Cambridge University Press, 2010). For a conventional IR view of sovereignty, see Daniel Philpott, *Revolutions in Sovereignty: How Ideas Shaped Modern International Relations* (Princeton. NJ: Princeton University Press, 2001). By contrast, see the early and important collection of essays in Thomas J. Biersteker and Cynthia Weber, eds., *State Sovereignty as Social Construct* (Cambridge, UK: Cambridge University Press, 1996).

2. Unfortunately, the writing of this book was completed before I had a chance to read and engage with geographer Stuart Elden's new book on this topic. Stuart Elden, *The Birth of Territory* (Chicago: University of Chicago Press, 2013).

3. Craig J. Calhoun, *Nationalism* (Minneapolis: University of Minnesota Press, 1997).

4. Henri Lefèbvre, *The Production of Space*, trans. Donald Nicholson-Smith (New York and Oxford: Wiley-Blackwell, 1991), p. 281.

5. Paul Allies quoted in Stuart Elden, "Land, Terrain, Territory," *Progress in Human Geography* 34, no. 6 (December 1, 2010), p. 801.

6. David Harvey, *The Limits to Capital*, revised ed. (London: Verso, 1982).

7. John A. Agnew, *Globalization and Sovereignty* (Lanham, MD: Rowman & Littlefield, 2009), pp. 21–22.

8. R. B. J. Walker, *Inside/Outside: International Relations as Political Theory* (Cambridge, UK: Cambridge University Press, 1993).

9. James J. Sheehan, "The Problem of Sovereignty in European History," *The American Historical Review* 111, no. 1 (February 1, 2006): 1–15; quotation from p. 4.

10. John Ruggie, "Territoriality and Beyond: Problematizing Modernity in International Relations," *International Organization* 47, no. 1 (1993): 139–174.

11. Turan Kayaoglu, "Westphalian Eurocentrism in International Relations Theory," *International Studies Review* 12, no. 2 (June 1, 2010): 193–217.

12. Zacher, "The Territorial Integrity Norm," 217.

13. Philpott, *Revolutions in Sovereignty*.

14. Biersteker and Weber, *State Sovereignty as Social Construct*.

15. Stephen D. Krasner, *Sovereignty: Organized Hypocrisy* (Princeton, NJ: Princeton University Press, 1999).

16. Edward Keene, *Beyond the Anarchical Society: Grotius, Colonialism and Order in World Politics* (Cambridge, UK: Cambridge University Press, 2002), pp. 40–59.

17. Tilly, *The Formation of National States in Western Europe*.

18. Jane Burbank and Frederick Cooper, *Empires in World History: Power and the Politics of Difference* (Princeton, NJ: Princeton University Press, 2010).

19. Sheehan, "The Problem of Sovereignty in European History"; quotation from p. 8.

20. Kratochwil, "Of Systems, Boundaries, and Territoriality."

21. Lauren Benton, *A Search for Sovereignty: Law and Geography in European Empires, 1400–1900* (Cambridge, UK: Cambridge University Press, 2010).

22. C. R. Pennell, *Bandits at Sea: A Pirates Reader* (New York: NYU Press, 2001). Sudipta Sen, *Distant Sovereignty: National Imperialism and the Origins of British India* (New York: Routledge, 2002).

23. Kayaoglu, "Westphalian Eurocentrism in International Relations Theory," p. 194.

24. Dipesh Chakrabarty, *Provincializing Europe: Postcolonial Thought and Historical Difference* (Princeton, NJ: Princeton University Press, 2000).

25. Anthony Pagden, *European Encounters with the New World: From Renaissance to Romanticism* (New Haven, CT: Yale University Press, 1994) and *Lords of All the World: Ideologies of Empire in Spain, Britain and France c. 1500–c. 1800* (New Haven, CT: Yale University Press, 1995). Nicolás Wey Gómez, *The Tropics of Empire: Why Columbus Sailed South to the Indies* (Cambridge, MA: The MIT Press, 2008).

26. Achille Mbembe, *On the Postcolony* (Berkeley: University of California Press, 2001).

27. James C. Scott, *The Art of Not Being Governed: An Anarchist History of Upland Southeast Asia* (New Haven, CT: Yale University Press, 2010), p. 64.

28. Ibid., p. 61.

29. Jordan Branch, "Mapping the Sovereign State: Technology, Authority, and Systemic Change," *International Organization* 65, no. 1 (2011): 1–36.

30. Holsti, *Taming The Sovereigns*, p. 111.

31. Michel-Rolph Trouillot, *Silencing the Past: Power and the Production of History* (Boston: Beacon Press, 1997). Liah Greenfeld, *Nationalism: Five Roads to Modernity* (Cambridge, MA: Harvard University Press, 1993).

32. Holsti, *Taming the Sovereigns*, pp. 84–85.

33. Peter Sahlins, *Boundaries: The Making of France and Spain in the Pyrenees* (Berkeley: University of California Press, 1991). Eugen Weber, *Peasants Into Frenchmen: The Modernization of Rural France, 1870–1914* (Stanford, CA: Stanford University Press, 1976).

34. John Torpey, *The Invention of the Passport: Surveillance, Citizenship and the State* (Cambridge, UK: Cambridge University Press, 1999), p. 24.

35. Frederick Cooper, *Colonialism in Question: Theory, Knowledge, History* (Berkeley: University of California Press, 2005), p. 169.

36. Trouillot, *Silencing the Past*.

37. Burbank and Cooper, *Empires in World History*.

38. Elden, "Land, Terrain, Territory," p. 804.

39. Agnew, *Globalization and Sovereignty*, p. 30.

40. Ibid.

41. Ibid., pp. 810, 812.

42. John A. Agnew and Stuart Corbridge, *Mastering Space: Hegemony, Territory and International Political Economy* (London and New York: Routledge, 1995), ch. 4.

43. Irit Rogoff, *Terra Infirma: Geography's Visual Culture* (New York and London: Routledge, 2000); both quotations from p. 75.

44. Edward Soja, quoted in Elden, "Land, Terrain, Territory." p. 803.

45. Kapil Raj, "Circulation and the Emergence of Modern Mapping," in *Society and Circulation: Mobile People and Itinerant Cultures in South Asia, 1750–1950*, eds. Claude Markovits, Jacques Pouchepadass, and Sanjay Subrahmanyam (Delhi: Permanent Black, 2006), p. 30.

46. C. A. Bayly, *Empire and Information: Intelligence Gathering and Social Communication in India, 1780–1870* (Cambridge, UK: Cambridge University Press, 2000), p. 21.

47. Ibid., pp. 23–25, 301–305. Sanjay Subrahmanyam, *The Career and Legend of Vasco Da Gama* (Cambridge, UK: Cambridge University Press, 1997).

48. Matthew H. Edney, *Mapping an Empire: The Geographical Construction of British India, 1765–1843* (Chicago: University of Chicago Press, 1997), p. 23. See also Bernardo A. Michael, *Statemaking and Territory in South Asia: Lessons from the Anglo-Gorkha War (1814–1816)* (London: Anthem Press, 2012).

49. Bernard S. Cohn, *Colonialism and Its Forms of Knowledge: The British in India* (Princeton, NJ: Princeton University Press, 1996).

50. Sumathi Ramaswamy, *The Goddess and the Nation: Mapping Mother India* (Durham, NC: Duke University Press, 2010), p. 53. Anderson, *Imagined Communities*.

51. Ramaswamy, *The Goddess and the Nation*. Quotations from pp. 70, 294.

52. Ashis Nandy, *The Intimate Enemy: Loss and Recovery of Self under Colonialism* (Delhi: Oxford University Press, 1983).

53. "Moderates" are opposed to "radicals" in nationalist historiography: They characterize what Partha Chatterjee has called the "moment of departure" in the development of Indian nationalism. Moderates were elite critics of the colonial state who worked for social reform and sought greater representation within the colonial system but stopped well short of demanding sovereign independence. Partha Chatterjee, *Nationalist Thought and the Colonial World: A Derivative Discourse?* (London: Zed Books, 1986).

54. Manu Goswami, *Producing India* (Chicago: University of Chicago Press, 2004), p. 8.

55. Ibid., p. 225.

56. Ibid., p. 166.

57. Ibid., p. 188.

58. Gyan Prakash, *Another Reason: Science and the Imagination of Modern India* (Princeton, NJ: Princeton University Press, 1999), p. 89.

59. Ibid., p. 91.

60. Goswami, *Producing India*; quotations from pp. 188, 269.

61. For an exceptional study of how caste was reformed under modernity, see M. S. S. Pandian, *Brahmin and Non-Brahmin* (Delhi: Permanent Black, 2008).

62. Foucault's concept of genealogy is knowledge work that

> ... displaces both the search for ultimate foundations and its opposite, nihilism, with a form of patient criticism and problematisation based in the present. Foucault's critical history forsakes the critique of the past in terms of the truth of the present but not the critical use of the history of reason to diagnose the practical issues, necessities, limits of the present.... [It is]

"critical" in proportion to its capacity to engage in the tireless interrogation of what is held to be given, necessary, natural, or neutral. (Mitchell Dean, *Critical and Effective Histories: Foucault's Methods and Historical Sociology* [London: Routledge, 1994], p. 20)

63. Mitchell, "Society, Economy, and the State Effect."

64. Krishna, following Heidegger, calls foreign policy a "spatialization of the self against an other . . . a *worlding*." Krishna, *Postcolonial Insecurities*, p. 29.

65. Walker, *Inside/Outside*, pp. 151–152.

66. The conventional understanding is well represented in Roy C. Macridis, *Foreign Policy in World Politics* (Englewood Cliffs, NJ: Prentice Hall, 1968).

67. Campbell, *Writing Security*, p. 36.

68. Ibid., p. 51.

69. Ibid., p. 81.

70. Ibid., p. 73. Emphasis added.

71. Mitchell, "Society, Economy, and the State Effect."

72. Michiel Baud and Willem van Schendel, "Toward a Comparative History of Borderlands," *Journal of World History* 8, no. 2 (1997): 211–242.

73. For "border games," see Peter Andreas, *Border Games: Policing the U.S.–Mexico Divide* (Ithaca, NY: Cornell University Press, 2000). As the extensive literature on borderlands has shown, entirely complementing the earlier discussion of inside/outside, in the process of demarcating space territorializing practices inevitably produce hierarchies of power and difference.

74. On "sovereign excess," see James D. Sidaway, "Sovereign Excesses? Portraying Postcolonial Sovereigntyscapes," *Political Geography* 22, no. 2 (February 2003): 157–178.

75. As Judith Butler notes in relation to gender, "The performance of gender produces retroactively the illusion that there is an inner gender core." See Judith Butler, *The Judith Butler Reader*, ed. Sara Salih (Oxford, UK: Blackwell Publishers, 2004), p. 253. Mitchell, "Society, Economy, and the State Effect."

76. Richard K. Ashley, "Foreign Policy as Political Performance," *International Studies Notes* 13, no. 2 (1987): 51–54.

77. Pierre Bourdieu, *Distinction: A Social Critique of the Judgement of Taste*, trans. Richard Nice (Cambridge, MA: Harvard University Press, 1984).

78. For the concept of the super-sign see Lydia He Liu, *The Clash of Empires: The Invention of China in Modern World Making* (Cambridge, MA: Harvard University Press, 2004).

79. Willem Van Schendel and Itty Abraham, eds., *Illicit Flows and Criminal Things: States, Borders, and the Other Side of Globalization* (Bloomington: Indiana University Press, 2005).

80. Lefèbvre, *The Production of Space*, p. 280.

81. William E. Connolly, *Identity, Difference: Democratic Negotiations of Political Paradox* (Minneapolis: University of Minnesota Press, 2002).

82. What follows is an extremely abbreviated account of a complex and lengthy moment in postwar international history, drawing on Pia Anjolie Oberoi, *Exile and Belonging: Refugees and State Policy in South Asia* (Delhi: Oxford University Press, 2006), ch. 1.

83. For an account of the partition of India and Pakistan through official documents, see Nicholas Mansergh and Penderel Moon, eds., *The Transfer of Power 1942–47: The Mountbatten Viceroyalty Formulation of a Plan 22 March–30 May 1947* (London: H.M.S.O., 1981).

84. B. S. Chimni, "The Geopolitics of Refugee Studies: A View from the South," *Journal of Refugee Studies* 11, no. 4 (January 1, 1998): 350–374.
85. Oberoi, *Exile and Belonging*, p. 1.
86. Ritu Menon and Kamla Bhasin, *Borders & Boundaries: Women in India's Partition* (New Brunswick, NJ: Rutgers University Press, 1998).
87. Ibid., p. 111.
88. Rada Iveković and Julie Mostov, eds., *From Gender to Nation* (Delhi: Zubaan, 2004).
89. Menon and Bhasin, *Borders & Boundaries*, p. 252.
90. Nicos Poulantzas, *State, Power, Socialism* (London: Verso, 2000). Bob Jessop, *State Theory: Putting the Capitalist State in Its Place* (University Park: Penn State University Press, 1990).
91. Vivek Chibber, *Locked in Place: State-Building and Late Industrialization in India* (Princeton, NJ: Princeton University Press, 2006). Peter B. Evans, *Dependent Development: The Alliance of Multinational, State, and Local Capital in Brazil* (Princeton, NJ: Princeton University Press, 1979).
92. These are the capitals of the eleven Asian and African countries (of a total of fifty-one states) that signed the San Francisco Treaty creating the United Nations Organization in 1945.

Chapter 2

1. E. J. Hobsbawm, *Nations and Nationalism since 1780: Programme, Myth, Reality* (Cambridge, UK: Cambridge University Press, 1992), p. 131.
2. Seth, *Marxist Theory and Nationalist Politics*, p. 56.
3. Kayaoğlu, *Legal Imperialism*. For China after 1949, see Yongjin Zhang, *China in International Society since 1949: Alienation and Beyond* (London and New York: Macmillan/ St. Martins Press, 1998).
4. Bimal Prasad, *The Origins of Indian Foreign Policy: The Indian National Congress and World Affairs, 1885–1947*, 2nd ed. (Calcutta and Allahabad: Bookland, 1962).
5. Susan Pedersen, "Back to the League of Nations, Review Essay."
6. Manela, *The Wilsonian Moment*.
7. Ibid., p. 219.
8. Krishna turns this relation around to propose that, for the postcolonial political strategist, the West is understood as "a space that has forever resolved the question of aligning territory with identity." Krishna, *Postcolonial Insecurities*, p. 223.
9. Anthony D. Smith, *The Antiquity of Nations* (London: Polity, 2004). E. Gellner, *Nations and Nationalism* (Oxford, UK: Blackwell, [1983] 2006).
10. Siba N'Zatioula Grovogui, *Sovereigns, Quasi Sovereigns, and Africans: Race and Self-Determination in International Law* (Minneapolis: University of Minnesota Press, 1996).
11. Sankaran Krishna, "Cartographic Anxiety: Mapping the Body Politic in India," *Alternatives: Global, Local, Political* 19, no. 4 (October 1, 1994): 507–521.
12. D. N. Verma, *India and the League of Nations* (Patna: Bharathi Bhavan, 1968), pp. 11–12.
13. This number was obtained by combining the figures for "identified burials" and "commemorated in memorials." Retrieved on March 5, 2014, from www.cwgc.org/ search-results.aspx?terms=IDENTIFIED%20BURIALS.
14. The dominions were Australia, Canada, New Zealand, and, South Africa.

15. Naoko Shimazu, *Japan, Race and Equality: The Racial Equality Proposal of 1919* (London: Routledge, 2002), p. 122.

16. Lanka Sundaram, "The International Status of India," *Transactions of the Grotius Society* 17 (January 1931): 35–54.

17. J. Onley, "The Raj Reconsidered: British India's Informal Empire and Spheres of Influence in Asia and Africa," *Asian Affairs* 40, no. 1 (2009): 44–62.

18. T. T Poulose, "India as an Anomalous International Person (1919–1947)," *British Yearbook of International Law* 44 (1970): 201.

19. Erez Manela quotes Margaret Macmillan saying Bikaner "said very little but gave nice dinner parties." Manela, *The Wilsonian Moment*, p. 159. For this quotation and further commentary on Sinha's and Bikaner's superb command of English and other reassuring characteristics, see "India Ready to Aid in Colonial Rule," *New York Times*, Feb. 3, 1919.

20. Manela, *Wilsonian Moment*, p. 161.

21. Uday Singh Mehta, *Liberalism and Empire: A Study in Nineteenth-Century British Liberal Thought* (Chicago: University of Chicago Press, 1999).

22. Verma, *India and the League of Nations*.

23. R. P. Anand, "The Formation of International Organizations and India: A Historical Study," *Leiden Journal of International Law* 23, no. 1 (March 2010): 5–21.

24. For a careful account of the debates over reparations, with a particular emphasis on Keynes's role, see Robert Skidelsky, *John Maynard Keynes: Hopes Betrayed: 1883–1920*, Vol. 1 (London: Macmillan, 1983), pp. 354–375.

25. Herbert Luthy, "India and East Africa: Imperial Partnership at the End of the First World War," *Journal of Contemporary History* 6, no. 2 (January 1, 1971): 55–85.

26. Shimazu, *Japan, Race and Equality*.

27. Hugh Purcell, "Paris Peace Discord," *History Today* no. July (2009): 40.

28. Billy Hughes ranted that this proposal would make his "White Australia" policy nothing short of a "pricked bladder." Ibid., p. 39.

29. Shimazu, pp. 117–136. See also Antoinette M. Burton, ed., *Gender, Sexuality and Colonial Modernities* (London and New York: Routledge, 1999).

30. Radhika Viyas Mongia, "Race, Nationality, Mobility: A History of the Passport," *Public Culture* 11, no. 3 (Fall 1999): 527–555.

31. The tendency to transform formal equivalence into racial difference to sustain the colonial order has been described by Partha Chatterjee as the "rule of colonial difference" (*The Nation and Its Fragments*). For a full-length analysis of the contradictions of imperial liberalism, see Mehta, *Liberalism and Empire*.

32. Shimazu, *Japan, Race and Equality*.

33. Chatterjee, *The Nation and Its Fragments*.

34. Hugh Tinker, *Separate and Unequal: India and the Indians in the British Commonwealth, 1920–1950* (Vancouver: University of British Columbia Press, 1976).

35. The Irish petition, "Official memorandum in support of Ireland's demand for recognition as a sovereign independent state. Presented to Georges Clemenceau and the members of the Paris Peace Conference by Sean T. O'Cealloigh and George Gavan Duffy," is available at www.difp.ie/viewdoc.asp?DocID=13 (Documents on Irish foreign policy, a project of the Royal Irish Academy, Department of Foreign Affairs, and National Archives of Ireland). Last accessed on October 30, 2011. For India, see "Self Determination for India" (London: The Indian Home Rule League, 1919, unpaginated). All following quotations are from these documents.

36. Kate O'Malley, *Ireland, India, and Empire: Indo-Irish Radical Connections, 1919–64* (Manchester, UK: Manchester University Press, 2008).
37. "Official memorandum in support of Ireland's demand for recognition."
38. "Self Determination for India."
39. "Official memorandum in support of Ireland's demand for recognition."
40. Ibid.
41. "Self Determination for India."
42. Ibid.
43. "Official memorandum in support of Ireland's demand for recognition."
44. "Self Determination for India."
45. "What Is a Nation?" in Homi K. Bhabha, ed., *Nation and Narration* (London and New York: Routledge, 1990), pp. 8–22.
46. "Self Determination for India."
47. Ronald B. Inden, *Imagining India* (Oxford, UK: Blackwell Publishers, 1990).
48. "Self Determination for India."
49. On the origins of the Aryan myth, see Thomas R. Trautmann, *Aryans and British India* (Berkeley: University of California Press, 1997).
50. "Self Determination for India." It would have done no harm, given the potential readership, to emphasize this point.
51. Ibid.
52. Ibid.
53. Ibid.
54. Hugo Grotius, *The Freedom of the Seas (Mare Liberum)*, trans. Ralph van Demen Magoffin (Washington, DC: Carnegie Endowment for International Peace, 1916). See also Peter Borschberg, *Hugo Grotius, the Portuguese, and "Free Trade" in the East Indies* (Honolulu: University of Hawaii Press, 2010).
55. For more on natural law, rights, and colonialism, see Mignolo, *The Darker Side of the Renaissance*. Pagden, *European Encounters with the New World*.
56. Keene, *Beyond the Anarchical Society*. Shogo Suzuki, *Civilisation and Empire: East Asia's Encounter with the European International Society* (London: Routledge, 2009).
57. Charles Henry Alexandrowicz, *An Introduction of the History of the Law of Nations in the East Indies* (Oxford, UK: Clarendon Press, 1967).
58. Grovogui, *Sovereigns, Quasi Sovereigns, and Africans*, p. 46.
59. Ibid.
60. David Strang, "Contested Sovereignty: The Social Construction of Colonial Imperialism," in *State Sovereignty as Social Construct*, ed. Thomas J. Biersteker and Cynthia Weber (Cambridge, UK: Cambridge University Press, 1996), p. 27.
61. Anghie, *Imperialism, Sovereignty and the Making of International Law*.
62. Gerrit W. Gong, *The Standard of "Civilization" in International Society* (Oxford, UK: Clarendon Press, 1984).
63. Strang, "Contested Sovereignty," p. 32.
64. Anand, "The Formation of International Organizations and India," p. 6.
65. Anghie, *Imperialism, Sovereignty and the Making of International Law*, p. 38.
66. Ibid.
67. Adas, *Machines as the Measure of Men*.
68. Anghie, *Imperialism, Sovereignty and the Making of International Law*, p. 37.

69. For a historian of Europe's critique of IR's disciplinary history, see Paul W. Schroeder, *The Transformation of European Politics, 1763–1848* (New York: Oxford University Press, 1996). Also, see the references in Kayaoglu, "Westphalian Eurocentrism in International Relations Theory."

70. Anand, "The Formation of International Organizations and India: A Historical Study," pp. 5–6.

71. Suzuki, *Civilisation and Empire*.

72. Nineteenth-century international lawyer Henry Wheaton, quoted in Anghie, *Imperialism, Sovereignty and the Making of International Law*, p. 54.

73. The following discussion is based on Kayaoğlu, *Legal Imperialism*.

74. Anghie, *Imperialism, Sovereignty and the Making of International Law*.

75. Ed Cohen, *A Body Worth Defending: Immunity, Biopolitics, and the Apotheosis of the Modern Body* (Durham, NC: Duke University Press, 2009).

76. Anghie, *Imperialism, Sovereignty and the Making of International Law*.

77. For a discussion of the trope of civilization and efforts to appropriate it by Asians, see Prasenjit Duara, *Sovereignty and Authenticity: Manchukuo and the East Asian Modern* (Lanham, MD: Rowman & Littlefield, 2004).

78. Lydia H. Liu, "The Desire for the Sovereign and the Logic of Reciprocity in the Family of Nations," *Diacritics* 29, no. 4 (1999): 150–177.

79. Quoted in Anghie, *Imperialism, Sovereignty and the Making of International Law*, p. 75.

80. Ibid., p. 76.

81. Keene, *Beyond the Anarchical Society*, 7.

82. Anghie, *Imperialism, Sovereignty and the Making of International Law*, p. 106.

83. Grovogui, *Sovereigns, Quasi Sovereigns, and Africans*.

84. Anghie, *Imperialism, Sovereignty and the Making of International Law*, p. 100.

85. Andrew J. Crozier, "The Establishment of the Mandate System, 1919–1925: Some Problems Created by the Paris Peace Conference," *Journal of Contemporary History* 14, no. 3 (July 1979): 483–513.

86. Eric Stokes, *The English Utilitarians and India* (Delhi: Oxford University Press, 1989).

87. P. Duara, "Asia Redux: Conceptualizing a Region for Our Times," *The Journal of Asian Studies* 69, no. 4 (2010): 963–983.

88. Needless to say, there were other political voices that drew different lessons from the humiliations of colonialism. Prominent among them were the nationalists who saw in the West's material and technological power the only means to prevent external domination from ever occurring again. For them, the only sensible response was to initiate domestic projects of industrialism and militarism as soon as possible. Further proof of the viability of this approach came from Japan's whole-scale and, in these eyes, successful, adoption of the Western path to international power. As Prasenjit Duara points out, projects of national revival built around materialism and militarism would come to trump rejuvenation through greater reliance on Asia's spiritual roots. See "The Discourse of Civilization and Decolonization," *Journal of World History* 15, no. 1 (March 2004).

89. A. Appadorai, *Asian Relations: Being Report of the Proceedings and Documentation of the First Asian Relations Conference, New Delhi, March–April, 1947* (New Delhi: Asian Relations Organization, 1948), pp. 28–29.

90. Itty Abraham, "Bandung and State Formation in Post-Colonial Asia," in *Bandung Revisited: The Legacy of the 1955 Asian–African Conference for International Order*, ed. See Seng Tan and Amitav Acharya (Singapore: NUS Press, 2008), pp. 48–67.

91. For a longer discussion of the diaspora problem, see Chapter 3.

Chapter 3

Parts of this chapter were originally published as Itty Abraham, "Bandung and State Formation in Postcolonial Asia," in *Bandung Revisited: The Legacy of the 1955 Asian–African Conference for International Order* (Singapore: NUS Press, 2008), pp. 48–67. It is reprinted here with permission of NUS Press.

1. Khachig Tölölyan, "The Nation-State and Its Others: In Lieu of a Preface," *Diaspora: A Journal of Transnational Studies* 1, no. 1 (1991): 3–7.

2. Dimitra Giannuli, "Greeks or 'Strangers at Home': The Experience of Ottoman Greek Refugees during Their Exodus to Greece, 1922–1923," *Journal of Modern Greek Studies* 13, no. 2 (1995): 271–287.

3. Maura Elise Hametz, *Making Trieste Italian: 1918–1954* (Woodbridge,UK: Boydell & Brewer, 2005).

4. Mark Mazower, *Salonica, City of Ghosts: Christians, Muslims and Jews 1430–1950* (New York: Knopf Doubleday Publishing Group, 2007).

5. Those were the lucky ones. The unlucky ones became stateless and were awarded Nansen passports to give them political identities and minimal civil protections.

6. By contrast, the Roma (Gypsies), resident in Europe for centuries, a migratory community originating in Rajasthan, are rarely if ever identified with India. For recent overviews of the South Asian diaspora, see Sunil S. Amrith, *Migration and Diaspora in Modern Asia* (Cambridge, UK: Cambridge University Press, 2011). Judith M. Brown, *Global South Asians: Introducing the Modern Diaspora* (Cambridge, UK: Cambridge University Press, 2006). Devesh Kapur, *Diaspora, Development, and Democracy: The Domestic Impact of International Migration from India* (Princeton, NJ: Princeton University Press, 2010). Latha Varadarajan, *The Domestic Abroad: Diasporas in International Relations* (New York: Oxford University Press, 2010). For modes of identification, see Sandhya Shukla, "Building Diaspora and Nation: The 1991 'Cultural Festival of India,'" *Cultural Studies* 11, no. 2 (1997): 296–315.

7. These three terms, often used synonymously, have different meanings. The first refers to Indian citizens normally resident outside the country, the second to former Indian citizens who have becomes naturalized citizens of another state, and the third to people who can trace their ethnic origins to today's territorial India.

8. Devji, *The Impossible Indian*.

9. Luthy, "India and East Africa."

10. Anirudha Gupta, "Ugandan Asians, Britain, India and the Commonwealth," *African Affairs* 73, no. 292 (July 1, 1974): 312–324.

11. To see how this history has been replaced by a new narrative by the Ministry of Overseas Indian Affairs, see Jen Dickinson, "Decolonising the Diaspora: Neo-Colonial Performances of Indian History in East Africa," *Transactions of the Institute of British Geographers* (2012), vol. 37, 4, 609–623, October 2012.

12. Gupta, "Ugandan Asians, Britain, India and the Commonwealth."

13. "The Indian Diaspora." Report of the High Level Committee on Indian Diaspora, Chairman L. M. Singhvi. New Delhi: Ministry of External Affairs. Retrieved on October 4, 2011, from http://indiandiaspora.nic.in/contents.htm.

14. Gao Ting, "Ethnic Chinese Networks and International Investment: Evidence from Inward FDI in China," *Journal of Asian Economics* 14, no. 4 (August 2003): 611–629. For a valuable analysis of Chinese transnationalism, see Aihwa Ong and Donald Macon Nonini, eds., *Ungrounded Empires: The Cultural Politics of Modern Chinese Transnationalism* (New York and London: Routledge, 1997). For a comprehensive diasporic history, see also Adam McKeown, "Conceptualizing Chinese Diasporas, 1842 to 1949," *The Journal of Asian Studies* 58, no. 2 (1999): 306–337.

15. Although the legal status of overseas Chinese has undergone considerable change during the twentieth century, neither Nationalist nor Communist governments broke ties entirely with their overseas compatriots. See Wang Gungwu, *The Chinese Overseas: From Earthbound China to the Quest for Autonomy* (Cambridge, MA: Harvard University Press, 2000).

16. For empirical detail on the socioeconomic profile of the Indian diaspora, see Kapur, *Diaspora, Development, and Democracy*.

17. For an early discussion of class in relation to the diaspora, see Leela Fernandes, "Nationalizing 'the Global': Media Images, Cultural Politics and the Middle Class in India," *Media, Culture & Society* 22, no. 5 (September 1, 2000): 611–628.

18. Between 1830 and 1930, "nearly 30 million Indians traveled overseas and some 24 million returned." Sugata Bose, *A Hundred Horizons: The Indian Ocean in the Age of Global Empire* (Cambridge, MA: Harvard University Press, 2006), p. 73.

19. Tinker, in turn, is quoting Lord John Russell. Hugh Tinker, *A New System of Slavery: The Export of Indian Labour Overseas 1830–1920*, 2nd ed. (London: Hansib, 1993).

20. Depending on context, I have used both the earlier and contemporary names for countries like Ceylon/Sri Lanka.

21. Quoted in Tinker, *A New System of Slavery*, p. 69.

22. Crispin Bates, ed., "Sojourners and Settlers: South Indians and Communal Identity in Malaysia," in *Community, Empire, and Migration: South Asians in Diaspora* (Delhi: Palgrave, 2001), pp. 185–205. For Chinese migration patterns, see McKeown, "Conceptualizing Chinese Diasporas, 1842 to 1949."

23. Radhika V. Mongia, "Historicizing State Sovereignty: Inequality and the Form of Equivalence," *Comparative Studies in Society and History* 49, no. 2 (2007): 384–411.

24. In the words of P. D'Espinay, Protector General of Mauritius, regulations designed to protect the island from "the refuse of the Indian bazaars and with such the germs of disorder." Ibid., p. 401. For the contradictions of liberal imperialism, see Mehta, *Liberalism and Empire*.

25. Tinker, *A New System of Slavery*, pp. 39–60. For a recent study, see Sunil S. Amrith, *Crossing the Bay of Bengal: The Furies of Nature and the Fortunes of Migrants* (Cambridge, MA: Harvard University Press, 2013).

26. Claude Markovits, *The Global World of Indian Merchants, 1750–1947: Traders of Sind from Bukhara to Panama* (Cambridge, UK: Cambridge University Press, 2000).

27. Ritu Birla, *Stages of Capital: Law, Culture, and Market Governance in Late Colonial India* (Durham, NC: Duke University Press, 2009). For the classic study of Chettiars, see David West Rudner, *Caste and Capitalism in Colonial India: The Nattukottai Chettiars*

(Berkeley: University of California Press, 1994). For Sindhi merchants, see Markovits, *The Global World of Indian Merchants, 1750–1947*.

28. K. N. Chaudhuri, *Trade and Civilisation in the Indian Ocean: An Economic History from the Rise of Islam to 1750* (Cambridge, UK: Cambridge University Press, 1985).

29. Ibid., p. 224.

30. G. Balachandran, "Circulation through Seafaring: Indian Seamen, 1890–1945," in *Society and Circulation: Mobile People and Itinerant Cultures in South Asia, 1750–1950* (Delhi: Permanent Black, 2003), pp. 89–130. Quotation from p. 91.

31. Ibid., p. 92.

32. Partha Sarathi Gupta and Anirudh Deshpande, eds., *The British Raj and Its Indian Armed Forces, 1857–1939* (Delhi: Oxford University Press, 2002).

33. Bose, *A Hundred Horizons.* p. 147.

34. Maia Ramnath, "Two Revolutions: The Ghadar Movement and India's Radical Diaspora, 1913–1918," *Radical History Review* 2005, no. 92 (Spring 2005): 7–30.

35. Harald Fischer-Tiné, "Indian Nationalism and the 'World Forces': Transnational and Diasporic Dimensions of the Indian Freedom Movement on the Eve of the First World War," *Journal of Global History* 2, no. 3 (2007): 325–344. Figures from pp. 328–329.

36. Fischer-Tiné, "Indian Nationalism and the 'World Forces.'"

37. Ramachandra Guha, *Gandhi before India* (London: Allen Lane, 2013).

38. For early semiofficial studies, see C. Kondapi, *Indians Overseas, 1838–1949* (Delhi: Indian Council of World Affairs, 1951) and Rammanohar Lohia and J. B. Kriplani, *Indians in Foreign Lands* (Allahabad: All India Congress Committee, 1938).

39. Tinker, *A New System of Slavery*, ch. 7.

40. Ibid., p. 321.

41. Ibid., p. 347.

42. Ibid., pp. 340–341.

43. Ibid., p. 341.

44. Tinker, *Separate and Unequal*.

45. Prasad, *The Origins of Indian Foreign Policy*, p. 69.

46. Manela, *The Wilsonian Moment*, ch. 8.

47. For more details, see Chapter 2.

48. Manela, *The Wilsonian Moment*, p. 166.

49. Iqbal Singh, *The Indian National Congress: A Reconstruction*, vol. 2: 1919–1923 (Delhi: Nehru Memorial Museum and Library, 1989), p. 119.

50. Sumit Sarkar, *Modern India: 1885-1947* (Delhi: Macmillan, 1983), ch. 5.

51. Prasad, *The Origins of Indian Foreign Policy*.

52. Ibid., pp. 72–73.

53. Ibid.

54. Ibid., p. 71.

55. Ibid., p. 77.

56. Ibid., pp. 76–86.

57. Gail Minault, *The Khilafat Movement: Religious Symbolism and Political Mobilization in India* (New York: Columbia University Press, 1982).

58. Judith M. Brown, *Gandhi's Rise to Power: Indian Politics 1915–1922* (Cambridge, UK: Cambridge University Press, 1972).

59. Quoted in Singh, *The Indian National Congress*, pp. 169–170.

60. Richard Gordon, "The Hindu Mahasabha and the Indian National Congress, 1915 to 1926," *Modern Asian Studies* 9, no. 2 (January 1, 1975): 145–203. Achin Vanaik

(personal communication) notes that another reason for the failure of Gandhi's strategy of bringing together Hindus, Sikhs, and Muslims was from his appeal to religious consciousness rather than seeking to *transcend* existing religious identification.

61. For an early but limited treatment of this issue, see Prasad, *The Origins of Indian Foreign Policy.*
62. Manela, *The Wilsonian Moment.*
63. Chatterjee, *Nationalist Thought and the Colonial World.*
64. Young, *Postcolonialism,* p. 176. Other meetings included the first Pan-Asiatic Congress at Nagasaki in 1926; the Pan-Asiatic Conference in Shanghai in 1927; All-Asia Education conference, Benares, 1930; All-Asia Women's conference, Lahore 1931; and the Pan-Asiatic Labour Congress, Colombo, 1934. See T. A. Keenleyside, "Nationalist Indian Attitudes towards Asia: A Troublesome Legacy for Post-Independence Indian Foreign Policy," *Pacific Affairs* 55, no. 2 (July 1, 1982): 210–230, p. 223. In addition, Imperial Japan held a conference on Greater East Asia in 1943 attended by Subhas Chandra Bose and representatives of Thailand, Manchukuo, China, Philippines, and Burma.
65. Onley, "The Raj Reconsidered,"
66. John Gallagher and Anil Seal, "Britain and India between the Wars," *Modern Asian Studies* 15, no. 3 (1981): 387–414.
67. Ibid., pp. 400-401.
68. This preferential treatment of Indian industry would not last long. For a comprehensive discussion, see Partha Sarathi Gupta, *Power, Politics, and the People: Studies in British Imperialism and Indian Nationalism* (Delhi: Permanent Black, 2001), part II, ch. 2. Malaviya's dissent from the report of the Indian Industrial Commission should be read as a document that prefigures much of postcolonial Indian industrial policy.
69. Anita Inder Singh, *The Limits of British Influence: South Asia and the Anglo-American Relationship, 1947–56* (London: Pinter Publishers, 1993), p. 25.
70. Gallagher and Seal, "Britain and India between the Wars."
71. Sundaram, "The International Status of India."
72. Poulose, "India as an Anomalous International Person (1919–1947)."
73. Ibid.
74. C. A Bayly and T. N. Harper, *Forgotten Armies: Britain's Asian Empire and the War with Japan* (London: Penguin, 2005).
75. D. R. SarDesai, *Indian Foreign Policy in Cambodia, Laos, & Vietnam* (Berkeley: University of California Press, 1968).
76. Jawaharlal Nehru, *India's Foreign Policy: Selected Speeches, September 1946–April 1961* (Delhi: Publications Division, Ministry of Information and Broadcasting, Government of India, 1961), p. 3.
77. The conference was not, strictly speaking, an international conference; rather it was a conference of Asian "cultural organizations." Reflecting India's incompletely sovereign status, the principal sponsor was the Indian Council of World Affairs, founded in 1943, rather than the government of India. For more details see Appadorai, *Asian Relations.*
78. For a longer discussion of the Asian Relations Conference, see A. Appadorai, "The Asian Relations Conference in Perspective," *International Studies* 18, no. 3 (July 1, 1979): 275–285.
79. Nehru, *India's Foreign Policy,* p. 250.

80. Michael Adas, "Contested Hegemony: The Great War and the Afro-Asian Assault on the Civilizing Mission Ideology," *Journal of World History* 15, no. 1 (2004): 31–63. Quotations from p. 61.

81. The following discussion draws on two earlier publications. Abraham, "Bandung and State Formation in Post-Colonial Asia"; and "From Bandung to NAM: Nonalignment and Indian Foreign Policy, 1947–65," *Commonwealth & Comparative Politics* 46 (April 2008): 195–219.

82. Abraham, "Bandung and State Formation in Post-Colonial Asia," p. 54.

83. Ibid.

84. Ibid., p. 55.

85. Ibid.

86. Ibid.

87. Ibid., p. 56.

88. Ibid.

89. Ibid., pp. 56–57. It would not be until the 1955 Bandung Conference that China would sign agreements with Thailand and Indonesia, countries with large overseas Chinese populations, resolving the dual nationality problem.

90. Ibid., p. 57.

91. Neil Smith, *American Empire: Roosevelt's Geographer and the Prelude to Globalization* (Berkeley: University of California Press, 2004), p. 177.

92. K. N. Chaudhuri, *Asia before Europe: Economy and Civilization of the Indian Ocean from the Rise of Islam to 1750* (Cambridge, UK: Cambridge University Press, 1990). Janet L. Abu-Lughod, *Before European Hegemony: The World System A.D. 1250–1350* (New York: Oxford University Press, 1989).

93. André Gunder Frank, *ReOrient: Global Economy in the Asian Age* (Berkeley: University of California Press, 1998), p. 98.

94. Ibid., p. 99.

95. Chaudhuri, *Trade and Civilisation in the Indian Ocean*, p. 359.

96. Ibid., p. 148.

97. Scott, *The Art of Not Being Governed*, p. 61.

98. There is a huge literature on the "construction of communalism" in India and other colonies. See Gyanendra Pandey, *The Construction of Communalism in Colonial North India* (Delhi: Oxford University Press, 1990). For a focus on the technologies of communal division, see Appadurai, *Modernity at Large*.

99. Anderson, *Imagined Communities*. Krishna, *Postcolonial Insecurities*.

100. Duara, "The Discourse of Civilization and Decolonization."

101. Appadorai, *Asian Relations*, p. 98. Emphasis added.

102. Ibid.

103. Nehru, *India's Foreign Policy*, pp. 127–128.

104. Ibid., p. 128.

105. This attitude would plague independent India's relations with Ceylon, later Sri Lanka, for decades. It would take until 1964 before an agreement reached between Mrs. Srimavo Bandarnaike of Sri Lanka and Indian premier Lal Bahadur Shastri would partially deal with the repatriation of people of Indian origin, as demanded by the Sri Lankans.

106. Nehru, *India's Foreign Policy*, p. 130.

107. Ramesh Thakur and Antony Wood, "Fiji in Crisis," *The World Today* 43, no. 12 (December 1, 1987): 206–211.

108. Under Rajiv Gandhi, India also intervened to restore the government of the Maldives following a military coup and sent a "peace-keeping" force to Sri Lanka.

109. Srinath Raghavan, *War and Peace in Modern India* (London: Palgrave Macmillan, 2010).

110. Deepak Nayyar, *Migration, Remittances, and Capital Flows: The Indian Experience* (Delhi: Oxford University Press, 1994).

111. Robina Mohammed and James D. Sidaway, "Spectacular Urbanization amidst Variegated Geographies of Globalization: Learning from Abu Dhabi's Trajectory through the Lives of South Asian Men," *International Journal of Urban and Regional Research* (2012).

112. Nayyar, *Migration, Remittances, and Capital Flows*.

113. Kapur, *Diaspora, Development, and Democracy*.

114. Angry reactions from persons of Indian origin living outside these "highly developed countries," including the Indian-origin Prime Minister of Trinidad, would embarrass the government into expanding the narrow terms of the Diaspora Report after a few years. See also Anupama Roy, "Between Encompassment and Closure: The 'Migrant' and the Citizen in India," *Contributions to Indian Sociology* 42, no. 2 (May 1, 2008): 219–248.

115. Varadarajan, *The Domestic Abroad*, p. 110.

116. Ibid.

117. Jason A Kirk, "Indian-Americans and the U.S.–India Nuclear Agreement: Consolidation of an Ethnic Lobby?" *Foreign Policy Analysis* 4, no. 3 (July 1, 2008).

118. Fernandes, "Nationalizing 'the Global.'"

119. Satish Deshpande, *Contemporary India: A Sociological View* (Delhi: Penguin Books, 2004), pp. 99–102.

120. Achin Vanaik, *The Furies of Indian Communalism: Religion, Modernity, and Secularization* (London: Verso, 1997).

121. Prema A. Kurien, *Kaleidoscopic Ethnicity: International Migration and the Reconstruction of Community Identities in India* (New Brunswick, NJ: Rutgers University Press, 2002).

122. Robin Cohen, *The New Helots: Migrants in the International Division of Labour* (London: Gower, 1987).

Chapter 4

1. Dean, *Critical and Effective Histories*. Foucault's use of the term is antihermeneutic; it "marks the advent of a materialist approach that respects the being of discourse, its materiality, its location in time and place, and seeks to account for it in terms of the conditions of its existence" (p. 17).

2. Abraham, "From Bandung to NAM."

3. The term *geopolitics* was coined by Rudolf Kjellén, a Swedish political scientist, in 1899. See Smith, *American Empire*, p. 275.

4. H. J. Mackinder, "The Geographical Pivot of History," *The Geographical Journal* 23, no. 4 (April 1, 1904): 421–437.

5. Gearóid Ó Tuathail, *Critical Geopolitics: The Politics of Writing Global Space* (Minneapolis: University of Minnesota Press, 1996), p. 76.

6. Ibid., p. 15.

7. Ibid., p. 34. Original italics.

8. Ibid., p. 37.

9. Hayden V. White, *Metahistory: The Historical Imagination in Nineteenth-Century Europe* (Baltimore, MD: Johns Hopkins University Press, 1975).

10. Tayyab Mahmud, "Colonial Cartographies and Postcolonial Borders: The Unending War in and around Afghanistan" (Seattle University School of Law, 2010); available at http://works.bepress.cam/tayyab_mahmud/1.

11. George Nathaniel Curzon, *Persia and the Persian Question: Volume 1* (London: Longman, 1892).

12. Although signs of aggressive geopolitical thinking in Japanese imperial behavior and a more defensive version in Thailand were visible in the early twentieth century, the combination of theory and practice brought together by Curzon was both distinct and turned out to be considerably longer lasting.

13. George N. Curzon, *Frontiers: The Romanes Lecture, 1907* (Oxford, UK: Clarendon Press, 1907). I have used the text of the lecture available from www.dur.ac.uk/resources/ibru/resources/links/curzon.pdf (retrieved on October 21, 2011). Page numbers cited refer to this PDF version.

14. Ibid., p. 16.

15. Ibid., p. 17.

16. Ibid., p. 1. For all the focus on natural philosophy, Curzon cannot resist lifting the eschatological veil just a little, authorizing "a few silent men, who may be found in the clubs of London, or Paris, or Berlin, when they are not engaged in tracing lines upon the unknown areas of the earth": people like himself, empire's éminences grises.

17. Ibid., p. 2. This argument would become the genesis for the earliest quantitative scholarship on borders and conflicts in the hands of the erstwhile biologist, Lewis Richardson.

18. This fear was of course the genesis of what Kipling would call the "Great Game." Peter Hopkirk, *The Great Game* (Oxford, UK: Oxford University Press, 1990).

19. Curzon, *Frontiers*, p. 8.

20. N. Maxwell, *India's China War* (New York: Random House, 1971).

21. Onley, "The Raj Reconsidered."

22. Ibid., pp. 44–45.

23. Bayly and Harper, *Forgotten Armies*.

24. Ibid., p. 37.

25. Quoted in Onley, "The Raj Reconsidered," p. 54.

26. For a discussion of Olaf Caroe and K. M. Panikkar as links between colonial and postcolonial geopolitical thought, see Peter John Brobst, *The Future of the Great Game: Sir Olaf Caroe, India's Independence, and the Defense of Asia* (Akron, OH: University of Akron Press, 2005).

27. K. M. (Kavalam Madhava) Panikkar, *India and the Indian Ocean: An Essay on the Influence of Sea Power on Indian History* (London: G. Allen & Unwin, 1962).

28. Christophe Jaffrelot, *The Hindu Nationalist Movement and Indian Politics: 1925 to the 1990s: Strategies of Identity-Building, Implantation and Mobilisation (with Special Reference to Central India)* (London: C. Hurst & Co. Publishers, 1996).

29. Paula Richman, ed., *Many Rāmāyaṇas: The Diversity of a Narrative Tradition in South Asia* (Berkeley: University of California Press, 1991).

30. Pandian, *Brahmin and Non-Brahmin*.

31. See Chapter 1.

32. For a recent critique, see Pierre-Yves Manguin, A. Mani, and Geoff Wade, *Early Interactions between South and Southeast Asia: Reflections on Cross-Cultural Exchange* (Singapore: ISEAS, 2011).

33. O. W. Wolters, *Early Southeast Asia: Selected Essays* (Ithaca, NY: Cornell SEAP Publications, 2008).

34. Quoted in SarDesai, *Indian Foreign Policy in Cambodia, Laos, & Vietnam*, note 12, p. 262.

35. Ibid., p. 8.

36. The absence of any serious discussion of geopolitics in the so-called debate on India's "strategic culture" exemplifies the taken for granted character of geopolitical thinking. The alleged lack of an Indian strategic tradition, first put forward by RAND Corporation counterinsurgency practitioner and military historian George Tanham, set forth a wave of handwringing in New Delhi in spite of the entirely misplaced problematic and weakness of evidence offered in support of the argument. Even K. Subrahmanyam, dean of Indian strategic thinkers, was surprisingly moved to respond to Tanham. He argued that British control over Indian defense for two centuries made the evidence of autonomous Indian thinking impossible to find. See George Kilpatrick Tanham, *Indian Strategic Thought: An Interpretive Essay* (Santa Monica, CA: Rand, 1992). A response by Indian writers can be found in *Securing India: Strategic Thought and Practice* (Delhi: Manohar Publishers & Distributors, 1996). See also K. Subrahmanyam, "Introduction," in *Defending India* (London/New York: Macmillan/St. Martin's Press, 1999), pp. viii–xxvi.

37. The eminent historian Romila Thapar, who was a student in London in 1953, recalls, over fifty years later, the fervor surrounding the publication of this book, especially among her Asian peers. Oral history interview, Washington, DC, 2005. Panikkar was a well-known writer, diplomat, and administrator who switched effortlessly between professions and masters spanning the period before and after Indian independence. Starting life as a journalist and Oxford-trained academic historian, he would go on to serve the Council of Princes and become *dewan* (prime minister) of two Princely States before being sent to China, Egypt, and France, as independent India's ambassador to those countries. K. M. Panikkar, *Asia and Western Dominance: A Survey of the Vasco Da Gama Epoch of Asian History, 1498–1945* (London: George Allen and Unwin, 1953).

38. Chakrabarty, *Provincializing Europe*.

39. Panikkar, *Asia and Western Dominance*, pp. 197–202. Panikkar closes the book with a chapter attacking Christian missionaries, followed by two chapters showing the "Oriental" influence on European culture and thought.

40. Ibid., pp. 13, 16.

41. Panikkar, *India and the Indian Ocean*. Alfred Thayer Mahan, *The Influence of Sea Power upon History 1660–1783* (Boston: Little, Brown, 1889).

42. Panikkar, *India and the Indian Ocean*. p. 84. For all the rhetorical bombast of this quotation, Panikkar was careful to add that India would be well served by collaborating with the British Commonwealth in this endeavor. He was, after all, writing while India was still a colony.

43. Panikkar, *Asia and Western Dominance*, p. 16.

44. In his later geopolitical writing, Panikkar would "switch sides" once again. In a pamphlet written in 1969, he would argue that invaders from abroad, once they crossed the Himalayas, had always gotten bogged down in the vast Gangetic flood plains. As a

result, northern India had become a zone of great racial mixing. The southern peninsula of India, India's Hindu "heart," on the other hand, remained relatively impervious to these invasions due to its own internal protective barrier, the Deccan "tablelands." Pannikar: "Thus even when the Gangetic plain fell under the domination of foreign culture, as it often did during the last 2,000 years, Hindu civilization was firmly entrenched in the South to retain the continuity and provide the inspiration for a general revival." In other words, the primary domestic fault line in India was the divide between a contaminated North and pristine South India. Kavalam Madhava Panikkar, *Geographical Factors in Indian History* (Delhi: Bharatiya Vidya Bhavan, 1969), p. 103.

45. Bharat Karnad, "India's Weak Geopolitics and What to Do about It," in *Future Imperilled: India's Security in the 1990s and Beyond*, ed. Bharat Karnad (Delhi: Viking, 1994), pp. 16–84. Quotation from p. 32.

46. Karnad, "India's Weak Geopolitics, p. 38. The source of this quote is telling—Karnad references Nehru's opening speech at the Asian Relations Conference (1947), hardly a moment when he would represent India in militaristic or belligerent terms!

47. Ibid., p. 38.

48. Achin Vanaik, *The Painful Transition: Bourgeois Democracy in India* (London: Verso, 1990).

49. Resistance to Indian demands would lead Sikkim to be annexed by India in 1975. Over the years, Nepal would become more successful in maintaining a small modicum of sovereignty but would be faced with economic blockades among other actions to force them back into line with Indian interests.

50. Keenleyside, "Prelude to Power."

51. M. S. Rajan, *India in World Affairs, 1954–56* (Delhi: Indian Council of World Affairs, 1964).

52. Curzon, *Frontiers*, p. 12.

53. Abraham, "From Bandung to NAM," p. 210.

54. C. Raja Mohan, *Crossing the Rubicon: The Shaping of India's New Foreign Policy* (New Delhi: Viking, 2004), p. 205.

55. Jaswant Singh, *Defending India* (Delhi: Macmillan India, 1999).

56. Jaswant Singh, *A Call to Honour: In Service of Emergent India* (Delhi: Rupa & Co., 2006).

57. Curzon, *Frontiers*, p. 21.

58. Ibid., p. 22. Unfortunately, he does not give any examples of these traditional "weapons of the weak." Cf. James C. Scott, *Weapons of the Weak: Everyday Forms of Peasant Resistance* (New Haven, CT: Yale University Press, 1985). Compare this account of vacillating natives with the more positive account of the vital importance of Indian surveyors in Edney, *Mapping an Empire*.

59. For a good discussion of the evolution of India's "China problem," see Raghavan, *War and Peace in Modern India*. See also Abdul Gafoor Abdul Majeed Noorani, *India–China Boundary Problem, 1846–1947: History and Diplomacy* (Delhi: Oxford University Press, 2011).

60. Bajpai to Patel, "Our Present Stand," November 3, 1950. Vallabhbhai Patel, *Sardar's Letters, Mostly Unknown*, ed. G. M. Nandurkar III (1950) (Ahmedabad: Sardar Vallabhbhai Patel Smarak Bhavan, 1983), p. 138.

61. Nehru notes that at one point the Indian ambassador had mistakenly used the word *sovereignty* rather than *suzerainty* in reference to Chinese claims over Tibet. Durga

Das, ed., *Sardar Patel's Correspondence, 1945–50*, vol. X (Ahmedabad: Navajivan Publishing House, 1974), p. 342.

62. During Curzon's viceroyalty, the first steps to bring Tibet into the British sphere of influence were set into motion, following the visit of Col. Younghusband and his troops to Lhasa (1903–1904). After Curzon left India, a treaty signed in Simla would create another geopolitical incision, the McMahon Line, which would serve to separate India from Tibet and imperial China.

63. Curzon, *Frontiers*, p. 17.

64. Tsering Shakya, *Dragon in the Land of Snows: The History of Modern Tibet since 1947* (New York: Random House, 2012), p. 54.

65. Ibid.

66. Jawaharlal Nehru, Note on China and Tibet, November 18, 1950. Patel, *Sardar's Letters, Mostly Unknown*, p. 150.

67. Vapal Pangunni Menon, *The Story of the Integration of the Indian States* (Bombay: Orient Longmans, 1961).

68. Prof. Kanti Bajpai feels that his grandfather, Sir Girija Shankar Bajpai, wrote many of the foreign policy memoranda now attributed to Patel (personal communication, November 11, 2012). Explicit textual similarities between Patel and Bajpai's correspondence and Patel's letters to Nehru lend strength to this claim, but it is beyond the scope of this study to pursue that line of argument any further.

69. Menon, *The Story of the Integration of the Indian States*.

70. Brobst, *The Future of the Great Game*.

71. Patel to Bajpai, "The Need for New Strategy," Patel, *Sardar's Letters, Mostly Unknown*, p. 140.

72. Patel to Bajpai, ibid., p. 141.

73. Bajpai to Patel, ibid., p. 142.

74. Patel to Nehru, November 11, 1950. Ibid., pp. 144–149.

75. Patel to Nehru, November 11, 1950. Ibid., p. 145.

76. Das, *Sardar Patel's Correspondence, 1945–50*, p. 337.

77. Patel to Nehru, November, 11, 1950. Patel, *Sardar's Letters, Mostly Unknown*, p. 146.

78. Patel reversed conventional understandings of communist tactics such as the popular front to argue this point. The logic of the popular front was a temporary alliance between Communists and other social forces that would support a struggle for national liberation as a short-term goal, in order for Communists to infiltrate power structures. Once in control, they could take over, eliminate their former allies, and institute a communist state. In the Northeast, Communism was a front for Chinese territorial nationalism.

79. Patel to Nehru, November 11, 1950. Patel, *Sardar's Letters, Mostly Unknown*, p. 146.

80. Das, *Sardar Patel's Correspondence, 1945–50*, pp. 342–347.

81. Ibid., p. 345.

82. Abraham, "Bandung and State Formation in Post-Colonial Asia."

83. Das, *Sardar Patel's Correspondence, 1945–50*, pp. 343–346.

84. Ibid., p. 345.

85. Lok Raj Baral, "Nepal–India Relations: Continuity and Change," in Dhruba Kumar, ed., *Nepal's India Policy* (Kathmandu: Centre for Nepal and Asian Studies, Tribhuvan University, 1992), p. 63.

86. By the end of the decade, Nehru's surprise at China's behavior would show that he had entirely forgotten making this prescient statement.

87. Ramachandra Guha, *Savaging the Civilized: Verrier Elwin, His Tribals, and India* (Chicago: University of Chicago Press, 1999).

88. Sanjay Chaturvedi, "Indian Geopolitics: 'Nation-State' and the Colonial Legacy," in *International Relations in India: The Region and the Nation*, ed. Kanti P. Bajpai and Siddharth Mallavarapu (Delhi: Orient Longmans, 2004), pp. 238–283.

89. This concluding section is not intended as a comprehensive political history of the Northeast. Its focus is on the Northeast as a site of Indian geopolitics and the shaping of this region in response to those policies. For a political overview, see Sanjib Baruah, *Durable Disorder: Understanding the Politics of Northeast India* (Delhi: Oxford University Press, 2007). For an ecological history, see Bengt G. Karlsson, *Unruly Hills: A Political Ecology of India's Northeast* (Delhi: Orient Black Swan, 2011). For a wide-ranging and informative introduction, see Bertil Lintner, *Great Game East: India, China and the Struggle for Asia's Most Volatile Frontier* (Delhi: Harper-Collins, 2012).

90. Giorgio Agamben, *Homo Sacer: Sovereign Power and Bare Life* (Stanford, CA: Stanford University Press, 1998).

91. Elizabeth Shannon Wheatley, "Ec(h)o-Tourism and the Whisper of the State: The 'Greening' of Indigenous Politics," in *International Relations and States of Exception: Margins, Peripheries, and Excluded Bodies*, ed. Shampa Biswas and Sheila Nair (New York: Routledge, 2010), p. 216.

92. The term was used by the colonial officer and historian of Assam, Sir Edward Gait, as quoted in Karlsson, *Unruly Hills*, p. 16.

93. Amalendu Guha, *Planter Raj to Swaraj: Freedom Struggle and Electoral Politics in Assam, 1826–1947* (Kolkata: Tulika Books, 1976). Yasmin Saikia, *Fragmented Memories: Struggling to Be Tai-Ahom in India* (Durham, NC: Duke University Press, 2004).

94. Lintner, *Great Game East*, pp. 51–54.

95. Bates, "Sojourners and Settlers."

96. Scott, *The Art of Not Being Governed*.

97. Sanjib Baruah, *India against Itself: Assam and the Politics of Nationality* (Philadelphia: University of Pennsylvania Press, 1999).

98. Ibid., p. 35. Regrettably, it is beyond the scope of this project to compare colonial and postcolonial representations of the Nagas with the Pathans of the Northwest Frontier Province (NWFP) and Federally Administered Tribal Areas (FATA) of present-day Pakistan.

99. Peter Robb, "The Colonial State and Constructions of Indian Identity: An Example on the Northeast Frontier in the 1880s," *Modern Asian Studies* 31, no. 2 (1997): 245–283.

100. Baruah, *India Against Itself*, pp. 28–29. Colonial frontier boundaries would include a bewildering patchwork of spatial distinctions, including partially Excluded Areas, assigned tracts, and unadministered territories, each with their own rules, residents, and boundaries.

101. Lintner, *Great Game East*, p. 55.

102. See Johannes Fabian, *Time and the Other: How Anthropology Makes Its Object* (New York: Columbia University Press, 2002).

103. For a brief history of legislation identifying the Northeast as a place apart, see Sanjib Baruah, "Citizens and Denizens: Ethnicity, Homelands, and the Crisis of Displacement in Northeast India," *Journal of Refugee Studies* 16, no. 1 (2003): 44–66.

104. Nari Rustomji, *Enchanted Frontiers: Sikkim, Bhutan, and India's Northeastern Borderlands* (Delhi: Oxford University Press, 1971).

105. Duncan McDuie-Ra, "Fifty-Year Disturbance: The Armed Forces Special Powers Act and Exceptionalism in a South Asian Periphery," *Contemporary South Asia* 17, no. 3 (2009): 255–270; Namrata Gaikwad, "Revolting Bodies, Hysterical State: Women Protesting the Armed Forces Special Powers Act (1958)," *Contemporary South Asia* 17, no. 3 (2009): 299–311.

106. The discussion of the Khasi states is based on Karlsson, *Unruly States*, pp. 254–255.

107. Lintner, *Great Game East*, p. 144.

108. Naorem Sanajaoba, *Manipur: Treaties & Documents* (Delhi: Mittal Publications, 1993), pp. 433–434.

109. Lintner, *Great Game East*.

110. Marcus Franke, *War and Nationalism in South Asia: The Indian State and the Nagas* (London: Taylor & Francis, 2009).

111. Mary P. Callahan, *Making Enemies: War and State Building in Burma* (Ithaca, NY: Cornell University Press, 2003).

112. AFSPA briefly applied in the Punjab, from 1983–1987, and extended to Jammu and Kashmir in 1990.

113. See Asian Human Rights Commission, *The Armed Forces Special Powers Act 1958 in Manipur and Other States of the Indian Northeast*. Hong Kong: Author, August 18, 2011. Retrieved on May 4, 2013, from www.humanrights.asia/resources/journals-magazines/article2/1003/the-armed-forces-special-powers-act-1958-in-manipur-and-other-states-of-the-northeast-of-india-sanctioning-repression-in-violation-of-india2019s-human-rights-obligations.

114. For a recent study, see the section on the Northeast in Paula Banerjee and Anasua Basu Ray Chaudhury, eds., *Women in Indian Borderlands* (Delhi: Sage Publications, 2011).

115. Arthur J. Dommen, "Separatist Tendencies in Eastern India," *Asian Survey* 7, no. 10 (October 1967): 726–739.

116. Sajal Nag, "A Gigantic Panopticon: Counter Insurgency Operations and Modes of Discipline and Punishment in Northeastern India" (Paper presented at *Development, Logistics, and, Governance: Fourth Critical Studies Conference*, Kolkata, 2011).

117. Dommen, "Separatist Tendencies in Eastern India," p. 735.

118. Nag, "A Gigantic Panopticon."

119. Ibid.

120. Ujjwal Kumar Singh, *The State, Democracy and Anti-Terror Laws in India* (New Delhi and Thousand Oaks, CA: Sage Publications, 2007).

121. Nasser Hussain, *The Jurisprudence of Emergency: Colonialism and the Rule of Law* (Ann Arbor: University of Michigan Press, 2003), p. 136.

122. Quoted in ibid., p. 21.

Conclusion

1. There is an additional aspect of this visit that is worth mentioning, namely the presence of chief ministers of Indian states bordering Bangladesh as members of the official delegation. This inclusion marks their recognition as stakeholders in affairs that were hitherto considered purely bilateral relations between Delhi and Dhaka. The

controversy over Chief Minister of West Bengal Mamata Bannerjee's absence from the delegation, and her refusal to accept the agreement over the Teesta River barrage, highlights the practical implications of this decentralization of federal sovereignty. For an insightful analysis of the importance of including Indian states in "inter-national" agreements, see Dipak Gyawali, "Missing Leg: South Asia's Hobbled Water Technology Choices," *Economic and Political Weekly* 36, no. 39 (2001): 3743–3758.

2. For the most comprehensive account of the enclave problem, see W. Van Schendel, "Stateless in South Asia: The Making of the India–Bangladesh Enclaves," *Journal of Asian Studies* (2002): 115–147.

3. "Historic Indo-Bangla Land Pact Next Month," *Business Standard*, August 10, 2011. It is also possible to see in this approach to India's neighbors a return to the style of foreign policy practiced during the I. K. Gujral period (1995–1997). Salman Haider, *A Framework for South Asian Peace and Security*, Senior Fellow Project Report (Washington, DC: United States Institute of Peace, 2006).

4. Atal Behari Vajapayee, "Nuclear Anxiety: Indian's Letter to Clinton on the Nuclear Testing," *The New York Times*, May 13, 1998. Retrieved on September 13, 2011, from www.nytimes.com/1998/05/13/world/nuclear-anxiety-indian-s-letter-to-clinton-on-the-nuclear-testing.html. Italics added.

5. Samina Ahmed and Varun Sahni, *Freezing the Fighting: Military Disengagement on the Siachen Glacier*, CMC Occasional Paper (Sandia, NM: Sandia National Laboratory, 1998).

6. V. R. Raghavan, *Siachen: Conflict without End* (Delhi: Viking, 2002).

7. Robert Wirsing, *India, Pakistan, and the Kashmir Dispute: On Regional Conflict and Its Resolution* (London: Palgrave Macmillan, 1998), p. 212.

8. "At Siachen, Casualties Come to All-Time Low," *Indian Express*, October 11, 2008.

9. Šumit Ganguly, *Conflict Unending: India–Pakistan Tensions since 1947* (New York and Washington, DC: Columbia University Press and Woodrow Wilson Center Press, 2001), p. 85.

10. For an overview, see Waheguru Pal Singh Sidhu and Jing Dong Yuan, *China and India: Cooperation or Conflict?* (Boulder, CO, and London: Lynne Rienner Publishers, 2003). Frank Wisner et al., *New Priorities in South Asia: U.S. Policy toward India, Pakistan, and Afghanistan: Chairmen's Report of an Independent Task Force Cosponsored by the Council on Foreign Relations and the Asia Society* (New York: Council on Foreign Relations, 2003).

11. Tina Harris, *Geographical Diversions: Tibetan Trade, Global Transactions* (Athens: University of Georgia Press, 2013).

12. Amitav Acharya, "Can Asia Lead? Power Ambitions and Global Governance in the Twenty-First Century," *International Affairs* 87, no. 4 (July 1, 2011): 851–869.

13. On the seas as a source of "territorial" conflict, see Philip E. Steinberg, *The Social Construction of the Ocean* (Cambridge, UK: Cambridge University Press, 2001).

14. Chen Jie, "China's Spratly Policy: With Special Reference to the Philippines and Malaysia," *Asian Survey* 34, no. 10 (October 1, 1994): 893–903. Ken Maclean, "In Search of Kilometer Zero: Digital Archives, Technological Revisionism, and the Sino-Vietnamese Border," *Comparative Studies in Society and History* 50, no. 4 (2008): 862–894.

15. For a detailed discussion of the Philippine claim, see Dapo Ankade, "Philippines Initiates Arbitration against China over South China Seas Dis-

pute," January 22, 2013. Retrieved on April 23, 2013, from www.ejiltalk.org/philippines-initiates-arbitration-against-china-over-south-china-seas-dispute/.

16. Shirin Tahir-Kheli, "Pakhtoonistan and Its International Implications," *World Affairs* 137, no. 3 (December 1, 1974): 233–245. Pakistan has recently renamed the North West Frontier Province (NWFP) as Khyber Pakhtoonkwha in an effort to address partially the long-standing demands of the Awami National Party and local nationalist sentiments.

17. Min Gyo Koo, "The Senkaku/Diaoyu Dispute and Sino-Japanese Political-Economic Relations: Cold Politics and Hot Economics?" *The Pacific Review* 22 (June 3, 2009): 205–232.

18. Kimie Hara, "50 Years from San Francisco: Re-Examining the Peace Treaty and Japan's Territorial Problems," *Pacific Affairs* 74, no. 3 (October 1, 2001): 361–382.

19. Greg Poulgrain, *The Genesis of Konfrontasi: Malaysia, Brunei, Indonesia, 1945–1965* (London: C. Hurst & Co. Publishers, 1998).

20. P. Cuasay, "Borders on the Fantastic: Mimesis, Violence, and Landscape at the Temple of Preah Vihear," *Modern Asian Studies* 32, no. 4 (1998): 849–890.

21. See the following pages for a longer discussion of China's approach to territorial disputes.

22. Quoted in Elden, "Land, Terrain, Territory," p. 801.

23. Prakash, *Another Reason*. Bhabha, *Nation and Narration*.

24. In this context, metaphors of national loss through tropes of partition and dismemberment have an ambivalent import. Although they seek to reinforce the mystified historical process that has inscribed national identity onto the prior control of territory, at the same moment they offer a glimpse into subordinated and suppressed histories that have been sacrificed on the state altar in the name of national unity. The territorialization of women's bodies after India's partition and independence is a perfect illustration of this point. It took nearly half a century for this revision of the official narrative of India's partition of India to enter the intellectual mainstream. Only by the 1990s was the Indian nation secure and stable enough to consider that other political outcomes than "India" were possible. By the beginning of the twenty-first century, even Hindu nationalists like Jaswant Singh could reevaulate the role of national "villains" like M. A. Jinnah. Jaswant Singh, *Jinnah: India, Partition, Independence* (Delhi: Oxford University Press, 2010).

25. Fravel, *Strong Borders, Secure Nation*. M. Taylor Fravel, "Regime Insecurity and International Cooperation: Explaining China's Compromises in Territorial Disputes," *International Security* 30, no. 2 (2005): 46–83.

26. Fravel, *Strong Borders, Secure Nation*.

27. India stands as an important exception to this argument.

28. Regarding offshore disputes, he proposes that delay is the most likely response, as it is the least-cost option; given the potential of future economic benefits, there is little or no incentive to compromise.

29. Fravel, "Regime Insecurity and International Cooperation," p. 59.

30. For the difficulties of applying the category "Han" without qualification, see Susan Debra Blum and Lionel M. Jensen, eds., *China Off Center: Mapping the Margins of the Middle Kingdom* (Honolulu: University of Hawaii Press, 2002). For modern Chinese nationalism as a project of Han Chinese replacing Manchu hegemony, see Liu, "The Desire for the Sovereign and the Logic of Reciprocity in the Family of Nations," p. 160.

31. Raghavan, *War and Peace in Modern India*. John W. Garver, *Protracted Contest* (Seattle: University of Washington Press, 2011). Xuecheng Liu, *The Sino–Indian Border Dispute and Sino–Indian Relations* (Lanham, MD: University Press of America, 1994).

32. Suzuki, *Civilisation and Empire*.

33. Duara, *Sovereignty and Authenticity*.

34. William A. Callahan, "The Cartography of National Humiliation and the Emergence of China's Geobody," *Public Culture* 21, no. 1 (Winter 2009): 141–173, especially pp. 145–146.

35. Ibid., p. 149.

36. Ibid., p. 145. See also Thongchai Winichakul, *Siam Mapped: a History of the Geo-Body of a Nation* (Honolulu: University of Hawaii Press, 1997).

37. Suisheng Zhao, *A Nation-State by Construction: Dynamics of Modern Chinese Nationalism* (Stanford, CA: Stanford University Press, 2004).

38. Gladney, "Representing Nationality in China: Refiguring Majority/Minority Identities."

39. Ibid., pp. 94–95.

40. McKeown, "Conceptualizing Chinese Diasporas, 1842 to 1949." Wang, *The Chinese Overseas*.

41. Wang, *The Chinese Overseas*.

42. McKeown, "Conceptualizing Chinese Diasporas, 1842 to 1949." Charles Keyes, "Presidential Address."

43. Zhang, *China in International Society since 1949*.

44. Callahan, "The Cartography of National Humiliation and the Emergence of China's Geobody."

45. Blum and Jensen, *China Off Center*.

46. Harris, *Geographical Diversions*.

47. Ganguly, *Conflict Unending*.

48. Jalal, *The State of Martial Rule*.

49. Burke and Ziring, *Pakistan's Foreign Policy*.

50. Khan, *The British Papers*.

51. Zaminder, *The Long Partition and the Making of Modern South Asia Refugees, Boundaries, Histories*.

52. Roy, *Mapping Citizenship in India*.

53. Abdul Ghani Sheikh, quoted in Aggarwal, *Beyond Lines of Control*, p. 221.

54. Samāddār, *The Politics of Dialogue*.

Bibliography

Abraham, Itty. "Bandung and State Formation in Post-Colonial Asia." In *Bandung Revisited: The Legacy of the 1955 Asian-African Conference for International Order*, edited by See Seng Tan and Amitav Acharya, pp. 48–67. Singapore: NUS Press, 2008.
———. "From Bandung to NAM: Non-Alignment and Indian Foreign Policy, 1947–65." *Commonwealth & Comparative Politics* 46 (April 2008): 195–219.
Abu-Lughod, Janet L. *Before European Hegemony: The World System A.D. 1250–1350*. New York: Oxford University Press, 1989.
Acharya, Amitav. "Can Asia Lead? Power Ambitions and Global Governance in the Twenty-First Century." *International Affairs* 87, no. 4 (July 1, 2011): 851–869.
Adas, Michael. *Machines as the Measure of Men: Science, Technology, and Ideologies of Western Dominance*. Ithaca, NY: Cornell University Press, 1990.
———. "Contested Hegemony: The Great War and the Afro-Asian Assault on the Civilizing Mission Ideology." *Journal of World History* 15, no. 1 (2004): 31–63.
Agamben, Giorgio. *Homo Sacer: Sovereign Power and Bare Life*. Stanford, CA: Stanford University Press, 1998.
Aggarwal, Ravina. *Beyond Lines of Control: Performance and Politics on the Disputed Borders of Ladakh, India*. Durham, NC: Duke University Press, 2004.
Agnew, John A. *Globalization and Sovereignty*. Lanham, MD: Rowman & Littlefield, 2009.
Agnew, John A., and Stuart Corbridge. *Mastering Space: Hegemony, Territory and International Political Economy*. London and New York: Routledge, 1995.
Ahmed, Samina, and Varun Sahni. *Freezing the Fighting: Military Disengagement on the Siachen Glacier*. CMC Occasional Paper. Sandia, NM: Sandia National Laboratory, 1998.
Alexandrowicz, Charles Henry. *An Introduction of the History of the Law of Nations in the East Indies*. Oxford, UK: Clarendon Press, 1967.
Amrith, Sunil S. *Decolonizing International Health: India and Southeast Asia, 1930–65*. London: Palgrave Macmillan, 2006.
———. *Migration and Diaspora in Modern Asia*. Cambridge, UK: Cambridge University Press, 2011.

———. *Crossing the Bay of Bengal: The Furies of Nature and the Fortunes of Migrants*. Cambridge, MA: Harvard University Press, 2013.
Anand, R. P. *New States and International Law*, 2nd edition. Gurgaon: Hope India Publications, 2008.
———. "The Formation of International Organizations and India: A Historical Study." *Leiden Journal of International Law* 23, no. 1 (March 2010): 5–21.
Anderson, Benedict Richard O'Gorman. *Imagined Communities: Reflections on the Origin and Spread of Nationalism*, 2nd edition. London: Verso, 1983.
Andreas, Peter. *Border Games: Policing the U.S.–Mexico Divide*. Ithaca, NY: Cornell University Press, 2000.
Anghie, Antony. *Imperialism, Sovereignty and the Making of International Law*. Cambridge, UK: Cambridge University Press, 2007.
Dapo Ankade, "Philippines Initiates Arbitration against China over South China Seas Dispute," January 22, 2013. Retrieved on April 23, 2013, from www.ejiltalk.org/philippines-initiates-arbitration-against-china-over-south-china-seas-dispute/.
Appadorai, A. *Asian Relations: Being Report of the Proceedings and Documentation of the First Asian Relations Conference, New Delhi, March–April, 1947*. New Delhi: Asian Relations Organization, 1948.
———. "The Asian Relations Conference in Perspective." *International Studies* 18, no. 3 (July 1, 1979): 275–285.
Appadurai, Arjun. *Modernity at Large: Cultural Dimensions of Globalization*. Minneapolis: University of Minnesota Press, 1996.
Arendt, Hannah. *The Origins of Totalitarianism*, new edition. New York: Harcourt Brace Jovanovich, 1968.
Arnold, David. *Colonizing the Body: State Medicine and Epidemic Disease in Nineteenth-Century India*. Berkeley: University of California Press, 1993.
Arnold, David, and Erich DeWald. "Cycles of Empowerment? The Bicycle and Everyday Technology in Colonial India and Vietnam," *Comparative Studies in Society and History* 53, no. 4 (2011): 971–996.
Ashley, Richard K. "Foreign Policy as Political Performance." *International Studies Notes* 13, no. 2 (1987): 51–54.
Asian Human Rights Commission, *The Armed Forces Special Powers Act 1958 in Manipur and Other States of the Indian Northeast*. Hong Kong: Author, August 18, 2011. Retrieved on May 4, 2013, from www.humanrights.asia/resources/journals-magazines/article2/1003/the-armed-forces-special-powers-act-1958-in-manipur-and-other-states-of-the-northeast-of-india-sanctioning-repression-in-violation-of-india2019s-human-rights-obligations.
"At Siachen, Casualties Come to All-Time Low." *Indian Express*, October 11, 2008.
Balachandran, G. "Circulation through Seafaring: Indian Seamen, 1890–1945." In *Society and Circulation: Mobile People and Itinerant Cultures in South Asia, 1750–1950*, pp. 89–130. Delhi: Permanent Black, 2003.
Banerjee, Paula, and Anasua Basu Ray Chaudhury, eds. *Women in Indian Borderlands*. Delhi: SAGE Publications, 2011.
Baruah, Sanjib. *India against Itself: Assam and the Politics of Nationality*. Philadelphia: University of Pennsylvania Press, 1999.
———. "Citizens and Denizens: Ethnicity, Homelands, and the Crisis of Displacement in Northeast India." *Journal of Refugee Studies* 16, no. 1 (March 1, 2003): 44–66.

———. *Durable Disorder: Understanding the Politics of Northeast India*. Delhi: Oxford University Press, 2007.
Bates, Crispin, ed. *Community, Empire, and Migration: South Asians in Diaspora*, pp. 185–205. London: Palgrave, 2001.
Baud, Michiel, and Willem van Schendel. "Toward a Comparative History of Borderlands." *Journal of World History* 8, no. 2 (1997): 211–242.
Bayly, Christopher A. *Imperial Meridian: The British Empire and the World, 1780–1830*. London: Longman, 1989.
———. *Empire and Information: Intelligence Gathering and Social Communication in India, 1780–1870*. Cambridge, UK: Cambridge University Press, 2000.
———. *The Birth of the Modern World: 1780–1914*. Oxford, UK: Blackwell Publishers, 2004.
Bayly, Christopher A., and T. N. Harper. *Forgotten Armies: Britain's Asian Empire and the War with Japan*. London: Penguin, 2005. {moved for alpha order}
Benton, Lauren. *A Search for Sovereignty: Law and Geography in European Empires, 1400–1900*. Cambridge, UK: Cambridge University Press, 2010.
Bhabha, Homi K., ed. *Nation and Narration*. London and New York: Routledge, 1990.
Bhagavan, Manu. *The Peacemakers: India and the Quest for One World*. Delhi: HarperCollins, 2012.
Biersteker, Thomas J., and Cynthia Weber, eds. *State Sovereignty as Social Construct*. Cambridge, UK: Cambridge University Press, 1996.
Birla, Ritu. *Stages of Capital: Law, Culture, and Market Governance in Late Colonial India*. Durham, NC: Duke University Press, 2009.
Blum, Susan Debra, and Lionel M. Jensen, eds. *China off Center: Mapping the Margins of the Middle Kingdom*. Honolulu: University of Hawaii Press, 2002.
Borschberg, Peter. *Hugo Grotius, the Portuguese, and "Free Trade" in the East Indies*. Honolulu: Hawaii University Press, 2010.
Bose, Sugata. *A Hundred Horizons: The Indian Ocean in the Age of Global Empire*. Cambridge, MA: Harvard University Press, 2006.
Bourdieu, Pierre. *Distinction: A Social Critique of the Judgement of Taste*. Translated by Richard Nice. Cambridge, MA: Harvard University Press, 1984.
Branch, Jordan. "Mapping the Sovereign State: Technology, Authority, and Systemic Change." *International Organization* 65, no. 1 (2011): 1–36.
Brenner, Neil. "Beyond State-Centrism: Space, Territoriality, and Geographic Scale in Globalization Studies." *Theory and Society* 28, no. 1 (February 1999): 39–78.
Brobst, Peter John. *The Future of the Great Game: Sir Olaf Caroe, India's Independence, and the Defense of Asia*. Akron, OH: University of Akron Press, 2005.
Brown, Judith M. *Gandhi's Rise to Power: Indian Politics 1915–1922*. Cambridge, UK: Cambridge University Press, 1972.
———. *Global South Asians: Introducing the Modern Diaspora*. Cambridge, UK: Cambridge University Press, 2006.
Brubaker, Rogers. *Nationalism Reframed: Nationhood and the National Question in the New Europe*. Cambridge: Cambridge University Press, 1996.
Burbank, Jane, and Frederick Cooper. *Empires in World History: Power and the Politics of Difference*. Princeton, NJ: Princeton University Press, 2010.
Burke, S. M., and Lawrence Ziring. *Pakistan's Foreign Policy: An Historical Analysis*. Karachi: Oxford University Press, 1990.

Burton, Antoinette M., ed. *Gender, Sexuality and Colonial Modernities*. London and New York: Routledge, 1999.
Butler, Judith. *The Judith Butler Reader*. Edited by Sara Salih. Oxford, UK: Blackwell Publishers, 2004.
Calhoun, Craig J. *Nationalism*. Minneapolis: University of Minnesota Press, 1997.
Callahan, Mary P. *Making Enemies: War And State Building in Burma*. Ithaca, NY: Cornell University Press, 2003.
Callahan, William A. "The Cartography of National Humiliation and the Emergence of China's Geobody." *Public Culture* 21, no. 1 (Winter 2009): 141–173.
Campbell, David. *Writing Security: United States Foreign Policy and the Politics of Identity*. Minneapolis: University of Minnesota Press, 1998.
Carter, D. B., and H. E. Goemans. "The Making of the Territorial Order: New Borders and the Emergence of Interstate Conflict," *International Organization* 65, no. 2 (2011): 275–309.
Chakrabarty, Dipesh. *Provincializing Europe: Postcolonial Thought and Historical Difference*. Princeton, NJ: Princeton University Press, 2000.
Chatterjee, Partha. *Nationalist Thought and the Colonial World: A Derivative Discourse?* London: Zed Books, 1986.
———. *The Nation and Its Fragments: Colonial and Postcolonial Histories*. Princeton, NJ: Princeton University Press, 1993.
Chaturvedi, Sanjay. "Indian Geopolitics: 'Nation-State' and the Colonial Legacy." In *International Relations in India: The Region and the Nation*, edited by Kanti P. Bajpai and Siddharth Mallavarapu, pp. 238–283. Delhi: Orient Longmans, 2004.
Chaudhuri, K. N. *Trade and Civilisation in the Indian Ocean: An Economic History from the Rise of Islam to 1750*. Cambridge, UK: Cambridge University Press, 1985.
———. *Asia before Europe: Economy and Civilization of the Indian Ocean from the Rise of Islam to 1750*. Cambridge, UK: Cambridge University Press, 1990.
Cheah, Pheng. *Spectral Nationality: Passages of Freedom from Kant to Postcolonial Literatures of Liberation*. New York: Columbia University Press, 2003.
Chibber, Vivek. *Locked in Place: State-Building and Late Industrialization in India*. Princeton, NJ: Princeton University Press, 2006.
Chimni, B. S. "The Geopolitics of Refugee Studies: A View from the South." *Journal of Refugee Studies* 11, no. 4 (January 1, 1998): 350–374.
Cohen, Ed. *A Body Worth Defending: Immunity, Biopolitics, and the Apotheosis of the Modern Body*. Durham, NC: Duke University Press, 2009.
Cohen, Robin. *The New Helots: Migrants in the International Division of Labour*. London: Gower, 1987.
Cohn, Bernard S. *Colonialism and Its Forms of Knowledge: The British in India*. Princeton, NJ: Princeton University Press, 1996.
Connolly, William E. *Identity\Difference: Democratic Negotiations of Political Paradox*. Minneapolis: University of Minnesota Press, 2002.
Cooper, Frederick. *Colonialism in Question: Theory, Knowledge, History*. Berkeley: University of California Press, 2005.
Cooper, Nicola. *France in Indochina: Colonial Encounters*. Oxford, UK: Berg, 2001.
Crozier, Andrew J. "The Establishment of the Mandate System, 1919–1925: Some Problems Created by the Paris Peace Conference." *Journal of Contemporary History* 14, no. 3 (July 1979): 483–513.

Cuasay, P. "Borders on the Fantastic: Mimesis, Violence, and Landscape at the Temple of Preah Vihear." *Modern Asian Studies* 32, no. 4 (1998): 849.

Curzon, George Nathaniel. *Persia and the Persian Question: Volume 1*. London: Longman, 1892.

———. *Frontiers: The Romanes Lecture, 1907*. Oxford, UK: Clarendon Press, 1907.

Das, Durga, ed. *Sardar Patel's Correspondence, 1945–50*. Vol. X. Ahmedabad: Navajivan Publishing House, 1974.

Dean, Mitchell. *Critical and Effective Histories: Foucault's Methods and Historical Sociology*. London: Routledge, 1994.

Der Derian, James. *On Diplomacy: A Genealogy of Western Estrangement*. Oxford, UK: Basil Blackwell, 1987.

Deshpande, Satish. *Contemporary India: A Sociological View*. Delhi: Penguin Books, 2004.

Devji, Faisal. *The Impossible Indian: Gandhi and the Temptation of Violence*. Cambridge, MA: Harvard University Press, 2012.

Dickinson, Jen. "Decolonising the Diaspora: Neo-Colonial Performances of Indian History in East Africa." *Transactions of the Institute of British Geographers*, 37, no. 4 (October 2012): 609–623.

Diehl, Paul Francis, ed. *A Road Map to War: Territorial Dimensions of International Conflict*. Nashville, TN: Vanderbilt University Press, 1999.

Dommen, Arthur J. "Separatist Tendencies in Eastern India." *Asian Survey* 7, no. 10 (October 1967): 726–739.

Duara, Prasenjit. *Sovereignty and Authenticity: Manchukuo and the East Asian Modern*. Lanham, MD: Rowman & Littlefield, 2004.

———. "The Discourse of Civilization and Decolonization." *Journal of World History* 15, no. 1 (March 2004).

———. "Asia Redux: Conceptualizing a Region for Our Times." *The Journal of Asian Studies* 69, no. 4 (2010): 963–983.

Edney, Matthew H. *Mapping an Empire: The Geographical Construction of British India, 1765–1843*. Chicago: University of Chicago Press, 1997.

Elden, Stuart. "Land, Terrain, Territory." *Progress in Human Geography* 34, no. 6 (December 1, 2010): 799–817.

———. *The Birth of Territory*. Chicago: University of Chicago Press, 2013.

Evans, Peter B. *Dependent Development: The Alliance of Multinational, State, and Local Capital in Brazil*. Princeton, NJ: Princeton University Press, 1979.

Fabian, Johannes. *Time and the Other: How Anthropology Makes Its Object*. New York: Columbia University Press, 2002.

Fernandes, Leela. "Nationalizing 'the Global': Media Images, Cultural Politics and the Middle Class in India." *Media, Culture & Society* 22, no. 5 (September 1, 2000): 611–628.

Fischer-Tiné, Harald. "Indian Nationalism and the 'World Forces': Transnational and Diasporic Dimensions of the Indian Freedom Movement on the Eve of the First World War." *Journal of Global History* 2, no. 3 (2007): 325–344.

Frank, André Gunder. *ReOrient: Global Economy in the Asian Age*. Berkeley: University of California Press, 1998.

Franke, Marcus. *War and Nationalism in South Asia: The Indian State and the Nagas*. London: Taylor & Francis, 2009.

Fravel, M. Taylor. "Regime Insecurity and International Cooperation: Explaining China's Compromises in Territorial Disputes." *International Security* 30, no. 2 (2005): 46–83.

———. *Strong Borders, Secure Nation: Cooperation and Conflict in China's Territorial Disputes*. Princeton, NJ: Princeton University Press, 2008.

Gaikwad, Namrata. "Revolting Bodies, Hysterical State: Women Protesting the Armed Forces Special Powers Act (1958)." *Contemporary South Asia* 17, no. 3 (2009): 299–311.

Gallagher, John, and Anil Seal. "Britain and India between the Wars." *Modern Asian Studies* 15, no. 3 (1981): 387–414.

Ganguly, Šumit. *Conflict Unending: India–Pakistan Tensions since 1947*. New York and Washington, DC: Columbia University Press and Woodrow WIlson Center Press, 2001.

Garver, John W. *Protracted Contest*. Seattle: University of Washington Press, 2011.

Gavrilis, George. *The Dynamics of Interstate Boundaries*. Cambridge, UK: Cambridge University Press, 2010.

Gellner, E. *Nations and Nationalism*. Oxford, UK: Blackwell Publishers, 2006.

Giannuli, Dimitra. "Greeks or 'Strangers at Home': The Experience of Ottoman Greek Refugees during Their Exodus to Greece, 1922–1923." *Journal of Modern Greek Studies* 13, no. 2 (1995): 271–287.

Gladney, Dru C. "Representing Nationality in China: Refiguring Majority/Minority Identities." *The Journal of Asian Studies* 53, no. 1 (February 1, 1994): 92–123.

Goertz, Gary, and Paul Diehl. *Territorial Changes and International Conflict*. London and New York: Routledge, 2002.

Gómez, Nicolás Wey. *The Tropics of Empire: Why Columbus Sailed South to the Indies*. Cambridge, MA: The MIT Press, 2008.

Gong, Gerrit W. *The Standard of "Civilization" in International Society*. Oxford, UK: Clarendon Press, 1984.

Gordon, Richard. "The Hindu Mahasabha and the Indian National Congress, 1915 to 1926." *Modern Asian Studies* 9, no. 2 (January 1, 1975): 145–203.

Goswami, Manu. *Producing India*. Chicago: University of Chicago Press, 2004.

Gourevitch, Peter. "The Second Image Reversed: The International Sources of Domestic Politics." *International Organization* 32, no. 4 (October 1, 1978): 881–912.

Greenfeld, Liah. *Nationalism: Five Roads to Modernity*. Cambridge, MA: Harvard University Press, 1993.

Grotius, Hugo. *The Freedom of the Seas (Mare Liberum)*. Translated by Ralph van Demen Magoffin. Washington, DC: Carnegie Endowment for International Peace, 1916.

Grovogui, Siba N'Zatioula. *Sovereigns, Quasi Sovereigns, and Africans: Race and Self-Determination in International Law*. Minneapolis: University of Minnesota Press, 1996.

Guha, Amalendu. *Planter Raj to Swaraj: Freedom Struggle and Electoral Politics in Assam, 1826–1947*. Kolkata: Tulika Books, 1976.

Guha, Ramachandra. *Savaging the Civilized: Verrier Elwin, His Tribals, and India*. Chicago: University of Chicago Press, 1999.

———. *Gandhi before India*. London: Allen Lane, 2013.

Gupta, Anirudha. "Ugandan Asians, Britain, India and the Commonwealth." *African Affairs* 73, no. 292 (July 1, 1974): 312–324.

Gupta, Partha Sarathi. *Power, Politics, and the People: Studies in British Imperialism and Indian Nationalism*. Delhi: Permanent Black, 2001.

Gupta, Partha Sarathi, and Anirudh Deshpande, eds. *The British Raj and Its Indian Armed Forces, 1857–1939*. Delhi: Oxford University Press, 2002.
Gyawali, Dipak. "Missing Leg: South Asia's Hobbled Water Technology Choices." *Economic and Political Weekly* 36, no. 39 (2001): 3743–3758.
Haider, Salman. *A Framework for South Asian Peace and Security*. Senior Fellow Project Report. Washington, DC: United States Institute of Peace, 2006.
Hametz, Maura Elise. *Making Trieste Italian: 1918–1954*. Woodbridge, UK: Boydell & Brewer, 2005.
Hara, Kimie. "50 Years from San Francisco: Re-Examining the Peace Treaty and Japan's Territorial Problems." *Pacific Affairs* 74, no. 3 (October 1, 2001).
Harris, Tina. *Geographical Diversions: Tibetan Trade, Global Transactions*. Athens: University of Georgia Press, 2013.
Harvey, David. *The Limits to Capital*. revised. London: Verso, 1982.
"Historic Indo-Bangla Land Pact Next Month," *Business Standard*, August 10, 2011.
Hobsbawm, E. J. *Nations and Nationalism since 1780: Programme, Myth, Reality*. Cambridge, UK: Cambridge University Press, 1992.
Holsti, Kalevi Jaakko. *Taming the Sovereigns: Institutional Change in International Politics*. Cambridge, UK: Cambridge University Press, 2004.
Hopkirk, Peter. *The Great Game*. Oxford, UK: Oxford University Press, 1990.
Hussain, Nasser. *The Jurisprudence of Emergency: Colonialism and the Rule of Law*. Ann Arbor: University of Michigan Press, 2003.
Huth, Paul K. *Standing Your Ground: Territorial Disputes and International Conflict*. Ann Arbor: University of Michigan Press, 1998.
Inden, Ronald B. *Imagining India*. Oxford, UK: Blackwell Publishers, 1990.
Indian Home Rule League. "Self Determination in India." London: Author, 1919.
Iveković, Rada, and Julie Mostov, eds. *From Gender to Nation*. Delhi: Zubaan, 2004.
Jaffrelot, Christophe. *The Hindu Nationalist Movement and Indian Politics: 1925 to the 1990s: Strategies of Identity-Building, Implantation and Mobilisation (with Special Reference to Central India)*. London: C. Hurst & Co. Publishers, 1996.
Jalal, Ayesha. *The State of Martial Rule: The Origins of Pakistan's Political Economy of Defence*. Cambridge, UK: Cambridge University Press, 1990.
Jessop, Bob. *State Theory: Putting the Capitalist State in Its Place*. University Park: Penn State University Press, 1990.
Jie, Chen. "China's Spratly Policy: With Special Reference to the Philippines and Malaysia." *Asian Survey* 34, no. 10 (October 1, 1994): 893–903.
Kapur, Devesh. *Diaspora, Development, and Democracy: The Domestic Impact of International Migration from India*. Princeton, NJ: Princeton University Press, 2010.
Karlsson, Bengt G. *Unruly Hills: A Political Ecology of India's Northeast*. Delhi: Orient Black Swan, 2011.
Karnad, Bharat. "India's Weak Geopolitics and What to Do about It." In *Future Imperilled: India's Security in the 1990s and Beyond*, edited by Bharat Karnad, pp. 16–84. Delhi: Viking, 1994.
Kayaoğlu, Turan. "Westphalian Eurocentrism in International Relations Theory." *International Studies Review* 12, no. 2 (June 1, 2010): 193–217.
Kayaoğlu, Turan. *Legal Imperialism: Sovereignty and Extraterritoriality in Japan, the Ottoman Empire, and China*. Cambridge: Cambridge University Press, 2010.
Keene, Edward. *Beyond the Anarchical Society: Grotius, Colonialism and Order in World Politics*. Cambridge, UK: Cambridge University Press, 2002.

Keenleyside, T. A. "Prelude to Power: The Meaning of Non-Alignment Before Indian Independence." *Pacific Affairs* 53, no. 3 (October 1, 1980): 461–483.

———. "Nationalist Indian Attitudes Towards Asia: A Troublesome Legacy for Post-Independence Indian Foreign Policy." *Pacific Affairs* 55, no. 2 (July 1, 1982): 210–230.

Keyes, Charles. "Presidential Address: 'The Peoples of Asia'—Science and Politics in the Classification of Ethnic Groups in Thailand, China, and Vietnam." *The Journal of Asian Studies* 61, no. 04 (2002): 1163–1203.

Khan, Roedad. *The British Papers: Secret and Confidential, India, Pakistan, Bangladesh Documents 1958-1969*. Karachi: Oxford University Press, 2002.

Kirk, Jason A. "Indian-Americans and the U.S.–India Nuclear Agreement: Consolidation of an Ethnic Lobby?" *Foreign Policy Analysis* 4, no. 3 (July 1, 2008): 275–300.

Kondapi, C. *Indians Overseas, 1838–1949*. Delhi: Indian Council of World Affairs, 1951.

Koo, Min Gyo. "The Senkaku/Diaoyu Dispute and Sino-Japanese Political-Economic Relations: Cold Politics and Hot Economics?" *The Pacific Review* 22 (June 3, 2009): 205–232.

Kowner, Rotem, ed., *The Impact of the Russo-Japanese War*. London: Routledge, 2007.

Krasner, Stephen D. *Sovereignty: Organized Hypocrisy*. Princeton, NJ: Princeton University Press, 1999.

———. "Revisiting 'The Second Image Reversed.'" Paper presented at the Conference in Honor of Peter Gourevich. San Diego, CA, 2010; retrieved on June 19, 2013, from http://empac.ucsd.edu/assets/006/11458.pdf.

Kratochwil, Friedrich. "Of Systems, Boundaries, and Territoriality: An Inquiry into the Formation of the State System." *World Politics* 39, no. 1 (1986): 27–52.

Krishna, Sankaran. "Cartographic Anxiety: Mapping the Body Politic in India." *Alternatives: Global, Local, Political* 19, no. 4 (October 1, 1994): 507–521.

———. *Postcolonial Insecurities: India, Sri Lanka, and the Question of Nationhood*. Minneapolis: University of Minnesota Press, 1999.

Krishnamurthy, J. "Indian Officials in the ILO, 1919–c.1947." *Economic and Political Weekly* 46, no. 10 (2011).

Kumar, Dhruba, ed. *Nepal's India Policy*. Kathmandu: Centre for Nepal and Asian Studies, Tribhuvan University, 1992.

Kurien, Prema A. *Kaleidoscopic Ethnicity: International Migration and the Reconstruction of Community Identities in India*. New Brunswick, NJ: Rutgers University Press, 2002.

Lefèbvre, Henri. *The Production of Space*. Translated by Donald Nicholson-Smith. New York and Oxford: Wiley-Blackwell, 1991.

Lintner, Bertil. *Great Game East: India, China and the Struggle for Asia's Most Volatile Frontier*. Delhi: Harper-Collins, 2012.

Liu, Lydia H. "The Desire for the Sovereign and the Logic of Reciprocity in the Family of Nations." *Diacritics* 29, no. 4 (1999): 150–177.

———. *The Clash of Empires: The Invention of China in Modern World Making*. Cambridge, MA: Harvard University Press, 2004.

Liu, Xuecheng. *The Sino–Indian Border Dispute and Sino–Indian Relations*. Lanham, MD: University Press of America, 1994.

Lohia, Rammanohar, and J. B. Kriplani. *Indians in Foreign Lands*. Allahabad: All India Congress Committee, 1938.

Luthy, Herbert. "India and East Africa: Imperial Partnership at the End of the First World War." *Journal of Contemporary History* 6, no. 2 (January 1, 1971): 55–85.

Mackinder, H. J. "The Geographical Pivot of History." *The Geographical Journal* 23, no. 4 (April 1, 1904): 421–437.
Maclean, Ken. "In Search of Kilometer Zero: Digital Archives, Technological Revisionism, and the Sino-Vietnamese Border." *Comparative Studies in Society and History* 50, no. 4 (2008): 862–894.
Macridis, Roy C. *Foreign Policy in World Politics.* Englewood Cliffs, NJ: Prentice Hall, 1968.
Mahan, Alfred Thayer. *The Influence of Sea Power upon History 1660–1783.* Boston: Little, Brown, 1889.
Mahmud, Tayyab. "Colonial Cartographies and Postcolonial Borders: The Unending War in and around Afghanistan." Seattle University School of Law, 2010; available at http://works.bepress.cam/tayyab_mahmud/1.
Manela, Erez. *The Wilsonian Moment: Self-Determination and the International Origins of Anticolonial Nationalism.* New York: Oxford University Press, 2007.
Manguin, Pierre-Yves, A. Mani, and Geoff Wade. *Early Interactions between South and Southeast Asia: Reflections on Cross-Cultural Exchange.* Singapore: ISEAS, 2011.
Mansergh, Nicholas, and Penderel Moon, eds. *The Transfer of Power 1942–47: The Mountbatten Viceroyalty Formulation of a Plan 22 March–30 May 1947.* London: H.M.S.O., 1981.
Markovits, Claude. *The Global World of Indian Merchants, 1750–1947: Traders of Sind from Bukhara to Panama.* Cambridge, UK: Cambridge University Press, 2000.
Markovits, Claude, Jacques Pouchepadass, and Sanjay Subrahmanyam, eds. *Society and Circulation: Mobile People and Itinerant Cultures in South Asia, 1750-1950.* Delhi: Permanent Black, 2006.
Maxwell, N. *India's China War.* New York: Random House, 1971.
Mazower, Mark. "Minorities and the League of Nations in Interwar Europe." *Daedalus* 126, no. 2 (Spring 1997): 47–63.
———. *Salonica, City of Ghosts: Christians, Muslims and Jews 1430–1950.* New York: Knopf Doubleday Publishing Group, 2007.
———. *No Enchanted Palace. The End of Empire and the Ideological Origins of the United Nations.* Princeton, NJ: Princeton University Press, 2009.
Mbembe, Achille. *On the Postcolony.* Berkeley: University of California Press, 2001.
McDuie-Ra, Duncan. "Fifty-Year Disturbance: The Armed Forces Special Powers Act and Exceptionalism in a South Asian Periphery." *Contemporary South Asia* 17, no. 3 (2009): 255–270.
McKeown, Adam. "Conceptualizing Chinese Diasporas, 1842 to 1949." *The Journal of Asian Studies* 58, no. 2 (1999): 306–337.
Mehta, Uday Singh. *Liberalism and Empire: A Study in Nineteenth-Century British Liberal Thought.* Chicago: University of Chicago Press, 1999.
Menon, Ritu, and Kamla Bhasin. *Borders & Boundaries: Women in India's Partition.* New Brunswick, NJ: Rutgers University Press, 1998.
Menon, Vapal Pangunni. *The Story of the Integration of the Indian States.* Bombay: Orient Longmans, 1961.
Michael, Bernardo A. *Statemaking and Territory in South Asia: Lessons from the Anglo-Gorkha War (1814–1816).* London: Anthem Press, 2012.
Mignolo, Walter. *The Darker Side of the Renaissance: Literacy, Territoriality, & Colonization,* 2nd edition. Ann Arbor: University of Michigan Press, 2003.

Minault, Gail. *The Khilafat Movement: Religious Symbolism and Political Mobilization in India*. New York: Columbia University Press, 1982.

Mitchell, Timothy. "Society, Economy, and the State Effect." In *The Anthropology of the State: A Reader*, edited by Aradhana Sharma and Akhil Gupta. Oxford, UK: Blackwell Publishers, 2006.

Mohammed, Robina, and James D. Sidaway. "Spectacular Urbanization amidst Variegated Geographies of Globalization: Learning from Abu Dhabi's Trajectory through the Lives of South Asian Men." *International Journal of Urban and Regional Research* (2012).

Mohan, C. Raja. *Crossing the Rubicon: The Shaping of India's New Foreign Policy*. New Delhi: Viking, 2004.

Mongia, Radhika V. "Race, Nationality, Mobility: A History of the Passport." *Public Culture* 11, no. 3 (Fall 1999): 527–555.

———. "Historicizing State Sovereignty: Inequality and the Form of Equivalence." *Comparative Studies in Society and History* 49, no. 2 (2007): 384–411.

Moseman, Andrew. "Tiny Island, Fought over by India and Bangladesh, Vanishes into Sea." *Discover Magazine*, March 25, 2010.

Mrázek, Rudolf. *Engineers of Happy Land: Technology and Nationalism in a Colony* Princeton, NJ: Princeton University Press, 2002.

Nag, Sajal. "A Gigantic Panopticon: Counter Insurgency Operations and Modes of Discipline and Punishment in Northeastern India." Kolkata, 2011.

Nandy, Ashis. *The Intimate Enemy: Loss and Recovery of Self under Colonialism*. Delhi: Oxford University Press, 1983.

Nayyar, Deepak. *Migration, Remittances, and Capital Flows: The Indian Experience*. Delhi: Oxford University Press, 1994.

Nehru, Jawaharlal. *India's Foreign Policy: Selected Speeches, September 1946–April 1961*. Delhi: Publications Division, Ministry of Information and Broadcasting, Government of India, 1961.

Noorani, Abdul Gafoor Abdul Majeed. *India–China Boundary Problem, 1846–1947: History and Diplomacy*. Delhi: Oxford University Press, 2011.

O'Malley, Kate. *Ireland, India, and Empire: Indo-Irish Radical Connections, 1919–64*. Manchester, UK: Manchester University Press, 2008.

Oberoi, Pia Anjolie. *Exile and Belonging: Refugees and State Policy in South Asia*. Delhi: Oxford University Press, 2006.

"Official Memorandum in Support of Ireland's Demand for Recognition as a Sovereign Independent State. Presented to Georges Clemenceau and the Members of the Paris Peace Conference by Sean T. O'Cealloigh and George Gavan Duffy." Dublin: Documents on Irish foreign policy, a project of the Royal Irish Academy, Department of Foreign Affairs, and National Archives of Ireland. Retrieved on October 30, 2011, from www.difp.ie/viewdoc.asp?DocID=13.

Ong, Aihwa, and Donald Macon Nonini, eds. *Ungrounded Empires: The Cultural Politics of Modern Chinese Transnationalism*. New York and London: Routledge, 1997.

Onley, J. "The Raj Reconsidered: British India's Informal Empire and Spheres of Influence in Asia and Africa." *Asian Affairs* 40, no. 1 (2009): 44–62.

Pagden, Anthony. *European Encounters with the New World: From Renaissance to Romanticism*. New Haven, CT: Yale University Press, 1994.

———. *Lords of All the World: Ideologies of Empire in Spain, Britain and France c. 1500–c. 1800*. New Haven, CT: Yale University Press, 1995.

Pandey, Gyanendra. *The Construction of Communalism in Colonial North India*. Delhi: Oxford University Press, 1990.
Pandian, M. S. S. *Brahmin and Non-Brahmin*. Delhi: Permanent Black, 2008.
Panikkar, Kavalam Madhava. *Asia and Western Dominance: A Survey of the Vasco Da Gama Epoch of Asian History, 1498–1945*. London: George Allen and Unwin, 1953.
———. *India and the Indian Ocean: An Essay on the Influence of Sea Power on Indian History*. London: G. Allen & Unwin, 1962.
———. *Geographical Factors in Indian History*. Delhi: Bharatiya Vidya Bhavan, 1969.
Patel, Vallabhbhai. *Sardar's Letters, Mostly Unknown*. Edited by G. M. Nandurkar III (1950). Ahmedabad: Sardar Vallabhbhai Patel Smarak Bhavan, 1983.
Pedersen, Susan. "Back to the League of Nations: Review Essay." *The American Historical Review* 112, no. 4 (October 2007): 1091–1116.
Pennell, C. R. *Bandits at Sea: A Pirates Reader*. New York: NYU Press, 2001.
Penrose, J. "Nations, States and Homelands: Territory and Territoriality in Nationalist Thought." *Nations and Nationalism* 8, no. 3 (2002): 277–297.
Philpott, Daniel. *Revolutions in Sovereignty: How Ideas Shaped Modern International Relations*. Princeton, NJ: Princeton University Press, 2001.
Poulantzas, Nicos. *State, Power, Socialism*. London: Verso, 2000.
Poulgrain, Greg. *The Genesis of Konfrontasi: Malaysia, Brunei, Indonesia, 1945–1965*. London: C. Hurst & Co. Publishers, 1998.
Poulose, T. T. "India as an Anomalous International Person (1919–1947)." *British Yearbook of International Law* 44 (1970): 201.
Prakash, Gyan. *Another Reason: Science and the Imagination of Modern India*. Princeton, NJ: Princeton University Press, 1999.
Prasad, Bimla. *The Origins of Indian Foreign Policy: The Indian National Congress and World Affairs, 1885–1947*, 2nd ed. Calcutta and Allahabad: Bookland, 1962.
Prashad, Vijay. *The Darker Nations: A People's History of the Third World*. New York: The New Press, 2007.
Purcell, Hugh. "Paris Peace Discord." *History Today* no. July (2009): 38–40.
Raghavan, Srinath. *War and Peace in Modern India*. London: Palgrave Macmillan, 2010.
Raghavan, V. R. *Siachen: Conflict without End*. Delhi: Viking, 2002.
Raj, Kapil. "Circulation and the Emergence of Modern Mapping," in *Society and Circulation: Mobile People and Itinerant Cultures in South Asia, 1750–1950*, eds. Claude Markovits, Jacques Pouchepadass, and Sanjay Subrahmanyam. Delhi: Permanent Black, 2006,
Rajan, M. S. *India in World Affairs, 1954–56*. Delhi: Indian Council of World Affairs, 1964.
Ramaswamy, Sumathi. *The Lost Land of Lemuria: Fabulous Geographies, Catastrophic Histories*. Berkeley: University of California Press, 2004.
———. *The Goddess and the Nation: Mapping Mother India*. Durham, NC: Duke University Press, 2010.
Ramnath, Maia. "Two Revolutions: The Ghadar Movement and India's Radical Diaspora, 1913–1918." *Radical History Review* 2005, no. 92 (Spring 2005): 7 –30.
Renan, Ernest. "What Is a Nation?" in Homi K. Bhabha, ed., *Nation and Narration*, pp. 8–22. London and New York: Routledge, 1990,
Richman, Paula, ed. *Many Rāmāyaṇas: The Diversity of a Narrative Tradition in South Asia*. Berkeley: University of California Press, 1991.
Robb, Peter. "The Colonial State and Constructions of Indian Identity: An Example on the Northeast Frontier in the 1880s." *Modern Asian Studies* 31, no. 2 (1997): 245–283.

Rogoff, Irit. *Terra Infirma: Geography's Visual Culture*. New York and London: Routledge, 2000.
Rosenau, James N., and Ernst-Otto Czempiel, eds. *Governance without Government: Order and Change in World Politics*. Cambridge, UK: Cambridge University Press, 1992.
Roy, Anupama. "Between Encompassment and Closure: The 'Migrant' and the Citizen in India." *Contributions to Indian Sociology* 42, no. 2 (May 1, 2008): 219–248.
———. *Mapping Citizenship in India*. Delhi: Oxford University Press, 2011.
Rudner, David West. *Caste and Capitalism in Colonial India: The Nattukottai Chettiars*. Berkeley: University of California Press, 1994.
Ruggie, John. "Territoriality and Beyond: Problematizing Modernity in International Relations." *International Organization* 47, no. 1 (1993): 139–174.
Rustomji, Nari. *Enchanted Frontiers: Sikkim, Bhutan, and India's Northeastern Borderlands*. Delhi: Oxford University Press, 1971.
Sahlins, Peter. *Boundaries: The Making of France and Spain in the Pyrenees*. Berkeley: University of California Press, 1991.
Saikia, Yasmin. *Fragmented Memories: Struggling to Be Tai-Ahom in India*. Durham, NC: Duke University Press, 2004.
Samāddār, Raṇabīra. *The Politics of Dialogue: Living Under the Geopolitical Histories of War and Peace*. London: Ashgate Publishing, Ltd., 2004.
Sanajaoba, Naorem. *Manipur: Treaties & Documents*. Delhi: Mittal Publications, 1993.
SarDesai, D. R. *Indian Foreign Policy in Cambodia, Laos, & Vietnam*. Berkeley: University of California Press, 1968.
Sarkar, Sumit. *Modern India: 1885–1947*. Delhi: Macmillan, 1983.
Schroeder, Paul W. *The Transformation of European Politics, 1763–1848*. New York: Oxford University Press, 1996.
Scott, James C. *Weapons of the Weak: Everyday Forms of Peasant Resistance*. New Haven, CT: Yale University Press, 1985.
———. *The Art of Not Being Governed: An Anarchist History of Upland Southeast Asia*. New Haven, CT: Yale University Press, 2010.
Securing India: Strategic Thought and Practice. Delhi: Manohar Publishers & Distributors, 1996.
Sen, Sudipta. *Distant Sovereignty: National Imperialism and the Origins of British India*. New York: Routledge, 2002.
Seth, Sanjay. *Marxist Theory and Nationalist Politics: The Case of Colonial India*. Delhi: Sage Publications, 1995.
Shakya, Tsering. *Dragon in the Land Of Snows: The History of Modern Tibet since 1947*. New York: Random House, 2012.
Sheehan, James J. "The Problem of Sovereignty in European History." *The American Historical Review* 111, no. 1 (February 1, 2006): 1–15.
Shimazu, Naoko. *Japan, Race and Equality: The Racial Equality Proposal of 1919*. London: Routledge, 2002.
Shukla, Sandhya. "Building Diaspora and Nation: The 1991 'Cultural Festival of India.'" *Cultural Studies* 11, no. 2 (1997): 296–315.
Sidaway, James D. "Sovereign Excesses? Portraying Postcolonial Sovereigntyscapes." *Political Geography* 22, no. 2 (February 2003): 157–178.
Sidhu, Waheguru Pal Singh, and Jing Dong Yuan. *China and India: Cooperation or Conflict?* Boulder, CO, and London: Lynne Rienner Publishers, 2003.

Singer, J. David. "The Level-of-Analysis Problem in International Relations." *World Politics* 14, no. 1 (1961): 77–92.
Singh, Anita Inder. *The Limits of British Influence: South Asia and the Anglo-American Relationship, 1947-56.* London: Pinter Publishers, 1993.
Singh, Iqbal. *The Indian National Congress: A Reconstruction.* Vol. 2: 1919–1923. Delhi: Nehru Memorial Museum and Library, 1989.
Singh, Jaswant. *Defending India.* Delhi: Macmillan India, 1999.
———. *A Call to Honour: In Service of Emergent India.* Delhi: Rupa & Co., 2006.
———. *Jinnah: India, Partition, Independence.* Delhi: Oxford University Press, 2010.
Singh, Ujjwal Kumar. *The State, Democracy and Anti-Terror Laws in India.* New Delhi and Thousand Oaks, CA: Sage Publications, 2007.
Skidelsky, Robert. *John Maynard Keynes: Hopes Betrayed: 1883–1920.* Vol. 1. London: Macmillan, 1983.
Smith, Anthony D. *The Antiquity of Nations.* London: Polity, 2004.
Smith, Neil. *American Empire: Roosevelt's Geographer and the Prelude to Globalization.* Berkeley: University of California Press, 2004.
Steinberg, Philip E. *The Social Construction of the Ocean.* Cambridge, UK: Cambridge University Press, 2001.
Stokes, Eric. *The English Utilitarians and India.* Delhi: Oxford University Press, 1989.
Stovall, Tyler Edward, and Georges Van den Abbeele, eds. *French Civilization and Its Discontents: Nationalism, Colonialism, Race.* Lanham, MD: Lexington Books, 2003.
Strang, David. "Contested Sovereignty: The Social Construction of Colonial Imperialism." In *State Sovereignty as Social Construct*, edited by Thomas J. Biersteker and Cynthia Weber, pp. 22–49. Cambridge, UK: Cambridge University Press, 1996.
Subrahmanyam, K. "Introduction." In *Defending India*, London/New York: Macmillan/ St. Martin's Press, 1999.
Subrahmanyam, Sanjay. *The Career and Legend of Vasco Da Gama.* Cambridge, UK: Cambridge University Press, 1997.
Sundaram, Lanka. "The International Status of India." *Transactions of the Grotius Society* 17 (January 1, 1931): 35–54.
Suzuki, Shogo. *Civilisation and Empire: East Asia's Encounter with the European International Society.* London: Routledge, 2009.
Swyngedouw, E. "Excluding the Other: The Production of Scale and Scaled Politics." *Geographies of Economies* (1997): 167–176.
Tahir-Kheli, Shirin. "Pakhtoonistan and Its International Implications," *World Affairs* 137, no. 3 (December 1, 1974): 233–245.
Tanham, George Kilpatrick. *Indian Strategic Thought: An Interpretive Essay.* Santa Monica, CA: Rand, 1992.
Thakur, Ramesh, and Antony Wood. "Fiji in Crisis." *The World Today* 43, no. 12 (December 1, 1987): 206–211.
Tilly, Charles, ed. *The Formation of National States in Western Europe.* Princeton, NJ: Princeton University Press, 1975.
Ting, Gao. "Ethnic Chinese Networks and International Investment: Evidence from Inward FDI in China." *Journal of Asian Economics* 14, no. 4 (August 2003): 611–629.
Tinker, Hugh. *Separate and Unequal: India and the Indians in the British Commonwealth, 1920–1950.* Vancouver: University of British Columbia Press, 1976.
———. *A New System of Slavery: The Export of Indian Labour Overseas 1830–1920*, 2nd ed. London: Hansib, 1993.

Tölölyan, Khachig. "The Nation-State and Its Others: In Lieu of a Preface." *Diaspora: A Journal of Transnational Studies* 1, no. 1 (1991): 3–7.
Tomlinson, B. R. *The Economy of Modern India, 1860–1970*. Cambridge, UK: Cambridge University Press, 1993.
Torpey, John. *The Invention of the Passport: Surveillance, Citizenship and the State*. Cambridge, UK: Cambridge University Press, 1999.
Trautmann, Thomas R. *Aryans and British India*. Berkeley: University of California Press, 1997.
Trouillot, Michel-Rolph. *Silencing the Past: Power and the Production of History*. Boston: Beacon Press, 1997.
Tuathail, Gearóid Ó. *Critical Geopolitics: The Politics of Writing Global Space*. Minneapolis: University of Minnesota Press, 1996.
Vajapayee, Atal Behari. "Nuclear Anxiety: Indian's Letter to Clinton on the Nuclear Testing." *The New York Times*, May 13, 1998. Retrieved on September 13, 2011, from www.nytimes.com/1998/05/13/world/nuclear-anxiety-indian-s-letter-to-clinton-on-the-nuclear-testing.html.
Van Schendel, Willem. "Geographies of Knowing, Geographies of Ignorance: Jumping Scale in Southeast Asia." *Environment and Planning D: Society and Space* 20, 6 (2002): 647–668.
———. "Stateless in South Asia: The Making of the India–Bangladesh Enclaves." *Journal of Asian Studies* (2002): 115–147.
Van Schendel, Willem, and Itty Abraham, eds. *Illicit Flows and Criminal Things: States, Borders, and the Other Side of Globalization*. Bloomington: Indiana University Press, 2005.
Vanaik, Achin. *The Painful Transition: Bourgeois Democracy in India*. London: Verso, 1990.
———. *The Furies of Indian Communalism: Religion, Modernity, and Secularization*. London: Verso, 1997.
Varadarajan, Latha. *The Domestic Abroad: Diasporas in International Relations*. New York: Oxford University Press, 2010.
Verma, D. N. *India and the League of Nations*. Patna: Bharathi Bhavan, 1968.
Gauri Viswanathan. *Masks of Conquest: Literary Study and British Rule in India*, reprint. Delhi: Oxford University Press, 1998.
Walker, R. B. J. *Inside/Outside: International Relations as Political Theory*. Cambridge, UK: Cambridge University Press, 1993.
Wang Gungwu. *The Chinese Overseas: From Earthbound China to the Quest for Autonomy*. Cambridge, MA: Harvard University Press, 2000.
Weber, Eugen. *Peasants Into Frenchmen: The Modernization of Rural France, 1870–1914*. Stanford, CA: Stanford University Press, 1976.
Wheatley, Elizabeth Shannon. "Ec(h)o-Tourism and the Whisper of the State: The 'Greening' of Indigenous Politics." In *International Relations and States of Exception: Margins, Peripheries, and Excluded Bodies*, edited by Shampa Biswas and Sheila Nair. New York: Routledge, 2010.
White, Hayden V. *Metahistory: The Historical Imagination in Nineteenth-Century Europe*. Baltimore, MD: Johns Hopkins University Press, 1975.
Winichakul, Thongchai. *Siam Mapped: A History of the Geo-Body of a Nation*. Honolulu: University of Hawaii Press, 1997.
Wirsing, Robert. *India, Pakistan, and the Kashmir Dispute: On Regional Conflict and Its Resolution*. London: Palgrave Macmillan, 1998.

Wisner, Frank, Nicholas Platt, Marshall M. Bouton, Dennis Kux, Mahnaz Z. Ispahani, Council on Foreign Relations. Independent Task Force on New Priorities in South Asia, Council on Foreign Relations, and Asia Society. *New Priorities in South Asia: U.S. Policy toward India, Pakistan, and Afghanistan: Chairmen's Report of an Independent Task Force Cosponsored by the Council on Foreign Relations and the Asia Society*. New York: Council on Foreign Relations, 2003.

Wolters, O. W. *Early Southeast Asia: Selected Essays*. Ithaca, NY: Cornell SEAP Publications, 2008.

Young, Robert J. C. *Postcolonialism: An Historical Introduction*. Oxford, UK: Blackwell Publishers, 2001.

Zacher, Mark W. "The Territorial Integrity Norm: International Boundaries and the Use of Force." *International Organization* 55, no. 2 (2001): 215–250.

Zaminder, Vazira Fazila-Yacoobali. *The Long Partition and the Making of Modern South Asia Refugees, Boundaries, Histories*. New York: Columbia University Press, 2010.

Zhang, Yongjin. *China in International Society since 1949: Alienation and Beyond*. London and New York: Macmillan/St. Martins Press, 1998.

Zhao, Suisheng. *A Nation-State by Construction: Dynamics of Modern Chinese Nationalism*. Stanford, CA: Stanford University Press, 2004.

Index

Abdul Ghani Sheikh, 163
Aborigine Protection Society, 82
Acton, Lord, 61
Aden, 53, 113
Afghanistan, 109, 111–12, 116, 144; as buffer state, 114, 121, 157
Africa: and Berlin Conference of 1884–1885, 51, 67; precolonial state power in, 25
Agamben, Giorgio, 130, 139
Agnew, John: on territorial states, 22, 28
Ahom kingdom, 131
Aksai Chin, 155
Albanians, 50
Alexandrowicz, C. A., 62–63, 64
Ali, Maulana Mohammed, 84
All-Asia Education Conference of 1930, 9
All-Asia Labour Congress of 1934, 9
All-Asia Women's Conference of 1931, 9
Allies, Paul, 20, 146
Amin, Idi, 75
Amoy (Xiamen) University, 152
Anderson, Benedict, 30; on anticolonial nationalist texts, 8
Anderson, Charles, 79
Andreas, Peter: *Border Games*, 171n73
Andrews, C. F., 82
Anghie, Anthony, 63, 64, 65, 67
anticolonial movements, 46–47, 49, 85–86, 145
Anti-Indenture League of Madras, 82
Appadurai, Arjun, 13

Arabia, 113
Arendt, Hannah: on imperialism, 9
Armed Forces Special Powers Act (AFSPA), 135–37, 138, 140, 187n112
Armenia, 68
Armenian diaspora, 73
Asian Relations Conference of 1947, 68–70, 89–93, 95–96, 129, 179n77, 184n46
Australia, 52, 55, 56, 98, 173n28; Indians resident in, 100, 105
Austro-Hungarian Empire, 6, 10, 24, 46, 50, 73
Ayutthaya, 93
Azerbaijan, 68

Bajpai, Girija Shankar, 123, 124, 125, 126, 129, 185n68
Bajpai, Kanti, 185n68
Baku Congress of Peoples of the East, 9, 85
Balachandran, G., 80
Baluchistan, 111
Bandarnaike, Srimavo, 180n105
Bandung Conference, 121, 129, 180n89
Bangladesh: creation of, 72; as East Pakistan, 37, 133, 157; labor migration from, 99–100; relations with India, 141, 145, 187n1
Bannerjee, Mamata, 188n1
Barkatullah, 81
Baruah, Sanjib, 132
Basra, 80

Bavadra, Timoci, 97
Bayley, C. A., 29
Bengali language, 37
Bengal Provincial Congress, 82
Benton, Lauren: on Bodin, 24; on territorial sovereignty, 24
Berlin Conference of 1884–1885, 51, 67
Bharatiya Janata Party (BJP), 104
Bharat Mata (Mother India), 30–31, 32–33, 108, 116, 123
Bhasin, Kamla: on abducted women, 40, 42
Bhutan, 120, 125, 126, 127–28, 157
Bierville Peace Conference of 1926, 9, 85
Bikaner, Maharaja of, 53, 173n19
Birla, Rita: on vernacular capitalists, 80
Bodin, Jean: *On Sovereignty*, 24
Bolan Pass, 112
borderlanders, 38
Borneo, 144
Bose, Sarat Chandra, 89
Bose, Subhas Chandra, 88, 179n64
Bose, Sugata, 80, 81; *A Hundred Horizons*, 177n18
Bowman, Isiah, 93
British Anti-Slavery Society, 82
British India: buffer states for, 121–22, 127–28, 157; and Burma, 17, 36–37, 84, 113; East India Company, 29–30, 33, 79, 109; foreign policy of colonial government, 84, 85–88, 98–99, 131–32, 134–35; Indian Army, 80–81, 87; Inner Line/Excluded Areas, 132, 134, 139, 186n100; legacies of, 16, 17, 92, 107–8, 110, 113, 114–15, 119–23, 122, 128–29, 130, 132–34, 135, 136, 137–40, 146, 156, 157, 158, 160, 161, 182n26, 183n36; majorities and minorities in, 31, 32–33; McMahon Line, 185n62; overseas Indians, 55–56, 57, 70, 78–83, 86, 91, 105, 131; and Paris Peace Conference, 46, 52, 52–62, 83–84, 173n35; partitioning of, 13, 71, 72, 99, 114, 139, 157–58, 161, 189n24; during World War I, 52, 75, 87, 88, 172n13
Brobst, Peter John: *The Future of the Great Game*, 182n26
Brunei, 143
Brussels anticolonial conference of 1927, 9, 85–86
Buddhism, 68, 117
buffer states, 121–22, 127–28, 138, 157, 185n63

Burbank, Jane: on empire states, 24; on post-Revolutionary France, 27
Burma, 88, 89, 93, 109, 111, 116, 117, 123, 131, 132; and British India, 17, 36–37, 84, 113; ethnic minorities after independence, 72, 95; Indians resident in, 36–37, 77, 79, 90, 91; relations with China, 148; relations with India, 69, 77, 135
Butler, Judith: on performance of gender, 171n75

Callahan, William, 150
Cama, Madame, 81
Cambodia, 117, 144, 148
Campbell, David: on foreign policy, 2–3, 34–35
Canada, 52, 81; immigration policies, 55–56; Indians resident in, 100, 105
Canton (Guangzhou), 80, 94
capitalism, 9, 44, 90, 101–4, 138
Caribbean, 74, 79, 100–101, 102
Caroe, Olaf, 114, 125, 182n26
caste, 16–17, 60, 77–78, 79–80, 100–101, 102, 103–5, 106, 156
Ceylon/Sri Lanka, 88, 89, 93, 109, 117; Indians resident in, 79, 92, 97, 180n105; relations with India, 77, 141, 180n105, 181n108; Sinhalese in, 69, 95; Tamils in, 77, 91, 95
Chakrabarty, Dipesh, 118
Chatterjee, Partha, 170n53; on rule of colonial difference, 173n31
Chaturvedi, Sanjay, 130
Chauduri, K. N., 80, 94
Cheah, Pheng: on spectral promises, 8
Chiang Mai, 113
China: Communist China, 122–30, 143–44, 147–55, 177n15, 185n78; as diasporic, 69, 76, 77, 79, 90–92, 93, 95, 151, 152–53, 177n15, 180n89; ethnic minorities in, 147, 149, 150–51, 152–53, 154; Guangzhou (Canton), 80, 94; Hong Kong, 80, 148, 149, 153; majority-minority relations in, 147, 149, 150–51, 152–53, 154; Manchuria, 150; nationalism in, 49, 127, 148, 149, 150–51, 153–54, 189n30; Nationalist China, 68, 69, 91–92, 124, 151, 152, 177n15; Qing Empire, 149–53, 154, 155, 157, 185n62, 189n30; relations with Burma, 148; relations with Cambodia, 148; relations with

INDEX

India, 113, 120, 122–30, 132, 139, 141–42, 143, 148, 149, 154–55, 184n61, 185n78, 186n86; relations with Indonesia, 180n89; relations with Japan, 144; relations with Laos, 148; relations with Mongolia, 148; relations with Taiwan, 144, 148, 152, 153; relations with Thailand, 180n89; relations with United States, 151; relations with Vietnam, 148; territorial disputes involving, 143–44, 147–55, 189n28; territoriality of, 148, 149–55; Tibet annexed by, 122, 123, 124–27, 129, 148, 149, 154–55, 184n61

citizenship: dual citizenship, 100–101, 102–3, 105; in France, 27; in Great Britain, 75; in India, 2, 16, 100–101, 102–3, 105, 106, 128, 139, 156, 158–60, 161; nation-states and unequal forms of, 2, 17–18, 51–52, 164; relationship to foreign policy, 17–18, 35, 43

civilization, 68–70, 150, 175n77; civilized/modern-backward/primitive hierarchy, 95–96, 132, 133, 138, 140, 156; and international law, 63–64, 65–67; and international recognition, 65–67

class: in India, 16–17, 77–78, 79–80, 99–101, 102, 103–5, 106, 156; in Marxism, 44; middle class, 8, 16–17, 78, 103–5, 106, 156; working class, 99–100, 101, 105, 106

Clemenceau, Georges, 57, 83

Clinton, Bill, 141

Cold War, 39, 121–22, 158

Communism, 89, 125, 126, 127, 129, 158, 185n78

Communist Party of India, 115

Cooper, Frederick: on empire states, 24; on post-Revolutionary France, 27

Corbridge, Stuart: on territoriality, 28

Croatians, 50

Curzon, George Lord, 82, 182n16, 184n58, 185n62; geopolitics of, 110–14, 120, 121, 123, 124, 125, 129, 131, 157, 182n12

Czechoslovakia, 74

Dalai Lama, 155
Danzig/Gdansk, 73
Das, Chittranjan, 84
Das, Taraknath, 81
Dayal, Har, 81
Dean, Mitchel: *Critical and Effective Histories*, 170n62
D'Espinay, P., 177n24

Devji, Faisal, 8

diaspora: Armenian diaspora, 73; Chinese diaspora, 69, 76, 77, 79, 90–92, 93, 95, 151, 152–53, 177n15, 180n89; defined, 16; foreign policy as, 16–17, 18, 73–106, 107, 156, 158–61; vs. geopolitics, 16, 107; and indentured labor, 57, 78–80, 81–83, 86, 91, 105, 131; Indian diaspora, 12, 14, 16–17, 18, 48, 57, 69, 70–71, 74–83, 86, 90–93, 96–98, 100–103, 114, 151, 156, 158–61, 176nn6,7,11, 177n18, 180n105, 181n114; Indian exiles, 81, 86; Indian students, 81, 86; Jewish diaspora, 73; labor migration, 99–100, 101, 105; and national self-determination, 73–74, 99; non-resident Indians (NRIs), 100–101, 102–5; Tibetan diaspora, 155

Diaspora Report of 2001, 100–103, 105, 181n114

dual citizenship, 100–101, 102–3, 105

Duara, Prasenjit, 175n88; *Sovereignty and Authenticity*, 175n77

Dubai: Indians resident in, 99

Duffy, George Gavan, 57

Durand Line, 144

Dutch East India Company (VOC), 62

East Timor, 72

Edney, Matthew H.: *Mapping an Empire*, 184n58

Egypt, 49, 89, 113

Einstein, Albert, 85

Elden, Stuart: on territory and territoriality, 13, 28

Elliott, C. S., 131–32

Elwin, Verrier, 130

emergency legislation, 137–38, 140, 156

English East India Company, 29–30, 33, 79, 109

ethnic minorities, 72, 93–96, 147, 149, 150–51, 152–53, 154

external sovereignty. *See* international recognition/personhood

federalism vs. nation-state, 48, 61
Fiji, 79, 82, 97–98, 102
Fischer-Tiné, Harald, 81
Food and Agriculture Organization, 10
foreign policy: as boundary-making practice, 2–3, 12, 13, 15–18, 21, 33–38, 41–44; as diaspora, 16–17, 18, 73–106, 107, 156, 158–60, 161;

foreign policy (continued)
  and discourses of danger, 34; as geopolitics, 16, 17–18, 36–38, 43, 95, 107–40, 156, 158, 160, 161, 162, 183n36, 186n89; relationship to citizenship, 17–18, 35, 43; role of identity and difference in, 34–35; state effect produced by, 3, 36. See also Indian foreign policy; territorial disputes
Foucault, Michel: on archeology, 181n1; on genealogy, 170n62
France: citizenship in, 27; empire of, 6, 23–24, 27, 46, 113, 117, 146; Indian exiles in, 81; Napoleon I, 27; popular sovereignty during Revolution, 26, 27
Frank, André Gunder, 94
Fravel, M. Taylor, 147–49, 154, 189n28
freebooters, 24
French Indochina, 113

Gait, Sir Edward, 186n92
Gallagher, John, 87
Gandhi, Mohandas K., 81–82, 83–85, 134, 179n60; on foreign policy, 84; and Khilafat movement, 84–85; in South Africa, 8, 75, 81, 86; during World War I, 84, 88
Gandhi, Rajiv, 98, 181n108
Ganguly, Sumit, 143
geopolitical hierarchies: center-periphery, 36–37; civilized/modern-backward/ primitive, 95–96, 132, 133, 138, 140, 156; insider-outsider, 16, 32, 33, 37–38, 43, 107, 139, 153, 171n73. See also majorities and minorities
geopolitics: of Curzon, 110–14, 120, 121, 123, 124, 125, 129, 131, 157, 182n12; defined, 16, 108–9, 181n3; vs. diaspora, 16, 107; foreign policy as, 16, 17–18, 36–38, 43, 89, 95, 107–40, 156, 158, 160, 161, 162, 183n36, 186n89; as imperial practice, 107, 108–15, 119–23, 156, 158, 160, 182nn16,17; and Indian Northeast, 17, 113, 122–40; of Nehru, 119–20, 121, 122–30; policy of nonalignment, 7, 108, 120–22; Scientific Frontiers, 123, 124, 129; space of exception in, 130, 138, 139–40. See also geopolitical hierarchies
Georgia, 68, 89
Germany, 6, 24, 74; East African colonies, 54, 75; Indian exiles in, 81; and Paris Peace Conference, 50, 54

Ghadar Party, 81
Gladney, Dru, 151
globalization, 77, 102–3
Gokhale, Gopal Krishna, 82
Golwalkar, Madhav Sadashiv, 115, 116, 117
Gomez, Nicolas Way, 25
Gong, Gerrit, 63
Gordon, Richard, 85
Goswami, Manu: on Bharat Mata, 32–33; on geography textbooks, 32; on technology and colonial state, 31
Gourevitch, Peter, 165n1
Great Britain, 124, 125, 127; citizenship laws, 75; Commonwealth, 56–57, 97; Empire, 6, 14, 17, 23–24, 27, 29–32, 46, 52–62, 70, 71, 74–75, 78–88, 99, 107–8, 121, 122, 123, 128, 131–32, 134–35, 136, 144, 146, 156, 158, 159, 161, 182n26, 183nn36,42, 185n62; Government of India Act, 132; Indians resident in, 100, 105; relations with South Africa, 56–57; Slavery Abolition Act, 6, 78. See also British India
Greater East Asia conference of 1943, 179n64
Greece, 73
Grotius, Hugo: on divisible sovereignty, 62; on international law, 62; Mare Liberum, 62, 63
Grovogui, Siba, 51, 63
Guha, Amalendu, 131
Gujarati trading community, 80
Gujral, I. K., 188n3
Gulf War, first, 105
Gupta, Aniruddha, 75
Gupta, Partha Sarathi: Power, Politics, and the People, 179n68
Guyana, 79, 97

Haiti, 27
Haji Pir pass, 141
Hall, William, 66
Hardinge, Lord, 82
Harvey, David: on accumulation by dispossession, 63; on territorial fix, 21
Hegdewar, Keshav Baliwar, 115
Hegel, G. W. F., 61
Hinduism, 68
Ho Chi Minh, 89
Hobsbawm, Eric: on the nation-state, 46
Hoi An, 94
Holsti, Kalevi J.: on antiterritorial revision, 26; on territorial sovereignty, 26–27

Holy Roman Empire, 23
Hong Kong, 80, 148, 149, 153
Hughes, Billy, 55, 173n28
Hugli, 94
humanitarian instinct, 163–64
Hussain, Nasser, 137–38, 139–40
Hydari, Sir Akbar, 134
Hyderabad monarchy, 72

imperialism, 8, 9–10, 11, 49, 68–69, 85; and buffer states, 17, 121–22, 138, 157, 185n62; doctrine of divisible sovereignty, 62; as expansionist, 107, 108–15, 120–21, 126, 129, 131–32, 185n62; and geopolitics, 107, 108–15, 119–23, 156, 158, 160, 182nn16,17; and international recognition/personhood, 1, 44–45, 47, 48, 51, 63–67; legacies of, 16, 17, 25, 51–52, 92, 107–8, 110, 113, 114–15, 119–23, 128–29, 130, 132–34, 135, 136, 137–40, 146, 149–52, 156, 157, 158, 160, 161, 182n26, 183n36; Lenin on, 46; and race, 10, 13–14, 54–57, 70, 79, 137, 173n31; rule of colonial difference, 79, 173n31, 177n24. *See also* British India
Imperial Legislative Council, 86
indentured labor, 57, 78–80, 81–83, 86, 91, 105, 131
India: Abducted Persons (Recovery and Restoration) Bill, 40–41; Armed Forces Special Powers Act (AFSPA), 135–37, 138, 140, 187n112; Article 7 of Constitution, 101; Bengal, 36–37, 39, 78, 79, 84, 109, 125; Bihar, 78, 79; Bombay, 84, 157; Buddhists in, 116; Calcutta, 17, 157; caste in, 16–17, 60, 77–78, 79–80, 100–101, 102, 103–5, 106, 156; Christians in, 116, 131, 133, 139, 183n39; citizenship in, 2, 16, 100–101, 102–3, 105, 106, 128, 139, 156, 158–60, 161; class in, 16–17, 77–78, 79–80, 99–101, 102, 103–5, 106, 156; Dalits in, 16, 103; Darjeeling, 125, 126; as diasporic, 12, 14, 16–17, 18, 36–37, 48, 57, 69, 70–71, 74–81, 90–93, 96–98, 100–103, 114, 151, 156, 158–60, 176nn6,7,11, 177n18, 180n105, 181n114; economic conditions in, 31–32, 59, 77, 79–80, 87, 99–100, 101–2, 105, 108, 131, 162, 179n68; Gujarat, 84; Hindus in, 21, 31, 32–33, 40–42, 60, 80, 85, 100–101, 104–5, 108, 123, 159, 160–61, 179n60, 189n24; Hyderabad, 124; independence, 13, 17, 71, 72, 74–75, 76–77, 87–88, 98, 99, 114, 133, 139; Jains in, 116; Jews in, 116; Junagadh, 124; Kalimpong, 125; Khasi states, 133–34, 187n106; Kohima, 131, 135; Maharashtra, 115; Maintenance of Internal Security Act (MISA), 137; Manipur kingdom, 134; Ministry of External Affairs, 76, 126, 127–28; Ministry of Overseas Indian Affairs, 176n11; Ministry of States, 130, 133–34; as multinational, 12, 15–16, 59–62, 70–71; Muslims in, 21, 32–33, 37, 40–41, 42, 54, 80, 84, 101, 104, 105, 115, 116, 158, 159, 161, 179n60; nationalism in, 12, 13, 21, 30–33, 36, 37, 48, 49, 52, 57–62, 74–75, 83–89, 107–8, 114, 115–17, 123, 170n53, 189n24; Native States, 53, 72, 99, 110, 111, 113–14, 124, 183n37; New Delhi, 17, 157; nuclear tests in 1998, 141; policy of reservations, 16–17, 103–4; Pravasi Bharatiya Divas/Overseas Indian Day, 105; Prevention of Terrorism Act (POTA), 137; Punjab, 37, 39, 109, 110, 111, 131, 142, 157, 187n112; refugees in, 39–40, 42; Scheduled Tribes in, 103; Sikhs in, 40–42, 56, 85, 109, 116, 159, 179n60; Sindh, 109, 111, 131; state boundaries of, 15–16, 17, 20, 21–22, 70 71, 75, 98, 99, 106, 114–15, 122–30, 155–56, 159, 162; Supreme Court, 137; Tamil Nadu, 78; Telengana, 126; territorial disputes involving, 141–43, 144, 145, 148, 149, 154 64; territorialization of women's bodies in, 13, 21–22, 38–43, 189n24. *See also* British India; Indian foreign policy; Northeast India
Indian Council for World Affairs, 68, 179n77
Indian foreign policy: nonalignment policy, 108, 120–22; regarding Asia, 88–93, 98–99; regarding Indian diaspora from 1947 to 1990, 74–78, 92–93, 96–99, 102, 105, 106, 151, 153, 180n105; regarding Indian diaspora since 1990s, 74, 75, 76–77, 78, 100–106, 156, 158–61, 181n114; relations with Bangladesh, 141, 145, 187n1; relations with Burma, 69, 77, 135; relations with Ceylon/Sri Lanka, 77, 141, 180n105, 181n108; relations with China, 113, 120, 122–30, 132, 139, 141–42, 143, 148, 149, 154–55, 184n61, 185n78, 186n86;

Indian foreign policy (*continued*)
  relations with Fiji, 97–98; relations with Gulf emirates, 105; relations with Himalayan states, 120, 124–25, 127–29, 157, 158, 184n49; relations with Pakistan, 4, 18, 37, 38, 99, 127, 141–43, 155–64, 188n3; relations with Saudi Arabia, 105; relations with Sri Lanka, 141; relations with United States, 102, 125
Indian Home Rule League, 57–60, 82
Indian Legislative Council, 82
Indian National Army (INA), 88
Indian National Congress, 82, 83–84, 85, 86, 88–89, 92–93, 124
Indian National Party, 81
Indian Sociologist, 81
India-U.S. nuclear agreement of 2005, 102
indigenous people, 95–96
Indonesia, 69, 72, 88–89, 91, 93, 95, 144
International Committee of the Red Cross, 6
International Court of Justice (ICJ), 11, 144
International Labor Organization (ILO), 10, 87
international law, 62–67; and civilization, 63–64, 65–67; and customary practice, 25; and extraterritoriality, 65, 72; and international space, 6–7; and natural law, 25, 62; positive vs. natural, 62–65; and race, 65; relationship to international recognition, 62, 64, 65–67, 70; and sovereignty, 65–67; and United Nations, 7
international recognition/personhood: as external sovereignty, 1–2, 14, 48; and imperialism, 1, 44–45, 47, 48, 51, 63–67; of India, 14, 47–48, 53, 57, 61–62, 88, 99; of PRC, 125, 149, 151–52; relationship to civilization, 64–67; relationship to international law, 62, 64, 65–67, 70; relationship to territorial sovereignty, 12, 14, 47–48, 61–62, 65–66, 70–72, 99, 145–46, 164
International Relations (IR) theory: foreign policy in, 2; levels of analysis in, 4, 5; second-image reverse problem, 165n1; territorial sovereignty in, 13, 22–28; and Treaty of Westphalia, 22–25, 64
international scale, 4–5, 9, 10–11, 48–49, 50
international space, 4–12; as field of struggle, 3, 4–6; and international law, 6–7; prior to 20th century, 5–6

Iraq, 113; Indians resident in, 99
Ireland, 14, 57–59, 173n35
irredentism, 37, 52, 73, 117, 125, 126
Italy, 6, 73

Jamaica, 79
Jamal al-din Al-Afghani, 8
Japan, 14, 65, 74, 175n88; geopolitics in, 182n12; Indian students in, 81; and Kurile Islands, 144; Manchuria annexed by, 150; racial equality proposal at Paris Peace Conference, 49, 54–57; relations with China, 144; Russo-Japanese War, 7, 85; and Senkaku/Diaoyu Islands, 144; Taiwan annexed by, 150; and Takeshima Islands, 144; during World War II, 157, 179n64
Javanese, 95
Jewish diaspora, 73
Jinnah, M. A., 189n24

Kachhateevu, 141
Kant, Immanuel, 11
Kanya Kumari, 116
Karakoram Pass, 142
Kargil War of 1999, 143
Karlsson, Bengt G.: *Unruly Hills*, 187n106
Karnad, Bharat, 119–20, 184n46
Kashmir, 111, 157, 187n112; India-Pakistan territorial dispute regarding, 5, 41, 99, 136, 141, 142, 143, 156, 158, 163–64; relaxation of border controls in, 143, 163–64
Kayaoglu, Turn: *Legal Imperialism*, 175n73; on Treaty of Westphalia, 25
Keene, Edward: on sovereignty, 23, 66–67
Kelat, 114
Keynes, John Maynard, 54
Khaireddin Barbarosa, 119
Khilafat movement, 84–85
Khyber Pass, 112
Kipling, Rudyard: *The Man Who Would be King*, 111–12
Kjellén, Rudolf, 181n3
Komagata Maru, 56
Konfrontasi conflict, 144
Korea, 49, 68; North Korea, 144; South Korea, 144
Korean War, 127
Krasner, Stephen, 165n1; on Treaty of Westphalia, 23

Krishna, Sankaran, 172n8; on foreign policy, 2–3
Krishnavarma, Shyamji, 81
Kurile Islands, 144
Kuwait: Indians resident in, 99

labor migration, 99–100, 101, 105
Lajpat Rai, Lala, 85
Lansbury, George, 86
Laos, 148
League Against Imperialism and for National Independence, 9, 86
League for the Abolition of Indentured Emigration, 82
League of Nations, 10–11, 38–39, 54–55, 85, 87
Lefèbvre, Henri, 20, 38
Lemuria, 14
Lenin, V. I., 9; on imperialism, 46
Lévi, Sylvain, 117
Lintner, Bertil, 132
Liu, Lydia He, 189n30; *The Clash of Empires*, 171n78
Lloyd George, David, 54
Lus Beyla, 114

Macau, 148, 153
Mackinder, Halford, 108, 109, 110, 120
Macmillan, Margaret, 173n19
Macridis, Roy C.: *Foreign Policy in World Politics*, 171n66
Mahan, Alfred, 118, 119
majorities and minorities: in British Burma, 72; in British India, 31, 32–33; in China, 147, 149, 150–51, 152–53, 154; ethnic minorities, 72, 93–96, 147, 149, 150–51, 152–53, 154; as geopolitical hierarchy, 17–18, 37–38, 51–52, 69–70, 90–96, 146, 150–51, 152–53, 154, 158–61, 164; in independent India, 158–61; irreducible alterity, 21, 32, 33; as super-sign, 37, 171n78; after World War I, 51, 73–74
Makino, Baron, 54
Malacca (Melaka), 80, 94, 113
Malaka, Tan, 8
Malaviya, Madan Mohan, 83, 85, 179n68
Malaya/Malaysia, 89, 93, 136, 143; Chinese residents of, 69, 90–91, 92, 95; Indian residents of, 77, 79, 88, 90–91, 100; *Konfrontasi* conflict, 144
Maldives, 181n108
Malhotra, Jyoti, 141

Mandate system, 67
Mandel Commission, 103
Manela, Erez, 173n19; on Paris Peace Conference, 49, 53; on Wilson's Fourteen Points speech, 49
mapmaking, 26, 51, 116, 146, 150; after partition of India, 139, 142; in British India, 21, 28–31; precolonial maps of India, 29–30, 33
Mare Liberum, 62, 63
Marxism, 26, 44, 46
Mauritius, 78–79, 102, 177n24
Mazower, Mark, 12
Mbembe, Achille: on itinerant territoriality, 25
McKinley, James, 110
Menon, Ritu: on abducted women, 40, 42
mercantilism, 31–32, 108
middle class, 8, 16–17, 78, 103–5, 106, 156
migration, 39, 99–100
Mill, John Stuart, 63
Mitchell, Timothy: on state effect, 36
Mohan, C. Raja, 119
Mongia, Radhika, 55–56, 79
Mongolia, 148
Montagu, Lord, 53–54
Montenegro, 50
Mother India, 30–31, 32–33, 108, 116, 123
Muscat and Oman, 113–14; Indians resident in, 99
Myanmar. *See* Burma

Naga National Council (NNC), 134–35
Nag, Sajal, 136
Naidu, Sarojini, 68–69, 75
Naoroji, Dadabhai: on colonial financial practices, 31–32
Nathu-La Pass, 143
national honor, 41, 42
national ID cards, 35
nationalism, 3, 8, 9, 15, 26, 44, 47, 49, 51, 145–46, 175n88; in China, 127, 148, 149, 150–51, 153–54, 189n30; Hindu nationalism, 108, 115–17, 123, 189n24; in India, 12, 13, 21, 30–33, 37, 48, 52, 57–62, 74–75, 83–89, 107–8, 114, 115–17, 123, 170n53, 189n24; national liberation movements, 46; national myths, 95, 146, 189n24
national self-determination: and diaspora, 18, 73–74, 99; and majority-minority populations, 18, 51–52, 73–74;

national self-determination (*continued*)
one people-one land-one state standard, 11–12, 20, 50, 51, 61–62, 145–46; and Paris Peace Conference, 11–12, 13–14, 46–52, 57–62, 83; and Wilson, 11, 12, 46–47, 50, 57–58, 60, 61, 70, 83, 93
nation-states: border games of, 35–36, 171n73; vs. empires, 4, 23, 24, 27, 51, 107; vs. federal states, 48, 61; as global norm, 46–48, 69, 70, 74, 145–46; and majority-minority relations, 17–18, 37–38, 51–52, 69–70, 73–74, 90–96, 146, 150–51, 152–53, 154, 158–61, 164; as national homelands, 18, 26–27, 33, 43, 47–48, 50, 51, 71, 73–74, 76, 77, 90, 93, 100, 108, 116, 146–47, 148, 149, 151, 153–54, 156; relationship to unequal forms of citizenship, 2, 17–18, 51–52, 164; state legitimacy, 1, 2, 11, 20, 42–45; territoriality of, 2, 4, 11–12, 15, 17–18, 19–21, 26–27, 33, 37, 42–43, 46, 47–48, 50, 51–52, 70–72, 73, 74, 75, 77, 93, 94–95, 98–99, 108, 115–17, 142–43, 145–47, 148, 149–50, 151, 153–54, 156, 162, 164. *See also* nationalism; national self-determination
Nehru, Jawaharlal, 69, 85–86, 88–90, 135, 184nn46,61, 185n68, 186n86; geopolitics of, 119–20, 121, 122–30; on India diaspora, 96–97; on nonalignment, 121
Nehru, Motilal, 83
neoliberalism, 77, 101–2
Nepal, 109, 114, 123, 126; relations with India, 120, 124–25, 127–28, 157, 184n49
Netherlands, 23–24, 27, 72, 91, 146
New Zealand, 52, 98, 100
Nobel Prizes, 11
nonaligned movement, 7, 108, 120–22
non-resident Indians (NRIs), 100–101, 102–5
nonstate actors, 24, 49
Northeast India, 154–55, 156, 157, 185n78, 186n89; Assam, 109, 110, 125, 126, 131, 160, 186n92; exceptional status of, 17, 108, 123, 130–40; and geopolitics, 17, 113, 122–40; Mizos, 132, 136–37; Nagas, 131–32, 134–36, 186n98; Sixth Schedule, 132, 133, 139, 140
North Korea (DPRK), 144

Oberoi, Pia, 39–40
Oberoi, Pia Anjolie: *Exile and Belonging*, 171n82
O'Cealloigh, Sean T., 57
Okakura Tenshin, 68
Olympic Games, 11
one people-one land-one state standard, 11–12, 20, 50, 51, 61–62, 145–46
Onley, James, 113
OPEC, 99–100
Opium Wars, 150
Oppenheim, L. F. L., 6, 64
orang asli, 95
Ottoman Empire, 46, 47, 113, 119; dismemberment of, 10, 50, 73, 84–85, 86
Ó Tuthail, Gearóid, 108–9
Overseas Citizens of India (OCI), 106

Pagden, Anthony, 25
Pakistan: Awami National Party, 189n16; creation of, 71, 72, 99, 114, 139, 157–58; East Pakistan, 37, 133, 157; and East Pakistan/Bangladesh, 37, 133; Federally Administered Tribal Area (FATA), 130, 186n98; Hindus in, 159, 160; labor migration from, 99–100; Lahore, 157; minorities in, 159, 160; Muslims in, 18, 158, 159, 160; nationalism in, 189n16; Northwest Frontier Province (NWFP), 157, 186n98, 189n16; Pathans in, 186n98; refugees in, 39–40; relations with Afghanistan, 144; relations with India, 4, 18, 37, 38, 99, 127, 141–43, 155–64, 188n3; relations with United States, 158; Sikhs in, 159, 160; territorialization of women's bodies in, 21–22. *See also* British India
Pan-Asiatic Conference of 1927, 9
Pan-Asiatic Congress of 1926, 9
Pan-Asiatic Labour Congress of 1934, 9
Panchsheel Agreement, 120
Panikkar, K. M., 95–96, 114, 126, 182n26; *Asia and Western Dominance*, 118, 119, 183nn37,39; *Geographical Factors in Indian History*, 183n44; *India and the Indian Ocean*, 118–19, 183n42; on northern vs. southern India, 183n44
Paris Peace Conference of 1919, 9, 46–62, 85; and ethnicity, 93; and Germany, 50, 54; Indian government at, 52–57; Indian nationalists' petition at, 52, 57–62, 173n35; Irish nationalists' petition at,

57–58, 173n35; Japan's racial equality proposal at, 49, 54–57; and national self-determination, 11–12, 13–14, 46–52, 57–62, 83–84
Parsis (Zoroastrians), 116
passports, 35, 56
Patel, Sardar Vallabhai, 122–30, 133, 139, 185nn68,78
patriarchy, 41, 42
Pearson, W. W., 82
Penang, 113
People of Indian Origin (PIO), 106
Permanent Court of International Justice, 87
Persia, 47, 65, 112, 113
Persian Gulf, 99–100, 101, 105, 106, 113
Peshawar, 131
Philippines, 100, 143, 144
Philpott, Daniel: on territorial sovereignty, 22–23
Phizo, 135
pirates, 24
Pires, Tome, 94
political geography, 22
political identity, 93, 146
Poulose, T. T., 88
Prakash, Gyan: on *Bharat Mata*, 32
Prasad, Bimla, 84
Prasad, Raja Shiva, 32
Pratap, Mahendra, 81
Preah Vihear temple, 144
Puranas, 32
Purcell, Hugh, 55

race: and imperialism, 10, 13–14, 54–57, 70, 79, 137, 173n31; and indigenous people, 95–96; Japan's racial equality proposal at Paris Peace Conference, 49, 54–57
Racial Equality Clause, 49, 54–57
Raghavan, V. K., 142
Rajasthani Marwari trading community, 80
Ramaswamy, Sumathi, 116; on *Bharat Mata* icon, 30–31
Rashtriya Swyamsevak Sangh (RSS), 115
Ratzel, Friedrich, 109, 118
remittances, financial, 99–100, 101, 105
Renan, Ernest, 59
Réunion, 78–79
Richardson, Lewis, 182n17
Rizal, José, 8
Robb, Peter, 131
Rogoff, Irit: on maps, 28, 31

Rolland, Romain, 85
Roma (Gypsies), 176n6
Romanticism, 26
Roosevelt, Theodore, 110
Rowlatt Act, 83–84
Roy, Anupama, 159–60
Roy, M. N., 9, 81
Ruggie, John: on territorial sovereignty, 22
Rumania, 50
Russia and Kurile Islands, 144
Russian Empire, 112, 157; Revolution, 46, 47; Russo-Japanese War, 7, 85

Salonika, 74
Saltoro Range, 142
Samaddar, Ranabir, 164
SarDesai, D. R., 89, 117
Sarvarkar, Vinayak Damodar, 81, 115, 116
Saudi Arabia: Indians resident in, 99, 105
Scott, James, 94; on manpower and political power, 25
Scott, James C.: *Weapons of the Weak*, 184n58
Seal, Anil, 87
Senkaku/Diaoyu Islands, 144
Serbia, 50
Servants of India Society, 82, 86
Seth, Sanjay, 46
Shan, 95
Shastri, Lal Bahadur, 180n105
Sheehan, James: on legal system expansion, 24; on the state and territorial sovereignty, 22, 24
Shimazu, Naoko, 52, 55
Siachen Glacier, 142–43, 162
Siam. See Thailand
Sikkim, 120, 125, 126, 127–28, 143, 157, 184n49
Simla Agreement, 142
Sindhi trading community, 80
Singapore, 53, 80, 88, 113; Indians resident in, 100
Singh, Jaswant, 122, 189n24
Singh, Manmohan, 162
Singh, V. P., 103
Singhvi, L. M., 76, 77
Sinhalese, 95
Sinha, Sir S. P., 53, 55, 173n19
Slovaks, 50
Slovenians, 50, 73
Smith, Neil, 93
socialism, 103–4

Soja, Edward: on mapmaking, 29
South Africa: immigration policies, 56; Indians resident in, 8, 55, 75, 81, 86, 97; Natal province, 79, 82; at Paris Peace Conference, 52; racial policies, 56–57, 97
South China Sea, 143–44
Southeast Asia, 117; vs. Europe, 25
South Korea and Dokdo Islands, 144
sovereignty. See international recognition/personhood; nation-states; territorial sovereignty; Treaty of Westphalia
Soviet Union, 7, 47, 112, 127
spatialization of difference, 17–18, 21
Spratly Islands, 143–44, 148
Sri Lanka. See Ceylon/Sri Lanka
Stalin, Joseph, 151
Straits Settlements, 17, 113
Strand, David, 63
Subrahmanyam, K., 185n36
Sukarno, 72
Sun Yat-Sen, 8, 150–51
Sun Yat-Sen, Madam, 85
Surat, 80, 94
Sweden, 6

Tagore, Rabindranath, 68
Taiwan, 143, 144, 148, 150, 151, 153
Tamil Chettiar trading community, 80
Tan Kah Kee, 152
Tanham, George, 183n36
territorial disputes: involving China, 143–44, 147–55, 189n28; importance of, 19, 168n1; involving India, 141–43, 144, 145, 148, 149, 154–64; Kashmir, 5, 41, 99, 136, 141, 142, 143, 156, 158, 163–64; Kurile Islands, 144; origins of, 12, 14–15, 72, 144–45, 146–47; involving Pakistan, 141–43, 155–64; persistence of, 4, 72, 142–43, 147, 148, 155, 156; resolution of, 4, 13, 15, 43, 143, 145, 147, 148, 154, 161–63; Senkaku/Diaoyu Islands, 144; Siachen Glacier, 142–43, 162; Taiwan, 144, 148, 152, 153; Takeshima/Dokdo Islands, 144
territoriality: as itinerant, 25; national homelands, 18, 26–27, 33, 43, 47–48, 50, 51, 71, 73–74, 76, 77, 90, 93, 100, 108, 116, 146–47, 148, 149, 151, 153–54, 156; of nation-states, 2, 4, 11–12, 15, 17–18, 19–21, 26–27, 33, 37, 42–43, 46, 47–48, 50, 51–52, 70–72, 73, 74, 75, 77, 93, 94–95, 98–99, 108, 115–17, 142–43, 145–47, 148, 149–50, 151, 153–54, 156, 162, 164; norm of antiterritorial revision, 26; as spatial strategy, 13. See also territorial disputes; territorial sovereignty; territory
territorial sovereignty, 19–21, 42–43, 94–95; of China, 148, 149–53, 154; of India, 14, 47–48, 61–62, 99, 153; in International Relations (IR), 13, 22–28; loss of territory as loss of state power, 12, 15, 19, 37, 43, 142–43, 145, 146–47, 162; relationship to international recognition/personhood, 12, 14, 47–48, 61–62, 65–66, 70–72, 99, 145–46, 164. See also international recognition/personhood; territorial disputes
territory: as hierarchically organized space, 5, 17, 21, 27–28, 36–37; and mapmaking, 21, 26, 28–31, 51–52, 116, 139, 142, 144, 145, 150; relationship to political community, 26, 146; relationship to state wealth, 23–24, 25–26; role in Hindu nationalism, 115–17; as technology, 28–33; as variable, 20–21, 27–28, 38, 43; wars over, 27, 41, 141. See also territorial disputes; territoriality
Thailand, 1, 47, 65, 69, 93, 100, 113, 144, 182n12
Thapar, Romila, 183n37
Tibet, 68, 121, 143, 157, 185n62; as buffer state, 114, 121, 157, 185n62; Chinese annexation, 122, 123, 124–27, 129, 148, 149, 154–55, 184n61
Tilak, Bal Gangadhar "Lokamanya," 57, 83, 85
Tilly, Charles, 23
Tinker, Hugh, 78, 82
Toraja, 95
Toynbee, Arnold, 129
trading companies, 24, 80, 118
Treaty of Augsburg, 23
Treaty of Punakha, 128
Treaty of Vienna, 26
Treaty of Westphalia, 22–25, 26, 64
Trieste, 73
Trigonometrical Survey of India, 29–30
Trinidad, 79
Turkey, 1, 65, 73, 87

Uganda: Indians expelled from, 75–76, 97
United Nations, 55, 69, 72, 87, 124, 172n92; and international law, 7; PRC

membership in, 125, 151; Refugee Convention of 1951, 39–40; and refugees, 38–40
United States, 6, 7, 110, 124, 127; immigration policies, 100; Indians resident in, 81, 100, 105; refugee policy, 39; relations with China, 151; relations with India, 102, 125; relations with Pakistan, 158
Universal Races Conference of 1911, 9, 85
UP (United Provinces) Congress, 82
Urdu language, 37

Vajpayee, Atal Bihari, 141–42
Vanaik, Achin, 120, 178n60
Varadarajan, Latha, 101–3, 104
Vattel, Emer de, 63
Veddas, 95
Victoria, Queen, 53
Vietnam, 69, 88–89, 94, 117, 143, 148
violence, 38, 42–43
Vitoria, Francisco de, 62

Wagah flaging-hoisting, 36
Walker, Rob: on foreign policy, 2–3, 33–34; on territorial sovereignty, 22

Wen Yuan-ning, 91
Westlake, John, 6, 66
West Papua/Irian Jaya, 72
Wheaton, Henry, 6
White, Hayden, 109
Wilson, Woodrow: chairman of Covenant Committee, 54–55; Fourteen Points, 12, 46–47, 49–51, 57–58, 145; and national self-determination, 11, 12, 46–47, 50, 57–58, 60, 61, 70, 83, 93
working class, 99–100, 101, 105, 106
World Congress of Religions of 1893, 167n23
World Health Organization, 10
World War I, 7, 10, 39, 46, 118, 145; British India in, 52, 75, 87, 88, 172n13. *See also* Paris Peace Conference of 1919
World War II, 39, 88, 157

Young India, 84
Yugoslavia, 74

Zacher, Mark: on territorial disputes, 168n1; on territory and foreign policy, 22
Zanzibar, 53, 113
Zhang Binglin, 68

Studies in Asian Security

Amitav Acharya, Chief Editor, American University

David Leheny, Chief Editor, Princeton University

How India Became Territorial: Foreign Policy, Diaspora, Geopolitics
By Itty Abraham
2014

Wronged by Empire: Post-Imperial Ideology and Foreign Policy in India and China
By Manjari Chatterjee Miller
2013

Looking for Balance: China, the United States, and Power Balancing in East Asia
By Steve Chan
2012

SPONSORED BY THE EAST-WEST CENTER, 2004–2011

Muthiah Alagappa, Founding Series Editor

Rethinking Japanese Public Opinion and Security: From Pacifism to Realism?
By Paul Midford
2010

The Making of Northeast Asia
By Kent Calder and Min Ye
2010

Islam and Nation: Separatist Rebellion in Aceh, Indonesia
By Edward Aspinall
2009

Political Conflict and Economic Interdependence across the Taiwan Strait and Beyond
By Scott L. Kastner
2009

(Re)Negotiating East and Southeast Asia: Region, Regionalism, and the Association of Southeast Asian Nations
By Alice D. Ba
2009

Normalizing Japan: Politics, Identity, and the Evolution of Security Practice
By Andrew L. Oros
2008

Reluctant Restraint: The Evolution of China's Nonproliferation Policies and Practices, 1980–2004
By Evan S. Medeiros
2007

Why Taiwan? Geostrategic Rationales for China's Territorial Integrity
By Alan M. Wachman
2007

Beyond Compliance: China, International Organizations, and Global Security
By Ann Kent
2007

Dangerous Deterrent: Nuclear Weapons Proliferation and Conflict in South Asia
By S. Paul Kapur
2007

Minimum Deterrence and India's Nuclear Security
By Rajesh M. Basrur
2006

Rising to the Challenge: China's Grand Strategy and International Security
By Avery Goldstein
2005

Unifying China, Integrating with the World: Securing Chinese Sovereignty in the Reform Era
By Allen Carlson
2005

Rethinking Security in East Asia: Identity, Power, and Efficiency
Edited by J. J. Suh, Peter J. Katzenstein, and Allen Carlson
2004

The authorized representative in the EU for product safety and compliance is:
Mare Nostrum Group
B.V Doelen 72
4831 GR Breda
The Netherlands

www.ingramcontent.com/pod-product-compliance
Lightning Source LLC
Chambersburg PA
CBHW020340240426
43662CB00048B/593